ALSO BY HEINRICH HARRER

Seven Years in Tibet

Return to Tibet

JEREMY P. TARCHER/PUTNAM

a member of

PENGUIN PUTNAM INC.

New York

THE WHITE SPIDER

THE WHITE SPIDER

The Classic Account of the Ascent of the Eiger

HEINRICH HARRER

Translated from the German by
HUGH MERRICK

With additional chapters by
HEINRICH HARRER AND KURT MAIX

Most Tarcher/Putnam books are available at special discounts for bulk purchases for sales promotions, premiums, fund-raising, and educational needs. Special books or book excerpts also can be created to fit specific needs. For details, write Putnam Special Markets, 375 Hudson Street, New York, NY 10014.

Jeremy P. Tarcher/Putnam
a member of
Penguin Putnam Inc.
375 Hudson Street
New York, NY 10014
www.penguinputnam.com

First published in Great Britain by Rupert Hart-Davis Ltd 1959
Revised edition 1965
Second revised edition published by Granada Publishing 1976

This translation copyright © Rupert Hart-Davis Ltd 1959

First published in the U.S.A. by E. P. Dutton & Co., Inc., 1960
Originally published by Ullstein A.G., Berlin, under the title:
Die Weisse Spinne
All rights reserved.

First Jeremy P. Tarcher/Putnam Trade Paperback edition 1998

Library of Congress Cataloging-in-Publication Data

Harrer, Heinrich, date.
[Weisse Spinne. English]
The white spider / by Heinrich Harrer.—1st Jeremy P.
Tarcher/Putnam trade pbk. ed.
p.   cm.
Originally published: London : Hart-Davis, 1976.
ISBN 0-87477-940-5
1. Mountaineering—Switzerland—Eiger—History.   2. Eiger
(Switzerland)—Description and travel.   I. Title.
GV199.44.S92E35313   1998   98-23179 CIP
796.52'2'0949454—dc21

Printed in the United States of America
3   5   7   9   10   8   6   4

This book is printed on acid-free paper. ∞

Book design by Deborah Kerner

Contents

ACKNOWLEDGMENTS FOR ILLUSTRATIONS

Map photograph *Gyger & Klopfenstein*

An aerial view of the Face *Swissair-Foto*

Harrer on the Hinterstoisser Traverse. Kasparek traversing
to the First Ice Field *The author's Eiger Archive*

The Second Ice Field *Sepp Jöchler*

1952. The French climbers on the upper part of the
"Spider" *Gaston Rébuffat*

1957. Rescue operations on the summit of the Eiger
Albert Winkler

Mittellegi Ridge

North East Face

Spider

Traverse of the Gods

Eigerwand Station 9403'

Grindelwald 3393'

Alpiglen 5300'

Grund 3093'

ger 13041'

Western Flank
(normal ascent route)

Mönch 13468'

Jungfrau 13677'

Jungfrau-Joch
12046'

Gallery window at
Kilometre 3·8

Eigergletscher
Station 7614'

8109'
Lauberhorn

Kleine
Scheidegg 6765'

Wengernalp
6147'

Wengen 4180'

THE WHITE SPIDER

"COME
BACK SAFE,
MY FRIENDS"

Writing a book about the North Face of the Eiger? Whatever
for?" The question was put to me by a man of some standing in Alpine circles. I was taken aback and slightly cross, so I gave him
a somewhat offhand answer: "For people to read, of course."

That started him off on a passionate tirade.

"Who's likely to read it? Don't you think the handful of climbers
who are really interested in that crazy venture have had quite enough
literature on the subject already? Or do you just want to join the sen-
sation-mongers, from whose ranks a serious climber like yourself
should keep as remote as possible?"

I answered him: "If all climbers shared your point of view, it
wouldn't be surprising to find the newspaper reports overflowing
with misstatements and exaggerations. I believe the public has a right
to authoritative information, especially when mountaineering problems become human ones. And I think it is a climber's duty to con-
tribute to the formation of public opinion in such matters."

And with that I dropped the unpleasant argument.

However, he had failed to shake my purpose to write a book about
the Eiger. I had already been engaged on the preliminary work for

months, indeed for years. My home was piled high with books, periodicals, newspaper cuttings—about two thousand of them in various languages—on the subject of the Eiger's North Face. I had written, and received replies to, innumerable letters. Every letter from a climber who had actually done the North Face was a personal document and, more than that, the documentation of a personality. I had no intention of allowing the history of the Eiger's North Face to become a mere calendar of climbs; its foreground theme was to be the men who had done those climbs.

This man, who was so shocked at the idea of my writing a book about the North Face of the Eiger, was akin to a certain type of climber, who plants himself on a pedestal of extreme exaltation and merely smiles superciliously at the nonsensical idea of writing for the layman about climbing. But one cannot ignore public opinion and at the same time expect it to judge one sympathetically and intelligently.

No less an authority than the late Geoffrey Winthrop Young, one of the grand old men of British climbing and outstanding in its literature, recognized the demands of the age and dealt with them in his article "Courage and Mountain Writing."[1] He understood well enough the general public's thirst for sensation, but he faced it squarely and yet refused to give in to it.

"The modern lay public," he writes, "is now ready to read mountain adventures among its other sensational reading. It still demands excitement all the time. The cut rope is no longer essential, and the blonde heroine has less appeal, now that she has to climb in nailed boots and slacks. It wants records, above all. Records in height, records in endurance, hair breadth escapes on record rock walls, and a seasoning of injuries, blizzards, losses of limbs and hazards of life. . . . I have suggested that the writers and producers of mountain books must also take some of the responsibility. . . ."

---

[1] *Berge der Welt* (Schweizerische Stiftung für Alpine Forschungen), (Zurich-Frankfurt: Buchergildel Gutenberg, 1955). English ed. *The Mountain World* (London: George Allen and Unwin, Ltd., 1955).

Responsibility with regard to the subject matter—responsibility with regard to the wishes of the reader. The key to a proper comprehension and understanding between the layman and the climber may well lie here.

And how is the climber to write? In Young's view: "If he is to be read by human beings, he must write his adventures exactly as he himself humanly saw them at the time. General or objective description, such as satisfied the slower timing of the last two centuries, now reads too slowly, and is dull."

But how can he avoid becoming a positive bore, if he intends to write a whole book about a single Alpine mountain face and the solitary route up it? Once again I will quote Young: "However well-known the peak, or the line of ascent, no mountain story need ever repeat itself, or seem monotonous. Both mountain surface and mountain climber vary from year to year, even from day to day."

There is no mountain, no mountain face anywhere, of which that can more truly be said than of the Eiger and its North Face. And all the men concerned—those who succeeded, or those who tried and failed—were all sharply defined personalities. No two of them were alike.

"A book about the Eiger? Whatever for?"

The question continued to rankle, though probably the man who asked it never intended to make me angry. Yet the barb persisted. And, though I needed neither an explanation nor a justification for my undertaking, I was greatly heartened to read the following words in an article by Albert Eggler, the well-known Alpine climber and leader of the Swiss Everest Expedition of 1956: "However, we Westerners more especially, who owe the improvements of our lifetime to the selfless devotion of a few exceptionally courageous and probably highly zealous men, ought not to be too hard on people who take on an assignment which in the end proves too big for them. Men who take unusual risks are not by any means the worst types. But what we could and should do is to open the eyes of young climbers in appropriate fashion to the very special dangers of the mountains. And in this direction, a great and worthwhile duty still lies before the Alpine clubs and Alpine publications generally."

But was the duty really worthwhile? Was it really a duty? And, if it was, dared I, could I perform it? I kept on remembering that question: "A book about the Eiger? Whatever for?" I am not usually the kind of person to dither about a selected target, or about a route, once I have recognised it as the right one. To spur me on, I had all the mass of writings and photographs, the notebooks, the letters, much of the material already sorted and arranged under the individual attempts on and ascents of the Face. But those misgivings aroused by a thoughtless remark were a poor source of driving power to start me on my work.

Then, one day, my old friend Kurt Maix called on me. In Austria there is no need to introduce Kurt. In his own country everyone who has anything to do with mountains or mountaineering knows him. His ability to describe things graphically has enabled him to interest laymen and those who know nothing of mountains in Alpine affairs, and to tell the devoted readers he has won for himself in this way everything he wants to, and everything he knows how to, about climbing and climbers. And that means plenty. For not only was he in his day a pretty sporting climber, but he continues to take a lively, indeed a passionate, interest in everything to do with mountains and mountaineers. He is no hack writer; every report on a climb, an expedition, a successful ascent, or an accident is a living experience for him. And though Maix is a journalist and writes by profession, he has never renounced his role as the mountaineer he remains at heart.

I was delighted to see Kurt again, but it was high time I was getting on with my book. After our first joyous greetings, I said to him: "I'm sorry I haven't much time for you. I'm up to my neck in work."

"So I hear," said Kurt. "They tell me you are writing a book about your African trip and Ruwenzori."

"No, not about Ruwenzori," I confessed.

"Then what is it about?"

I hesitated a little. Perhaps I was afraid of another answer like the one which had made me so angry a few days ago. Then I blurted out: "About the North Face of the Eiger."

Kurt looked surprised for a moment; then he said, with obvious delight: "But that's grand news!"

Still a little dubious, I asked him: "What's grand about it?"

"Why, that you're the one who's going to write the book about the Eiger. Not only because you were one of the party which made the first ascent. But because a book of yours will have more effect on our youngsters than a thousand warnings from elsewhere. They'll believe *you*."

"Certainly, there will have to be warnings," I said.

Kurt shook his head vigorously. "No," he said, "I don't mean that you will warn them in the ordinary sense. You won't raise a minatory finger, with a superior smile. All you will need to do is to present the Face as it actually is. Its history is more than a record of mountaineering disasters and successes. It is a history of human development and human tragedies. Someone had to write this book about the Eiger sometime. I would have done it myself, if—"

"If what?"

"If I were properly qualified to do it. But this is a book which can only be written by someone with personal experience of the Face. General mountaineering knowledge, imagination, reconstructions, and a study of the sources, all these aren't sufficient here."

I remembered a broadcast I had heard, the previous year. Fischer-Karwin, the Austrian Radio's star interviewer, had been asking Kurt Maix for his views about the mountaineering accidents of the summer of 1957. Kurt had answered: "I refuse to lump the tragedies on the Eiger Wall together with other accidents which resulted from carelessness or insufficient experience. Anyone who makes headway on the North Face of the Eiger and survives there for several days has achieved and overcome so much—whatever mistakes he may

5

have committed—that his performance is well above the compre-hension of the average climber."

And now here was Kurt, thrilled at my determination to write the book. His enthusiasm was infectious and convincing. Had I really been annoyed a few days ago by a thoughtless remark? I had already forgotten about it. Suddenly, I saw a strange picture before my eyes. I was standing at the bottom of a high and difficult moun-tain face, intending to climb it solo. Then I was joined by another solitary climber who, too, stood looking up the face, just as I had stood, searching, studying, assessing. An unexpected meeting, a brief word of greeting, and a decision was born to climb the face as a pair.

Following a spontaneous impulse, I asked Kurt: "Will you help me with the book? There is so much basic material that it needs con-tinual revision and sifting. Thoughts and questions keep on cropping up which call for definite answers. It is often very hard to provide the right answer oneself. Could you stay for a few days?"

Kurt stayed for many days. We worked like demons, from morn-ing till night. We wallowed in reports and statements, made notes, headings, began to write things down, mostly each working on his own. But we both looked forward to the evenings, when we joined up again and shared the experiences and fresh knowledge the day had brought. Those evenings frequently extended far into the night, oc-cupied by long conversations which always seemed too short. Everything always revolved about the North Face of the Eiger. Yet it was a focus from which our thoughts could range outwards in all directions. And from some small occurrence on the Face we often travelled directly to life's most serious problems. Memories which I had long since thought deeply overlaid came vividly to life again. A great deal of what was eventually set down and developed in the book arose out of our nightly talks. They were good days, those, with Kurt as my companion, and both of us spiritually in the shadow of the Eiger's Face.

I have always been disappointed when climbers who lead a first ascent on a difficult climb fail to acknowledge the support of the second man on the rope. One loses nothing by reporting that the rope moved through the safeguarding hands of one's partner while one was mastering an overhang. And now that the book about the North Face of the Eiger is finished, I would like to shake hands with Kurt Maix, just as I would on reaching a summit.

But there are many others besides Kurt whom I must thank for their share in the completion of this book. Their role has been that of the porters and teammates on an expedition, who pitch camps and shuttle loads, so that the assault party can push on up to the top. The late Othmar Gurtner, that great Swiss mountaineer, author, and editor, provided me, out of his rich store of knowledge, with endless facts, basic sources, and special Eiger documentation. How grateful I was for my acquaintance with Guido Tonella, who wields his pen for truth and justice as bravely as any Cavalier of old his sword. How gratefully I recognised in my correspondence with Lionel Terray and Gaston Rébuffat that brotherly comradeship which unites all climbers. And what thanks I owe to all the others who helped me, by their letters and reports, in my labours of compiling this book. Anderl Heckmair, Erich Vanis, Erich Waschak, Sepp Jöchler, Karl Blach, Sepp Larch, Jean Fuchs, Karl Gramminger, Alfred Hellepart. . . . Technical considerations alone prevent my naming all the others to whom my thanks are due. And then there are the dead, whose memories, whose achievements, and whose letters survive as living witnesses of strong and good men: Fritz Kasparek, Ludwig Vörg, Hans Schlunegger, Karl Reiss, Jürgen Wellenkamp, Hermann Buhl, and Louis Lachenal.

As I write these lines, the summer of 1958 has begun. It is five years since the last party succeeded in climbing the North Face of the Eiger—the twelfth to reach the top safe and sound. So far there has been no thirteenth. I know that within the next few weeks some keen young climbers will be trying to break the barrier of tragedy that seems to hang over the thirteenth climb of the Face. They are continually in my thoughts.[1]

Easy enough to say it; but I mean it in all sincerity. I mean it as seriously as I mean the warning every reader of this book can draw from its pages. Obviously I could not fail to do justice to the rare beauty and the unique size of this mighty Face and of the route which leads up it; that would have been letting myself down. But I can only hope that Kurt Maix was right when he said: "No one who reads your book can fail to know, afterwards, whether he belongs on the Face or not. . . ."

A few days ago two climbers came to see me. One of them was young Brandler, the very same Brandler who in 1956 saw Moosmüller and Söhnel go plunging to their death near the Difficult Crack. In those two years since Moosmüller's falling body brushed past him, a boy has grown into a man who knows what responsibility means. He has worked hard and become a good mountaineer, not only an exceptional rock climber. This summer he wants to try the Face again. His rope mate is to be Hias Noichl, that outstanding Tirolean mountaineer and long-distance ski runner. Brandler asked my advice about equipment for the climb. Ought I to have dodged the responsibility, by warning him and begging him not to try the Face again?

I could see that both were well trained and well prepared for an attempt on the Face. I could see that the character and skill of both men would make for a harmonious rope of two. I gave young Brandler as much advice as I could. We spoke in a matter-of-fact way without a touch of sentiment. Even when we said goodbye, I refrained from voicing the hope against hope which had been welling up within me all the time—"Come back safe, my friends. . . ."

But I watched them both for a long time, as they went farther and farther away down the road. . . .

---

[1]The success of Kurt Diemberger and Wolfgang Stefan is described in the Epilogue.—Translator's note.

THE "WHITE
SPIDER"

It is common form to congratulate people on their birthdays. It is also customary to pay a suitable tribute to buildings, cities, and associations when they reach a certain age. Biographies and autobiographies are written, and historical records, from the most comprehensive tomes to the smallest pamphlet. Why, then, not write a book to celebrate the birthday of a mountain, or even of a face of that mountain?

Admittedly, it is not the birthday celebration of the mountain or the face itself, but the remembrance of the day that first brought a human being into direct personal contact with it—the remembrance of the first ascent of a peak or the first successful climb of a face.

The 13,041-foot summit of the Eiger, in the Bernese Oberland, was first trodden by the foot of man just a hundred years ago, in 1858. Its North Face was climbed for the first time only twenty years ago, in 1938, and it was the climbing of this Face that first made the Eiger world-famous. Thanks to this, its name has become better known than that of the Matterhorn or Mont Blanc. It has become familiar to millions of readers of innumerable newspaper reports; it has been mentioned hundreds of times on the radio. It became the epitome of everything tragically sensational that mountaineering had to offer the reader. When millions, who had never seen either the mountain or the Face, formed their own picture of it, it could hardly help being a caricature. What I propose to do here is to draw a true picture of it; one which will be hardly less exciting, but whose drama will be based on truth and fact, not on the uninformed imaginings of some pen-pusher. For the true story of the Eiger's North Face is even more terrible and more glorious than men have yet been able to discover.

I am one of the party of four who, in July 1938, just sixty years ago, first succeeded in climbing the North Face. My memory of it is like a birthday celebration of my own, and has accompanied me to this day without ever diminishing in strength. Not even my great experience in Tibet, which gave such a decisive twist to my life, has ever succeeded in canceling it out; nor did the memory ever fade during the thirteen years I spent in Asia.

I do not think any one of us who climbed that 6,000-foot bastion of rock and ice was at any time in fear of his life. But after our safe return from the venture we felt more conscious of the privilege of having been allowed to live; and this feeling of awareness has never left me since that climb of the mighty North Face. Maybe my memory of the Eiger's Face has often given me the strength, the patience, and the confidence to cope with apparently hopeless and dangerous situations, and helped me to believe in life at times when all the circumstances seemed most hostile to life itself.

Self-confidence is the most valuable gift a man can possess, but it is not a gift freely granted. The blindly arrogant possess it least of all. To possess this true confidence, it is necessary to have learned to know oneself at moments when one was standing on the very frontier of things, times when one could even cast a glance over to "the other side." And then one had to examine oneself with unsparing clarity to establish what one felt, thought, or did at such a moment.

On the "Spider" in the Eiger's North Face I experienced such borderline situations, while the avalanches were roaring down over us, endlessly. This sector of the Eiger's upper wall has won its name from its external likeness to a gigantic spider. Seldom has an exterior attracted a name at the same time suits the inner nature of the object named so completely. The "Spider" on the Eiger's Face is white. Its body consists of ice and eternal snow. Its legs and its predatory arms, all hundreds of feet long, are white, too. From that perpetual, fearfully steep field of frozen snow nothing but ice emerges to fill gullies, cracks, and crevices. Up and down. To left, to right. In every direction, at every angle of steepness.

And there the "Spider" waits.

Every climber who picks his way up the North Face of the Eiger has to cross it. There is no way around it. And even those who moved best and most swiftly up the Face have met their toughest ordeal on the "Spider." Someone once compared the whole Face to a gigantic spider's web catching the spider's victims and feeding them to her. This comparison is unfounded, exaggerated, and merely a cheap way of making the flesh creep. Neither the savage wall nor the lovely mountain have deserved this slur. Nor have the climbers; for climbers are not flies and insects stumbling blindly to their fate, but men of vision and courage. All the same, the "White Spider" seems to me to be a good symbol for the North Face. The climber has to face its perils on the final third of the wall, when he is tired from many hours and days of exhausting climbing and weakened by chilly bivouacs. But there is no rest to be had there, no matter how tired you are.

He who wishes to survive the spate of avalanches that sweep the "Spider" must realise that there is no escape from this dangerously steep obstacle; he must know how to blend his strength with patience and reflection. Above the "Spider" begin the overhanging, iced-up exit cracks; that is where sheer strength tells. But here the man who abandons patience and good sense for fear-induced haste will surely finish up like the fly that struggles so long in the spider's web that it is caught through sheer exhaustion.

The "White Spider" on the Eiger is the extreme test not only of a climber's technical ability, but of his character as well. Later on in life, when fate seemed to spin some spider's web or other across my path, my thoughts often went back to the "White Spider." Life itself demanded the same methods, the same qualities, when there no longer seemed to be any possible escape from its difficulties, as had won us a way out of the difficulties of the Eiger's North Face—common sense, patience, and open-eyed courage. Haste born of fear and all the wild stunts arising from it can only end in disaster.

I remember a saying of Schopenhauer's: "Just as the wayfarer only surveys and recognises the road he has come when he reaches some high place and can look back over it in its entirety, so we ourselves are only able to recognise and value a stage in our life when it is over." The North Face of the Eiger and the crossing of the "White Spider" were for me an expedition and a stage in my life at one and the same time, though I only realised it a good deal later. Today I have no doubt whatever about the invaluable contribution a difficult and, in the eyes of many, an incredibly dangerous climb on a mountain can make to a man's later life. I do not believe in a blind fate that dominates us; nor can I unreservedly agree with Schopenhauer's statement—"Fate shuffles the cards, we play them." I am quite certain that we have a hand in the shuffling.

There is nothing new to be said about the behaviour of man in exceptional circumstances of danger or crisis. It has all been thought and said already. But if I had to write an entry in the autograph album of the worshippers of blind chance and inevitable fate I could not find better words than those used by the Athenian Menander more than two thousand years ago. "A man's nature and way of life are his fate, and that which he calls his fate is but his disposition." This truth was brought home to me clearly for the first time on the slope of the "White Spider." Perhaps all four of us were the fortunate owners of a disposition that was the basic factor in our successful climb; training, scientific preparations, and equipment being only very necessary adjuncts.

THE NORTH FACE of the Eiger was described for the first time in Alpine literature by A. W. Moore, whose splendid book *The Alps in 1864* [1] does full justice to its savage grandeur. Moore, with his guides and companions—among whom there was a lady, Miss Walker—made the third ascent of the Eiger on July 25, 1864; then they climbed a little way farther, along the Northwest Ridge, from which they could look straight down the precipitous North Face.

"Of the thousands," Moore writes, "who annually pass under the shadow of this magnificent wall, which in height and steepness alike excels the corresponding face of the Wetterhorn, few can have failed to be impressed with its rugged and precipitous character. But grand and striking as is the view of the cliffs from below, no one who has not looked down them as we now did can appreciate them properly. Except in the Dauphiné, I have never seen so sheer and smooth a precipice. A stone dropped from the edge would have fallen hundreds of feet before encountering any obstacle to its progress. It is rather remarkable (and fortunate) that while the northern face of this great mass of rock is cut away abruptly, in such an inaccessible manner, its western face should be so comparatively easy and practicable. . . ."

"Inaccessible"—it never occurred to Moore that there could be even the possibility of making a way up this wall, in which the eye can detect no holds at all. E. H. Stevens, who produced the new edition of Moore's book in 1939, added a footnote to the above description of that terrific Face. It reads: "This is the terrible 'Eigerwand' (the western section of the North Face) which in the last two or three years has been the scene of such shocking disasters to several parties attempting, with reckless and ill-considered daring,[2] to solve this last

---

[1] A. W. Moore, *The Alps in 1864*, ed. E. H. Stevens (Oxford: Basil Blackwood, 1939).
[2] The author in his original has rendered these words as "resulting from a sick mind."—Translator's note.

and greatest of Alpine problems. The ascent was finally achieved in 1938."

As one who belonged to the party that succeeded in the first ascent of the Face in 1938, I should like to observe—with due respect for our critic's judgment—that I neither felt mentally deranged twenty years ago nor consider myself mad now.

It has been widely deplored that the very creed of mountaineering should have been debased by the climbs and attempts on this particular Face, in that it has become an arena, a natural stage, on which every movement of the actors can be followed. And the applause accorded to successful climbers on their return is argued as another outward sign of their inward decay. . . .

Nobody regrets it more than the men themselves who climb on the Eiger's North Face. They desire nothing more than peace and quiet; they do not want to be looked at. They long for the days of their grandfathers when nobody took any notice of climbers or bothered to watch them. Full of nostalgia for those good old days, I read the end of Moore's account of his first climb of the mountain, the return to Wengern Alp. Alas, my yearnings for peace and quiet and a tranquil ending to that fine performance were not to be granted, even then. This is what I read: "Hence, running over the easy rocks and smooth snow, we got to the *gazon* at 2:40, and after a rapid walk over the pastures, amidst the firing of guns at the hotel, which was commenced as soon as we appeared in sight, at 3:10 P.M. once more arrived at the Wengern Alp, where we were received with an amount of enthusiasm and handshaking that was quite overpowering. . . ."

That happened on July 25, 1864, at the height of the "golden age" of Alpine climbing. Am I really supposed to be disappointed because the climbers of the day were just human beings, with all the human weaknesses and follies? All I can do is to record, with a smile of amusement, that when we got back nobody fired off any guns to greet us. They certainly had more feeling for style and dramatic effects a hundred years ago!

When was the Eiger first climbed, then?

We know now that it was on August 11, 1858. But when I looked for a report about this still considerable achievement of a first ascent in the contemporary issues of the *Alpine Journal*, I had no luck at all. It was said that a Mr. Harrington or Harington had reached the summit with some guides. This was the only mention of the name Harrington, and small wonder; for the name of the first man to climb the Eiger was not Harrington at all, but Barrington. Mr. Charles Barrington.

It was not till 1883, twenty-five years after his first ascent, that Barrington wrote his long-overdue report in the shape of a letter to the editor of the *Alpine Journal*. From this article-in-form-of-a-letter we learn that Barrington—himself not even a member of the Alpine Club, which was just one year old at the time of his climb—arrived at Grindelwald early in August 1858 and engaged two celebrated guides, Christian Almer and Peter Bohren, the latter being characterised by his nickname of the "Wolf of the Glaciers." On August 6 they climbed to the Strahlegg and on the 9th ascended the Jungfrau from the cave in the Faulberg, returning to Grindelwald the same evening. Glacier burn must have played havoc with Barrington's face, for he describes, in his humorous way, how he spent the night, "sleeping with a beefsteak on my face. . . ."[1]

But young Mr. Charles was by no means satisfied with his Alpine performances. With all the liberality of a man who hasn't a farthing in his pocket, but still inquires the price of the world, he asked what else there was to do. Good advice costs little, its implementation is expensive. "You could do the Matterhorn—or the Eiger. Neither has been climbed as yet," came the answer.

The Matterhorn was way over there in the Valais and would doubtless cost much more. At Grindelwald the Eiger was right in front of one's nose and there was enough money for it. So the Eiger

[1] A. J., February 1883.

be it! About midnight on August 10 Charles and his guides arrived at Wengern Alp. Barrington lay down on a sofa and slept for three hours. At 3 A.M. on the 11th, Barrington, Almer, and Bohren left the inn and started off for the Eiger. As soon as they reached the rocks, Barrington, according to his own account, took over the lead. Thanks to young Charles's delight in rock climbing, they went up, not by the normal route in use today, but almost straight up the crest of the Northwest Ridge, and reached the summit well before noon. On the descent, they followed the Couloir and went on down the slope over which the usual ascent route runs today. They still had a few adventures to contend with. Twice they were almost swept away by avalanches; fortunately it was only "almost," and four hours after leaving the summit the three men were all safely back at Wengern Alp. Barrington ends his account thus: "Thus ended my first and only visit to Switzerland. Not having money enough to try the Matterhorn, I went home. . . . Had I not been as fit as my old horse 'Sir Robert Peel' when I won the 'Irish Grand National' with him, I would not have seen half the course. . . ."

He was a true sportsman—a word with which the English chronicler acknowledges alike Charles Barrington's exploits and the tone of his report. So it seems that the racing motif as one of the mainsprings of the Alpine urge is by no means the contribution of modern, decadent youth. It has smouldered unseen in the youth of every age, whenever that youth is as "fit as Sir Robert Peel," and has always stirred mountaineers, starting with the Balmat-Paccard conflict, and continuing through the rivalry of Whymper and Carrel, to Buhl versus Rébuffat among the young men of today. The unique thing about the urge to climb is that it springs from many other bodily, spiritual, and ethical motives besides its purely "sporting" basis. It is impossible to classify mountaineering, or to integrate it with a stratum of the cultural life of today. It must be accorded its own unique place, just as the waywardness of mountaineers cannot be eradicated from the scheme of things.

The history of the Eiger is a typical piece of Alpine history. First came this Charles Barrington who, in all the simplicity of his uninformed upward urge, "bagged" the peak, merely because the Matterhorn was too expensive. Just a year later we find here one of the most gifted brains and sensitive spirits which has ever climbed in the Alps, a nature as far removed from "Sir Robert Peel" as it could possibly be. This was Leslie Stephen,[1] who traversed the Eigerjoch in 1859 with George and William Matthews and three guides.

The Southwest Ridge was climbed in 1874, the South Ridge in 1876. In 1885 some Grindelwald guides succeeded in descending the Mittellegi Ridge, always the shortest direct route between their village and the Eiger's summit, had it not been so difficult. They roped down the great rock pitch in the upper part of the ridge.

Nineteen twelve brought the triumph of science, for in that year the Jungfrau Railway was completed. The line runs for miles in the very heart of the mountain, through the Eiger's rocky core. Only two windows open out from the tunnel into the air of the North Face; and these were destined to play their part one day in the tragedies yet to be enacted on that grim precipice.

It was not till 1921 that the Mittellegi Ridge was at last ascended. Once again the success was scored by three Grindelwald guides, Fritz Amatter, Samuel Brawand, and Fritz Steuri senior, accompanied by a tourist, a very youthful Japanese, Yuko Maki. Thirty-five years later he was destined to lead a successful Japanese attempt on the eighth-highest mountain in the world, 26,650-foot Manaslu. Yuko Maki was the first to forge a direct link, so to speak, between the Eiger and the Himalaya. Later on, it was of course perfectly natural for the names of many of those who have climbed the North Face of the Eiger to appear and reappear in the story of the world's highest peaks.

Nineteen thirty-two saw the last great first ascent in the classical

[1] Leslie Stephen, *The Playground of Europe.*

style on the Eiger, When Dr. Hans Lauper and Alfred Zürcher, those outstanding Swiss climbers, with two world-famous Valaisian guides, Josef Knubel and Alexander Graven, reached the summit of the Eiger by the Northeast Face.

Every side of this mighty peak had now been climbed, except one only: the absolutely unclimbable, the "impossible" Eiger Wall, which receives and retains the bad weather as it comes raging in on the mountain from the north and northwest; the wall, high up on which the "White Spider," with its slender arms, hundreds of feet long, all of snow and ice, seems to be waiting, clawing the rocks.

Waiting?

It was not the "Spider" that was waiting. It was men who were waiting—the young men. They were waiting and biding their time. For now there was no longer a Matterhorn to be climbed for the first time, there were no more virgin summits such as the pioneers of the "Golden Age" could select at will. The last of the great faces had gone, too. In 1931, the brothers Schmid had scaled the North Face of the Matterhorn and in 1935 the North Wall of the Grandes Jorasses had fallen to Peters and Maier.

But what about the great Face of the Eiger—the wall over which the "White Spider" brooded?

Was it really impossible, or was there perhaps, after all, a way to its top?

No one who had not tried could answer that question. Someone had to come and be the first to try it.

And in the summer of 1935 someone came.

THE FIRST
ATTEMPT ON THE
NORTH FACE

I t is not only the young who are "ready with words." The broad mass of the public is ever ready to express a glib opinion about events and matters that it does not and cannot understand. It passes judgment and condemns, giving the descriptions of "folly" and "a gamble for life" to what are in truth "a love of adventure" and "the preservation of life." Modern science and psychology have also provided a phraseology in support of its criticism and condemnation. "Inverted inferiority complexes," "Self-justification of the maladjusted," "Mock heroism of failures in life"—one could produce a list, pages long, of the expressions that have been used to delineate at once the good sense and the nonsense of mountaineering and to damn it at the same time.

But are we really supposed to believe, for example, that in 1888 Fridtjof Nansen set out to cross the inland ice of Greenland on skis because he was suffering from an inferiority complex? Or that the great Norwegian explorer and campaigner for peace undertook that remarkable journey simply to serve the cause of science? What lured him on was, of course, the great adventure, the eternal longing of every truly creative man to push on into unexplored country, to discover something entirely new—if only about himself. In that lies the detonating spark, the secret source of strength, which enables men to achieve the extraordinary. Is it good sense or nonsense? Who can decide? Who dares to deliver judgment? Should the adventurer outlive and survive his adventure, and should it result in a tangible, easily comprehensible success, the public is generous with its applause. It is only too ready to haul into the glare of publicity and set upon a hero's pedestal—after he has succeeded—the very man it previously scorned, condemned to ridicule, accused of irresponsibility. Contempt and hero worship are equally unhealthy and both can lead to mischief. But ever since men have existed, the enterprising and daring men have had to translate their "out-of-the-ordinary" ideas into deeds somewhere between the two extremes of scorn and rejection on the one hand and recognition and adulation on the other. And it will always be so.

Where mountaineering is concerned, there is an additional difficulty. With the best will in the world no one can inject a secret element of general usefulness to mankind into a climb of the Eiger's North Face. Such a climb must remain a personal triumph for the climber himself. And however many considerations of material weight one may adduce, they do not bear comparison with the risk, the indescribable labors and difficulties, which demand the very uttermost ounce of physical, spiritual, and mental resistance. To win fame at the expense of that horrific wall? Of course, ambition plays a great part in such a venture. Yet, a mere fraction of the energy evoked, coupled with the cool judgment required, would lead to outstanding success, to fame and an assured livelihood in any calling, or any less dangerous form of sporting activity you may name.

Self-examination? Compensation for an inferiority complex? A climber who dares to tackle the North Face of the Eiger must have examined and proved himself a hundred times in advance. And suppose he has at some time suffered from complexes—and where is the man who has not, unless he is satisfied with the dull existence of a mere vegetable?—he must have found the right adjustment long before he gets there. A climb of the North Face as a counterbalance to hysteria? A hysteric, an unstable character, would go to pieces at the very sight of the Wall, just as surely as every mask of the kind men wear before one another in the daily round of life falls away in the face of this menacing bastion of rock and ice.

Let us grant courage and the love of pure adventure their own justification, even if we cannot produce any material support for them. Mankind has developed an ugly habit of only allowing true courage to the killers. Great credit accrues to the one who bests another; little is given to the man who recognises in his comrade on the rope a part of himself, who for long hours of extreme peril faces no opponent to be shot or struck down, but whose battle is solely against his own weakness and insufficiency. Is the man who, at moments when his own life is in the balance, has not only to safeguard it but, at the same time, his friend's—even to the extent of mutual self-sacrifice—to receive less recognition than a boxer in the ring, simply because the nature of what he is doing is not properly understood? In his book about the Dachstein,[1] Kurt Maix writes: "Climbing is the most royal irrationality out of which Man, in his creative imagination, has been able to fashion the highest personal values." Those personal values, which we gain from our approach to the mountains, are great enough to enrich our life. Is not the irrationality of its very lack of purpose the deepest argument for climbing? But we had better leave philosophical niceties and unsuitable psychoanalysis out of this.

First, let us take a glance at the two men who in mid-August 1935 took up their quarters in a cow hut among the meadows of Alpiglen, which they proposed to use as their base—the first two ever to dare an attempt on that mighty Face, Max Sedlmayer and Karl Mehringer. They were wiry, well-trained types, men with frank, wholesome

---

[1] Kurt Maix, "Im Banne der Dachstein Südwand," in *Das Bergland Buch* (Salzburg, 1952).

faces. Not theirs the steely iron-hard features of legendary heroes, or of film stars of a certain stamp. One would hardly have noticed them in the ordinary way, probably because they were just that little bit more reserved, quieter, and likeable than the average young man. Their calm and relaxed demeanor marked them out as people who had a firm standing in everyday life, men who had no need either to justify themselves by an unusually perilous venture, which might cost them their lives, or to await the applause of the masses to tell them who they were.

The very way in which Sedlmayer and Mehringer went about the reconnaissance of the Face spoke volumes for their character. They approached their mountain calmly and without fuss. There was no challenging smile on their faces, no show of conceit. They knew well enough the measure of their undertaking and went about their preparations in all seriousness. Of course, the real preparation, the spiritual mentality, the long years of hard training, the sober assessment of their own capabilities, all these already lay far behind them. They were not world-famous; only a narrow circle of friends knew them. These sternest of critics, all members of the climbing elite, knew that Sedlmayer and Mehringer were among the best, the most careful, the toughest, and most penetrative of climbers, tested and tried a hundred times over on the severest of climbs.

But even if you choose a herdsman's hut as your base, you cannot keep your most secret plans secret in a tourist center. The rumor filtered through that there were two men intending to attempt the North Face of the Eiger. There were plenty of well-intentioned, warning voices. But what is the use of warnings and advice? Nobody knew anything about the Face then; all that was known was its grim, ever-changing countenance—ice, rock, snow . . . avalanches . . . volleys of falling stones. An unfriendly, merciless countenance. All anybody could say was: "Don't climb the Face, it is horrible." But was its horror stronger than man's willpower, than his capacity? Who could answer that question? Nobody had yet been on the Face.

Sedlmayer and Mehringer would be the first. And they were preparing themselves for this climb as for no other climb in their lives. They knew that this was no mere case of a difficult first ascent, but of a positive irruption into the Vertical, which the two of them were making. How long would it last? Two or three days, or more? They took provisions along for six days. Their equipment, too, was the best yet seen at that time. The worst of it was that they didn't yet know what was most essential for the Eiger's North Face; was that Face of ice, was it of rock? Not even long study through a strong telescope could answer that question, for the Face continually altered its appearance from day to day, nay, from hour to hour. The only unalterable features were its pitiless magnificence and its utter unapproachability. All experience won from other mountains seemed useless here. Experience of this gigantic wall could only be gained on the Face itself.

The weather would be the decisive factor. The two Munich men knew that only too well. But they also knew that the famous period of settled weather for which they ought, by the strictest of basic climbing rules, to wait, apparently didn't exist where the North Face of the Eiger was concerned. It might be perfectly fine for miles around; the Eiger and the North Face have their own particular weather. Quite a small cloud, caught in the huge, perpendicular upthrust of the Wall's concave basin, can kindle a fearsome storm of hail, snow, and raging winds, while the visitors in Grindelwald, just below down there, are comfortably sunbathing on their *chaises-longues*. Every shred of weather working up from the plains fights its savage opening engagement on that Face. Even the clouds that have already dumped their load of rain on their approach to the hills, join up again on the Eiger's Face with redoubled strength, to fight a last desperate rearguard action before drifting off to float about the other summits as exhausted, harmless tatters of mist. Or else the mere contrast between the cold air trapped on the Face and the sun-warmed air external to it forms a cloud pregnant with tension of its own making, to whip rain, snow, and ice into the Eiger's flanks.

These two men, who believed they had spotted a route—probably the only possible one—up the Face, had noted all this. The lowest point of the Face was at about 6,900 feet. The first 800 feet of the climb—although steep and exposed to falling avalanches and stones—looked difficult but not impossibly so. With field glasses it was possible to distinguish some holes in the rock up there—the windows of Eigerwand Station on the Jungfrau Railway, which winds its upward way for miles in the heart of the mountain. About 400 yards to the west there is yet another such gallery window in the Face, the window at the 3.8-kilometre mark from which, during the construction of the line, they used to dump the rubble down the outside of the mountain. Of course, one could take the train to Eigerwand or the window at Kilometer 3.8 and start the climb from there; but one might just as well climb the Eiger by the normal route and only look at the Face. No, the railway inside the mountain was meant for the rest of the world. For the men interested in the climbing of the Face, only one thing counts—a climb, unquestionable in the eyes of sporting and climbing circles, from the lowest point to the 13,041-foot summit of the Eiger.

Sedlmayer and Mehringer studied the Face for days on end, prepared their gear for the climb, lay there for hours on the Alp, looking through field glasses. Above the railway window in the Face a vertical rock step went surging up for more than six hundred feet. Could it be climbed? That could only be decided once you got up there. Above the step gleamed an ice field, the First Ice Field, as it is now called. How high was it? How steep? Very hard to decide those questions from down below.

Above that again a second rock pitch, followed by a huge sheet of snow and ice, which one would have to ascend diagonally to the left. Then there was a third ice field, whose rock and ice outlines had a strange shape, almost that of a huge hawk beating upwards with outspread wings. To reach the beak of this hawk one would have to climb a sharp arête leaning against the perpendicular summit wall at that point—a ridge later christened the "Flatiron" by its climbers. Could all this be climbed? From the ridge one would have to traverse leftwards across that steep, third ice field, from whose farther end an abrupt ramp goes surging diagonally to the left across the Face toward the Mittellegi Ridge. Could it be climbed right up to its top? Could one traverse off it to the right onto the huge snowfield which throws out slender snow and ice runnels in every direction like a huge spider crouching above the gulf 5,000 feet beneath? And finally: could one climb from the "Spider" to the Summit through the cracks and couloirs above?

Nobody who had not tried it himself could give a definite answer.

Max Sedlmayer and Karl Mehringer left their shelter in the herdsman's hut at Alpiglen during the night of August 20–21, 1935. At 2 A.M. on the 21st—a Wednesday—they started to climb the Face. As soon as daylight came, queues gathered around the telescopes at Grindelwald and Kleine Scheidegg. All day long people watched the intrepid Munich pair; the criticism of the know-it-alls died away into silence, quenched by admiration and sheer wonder. The two men were climbing magnificently, in spite of the steepness of the Face, in spite of their heavy rucksacks. One could see clearly as they belayed each other, as they roped their rucksacks up difficult pitches after them. Not an ill-judged step or an unconsidered movement. Even the guides, watching everything that goes on in their own sector of the mountains with a suspicious and critical eye, had to admit that they were watching two master climbers at work.

Following a perfect line of ascent, straight up towards the summit, hardly stopping to rest, Sedlmayer and Mehringer were gaining height steadily, like some perfectly functioning machine, rope length by rope length, almost as if they were giving an exhibition at a climbing school. By dusk, they had disposed of the whole lower section of the Face. At 9,500 feet, 2,600 feet above the point where they started to climb, they bivouacked, well above the windows of Eigerwand Station, whose lights shone down almost like stars.

Thursday dawned. Even the sceptics were now almost convinced that the bid was going to succeed. Indeed, many were striking bets that the pair would reach the summit this very day, early in the afternoon. But the Face is terribly deceptive. It was still a long way to the top, and the route as difficult as it was unexplored. The spectators, avid for sensations, showed their disappointment. Their gladiators are a lazy lot. There is only that ridiculous little belt of rock; how high can it be? They turn down their thumbs, shaking their heads angrily. Why, it can't be much more than sixty feet!

But no. It wasn't sixty feet, it was more than three hundred. Three hundred feet of vertical rock, up which two heavy rucksacks as well as two men had to come. And these two men were climbers, not gladiators. They tackled the cliff, which was of such a degree of severity that it would have graced some tower in the Dolomites more fittingly than this ghastly Face of the Eiger, belaying and safeguarding one another, neither of them aware that they were being, nor in the least desiring to be, watched. Their thoughts were far from the rest of the world, not through any feeling of superiority, but simply because the mountain had taken complete possession of them and because they were constrained to fight with every fiber of their being, with all the awareness of men in mortal danger, to master the difficult pitch. Stones and fragments of ice began to fall from above; so steep is the cliff that they went whistling far out over their heads. After long hours of punishing work they reached the top of the step in the wall. But by then it was afternoon.

It took the whole afternoon to cross that first, steep ice field—the one that looks so ludicrously short from below. Again and again they could be seen covering their heads with their rucksacks or using them to give some kind of cover as they moved on. The mountain artillery was at work.

At dusk they bivouacked at the upper rim of the First Ice Field.

It was impossible to see from below whether they had room to sit; there could be no question of lying down. They looked as if they were glued to the Wall. It was a very long night, but the weather continued to hold.

All through Friday the spectators watched Sedlmayer and Mehringer, who hardly seemed to be gaining height anymore. The traverse from the First to the Second Ice Field seemed to be very difficult, too. The huge size of this field could be gauged by the tiny size of the dots that were men, by the short distances which were nonetheless rope lengths of a hundred feet. Again and again the climbers were forced to halt, clearly to shelter against falling stones and ice fragments. The roping up of the rucksacks took up much time. Slowly, terribly slowly, they gained height, as the hours raced by like minutes; but still they moved upward toward the left-hand rim of the Second Ice Field. Everyone was asking: "Where will they bivouac?" No one was destined to see, for a curtain of mist sank slowly down the mountain face, to sever one world from another.

During the night, the weather broke. A strong gale tore across the ridges, rain pattered down on the valleys and, up above, the wind chased the hailstones along the mountainsides. At first it was just a thunderstorm; but the crashing of the thunder was shot through with the crackle and rattle of falling stones and ice. So great was the din up on the stormbound Face that the peaceful sleep of tourists at Alpiglen and above on the Kleine Scheidegg was disturbed.

This appalling weather lasted the whole of Saturday. To the hammering of the falling stones was added the rushing roar of avalanches. The cold grew intense. The night temperature down at the Kleine Scheidegg fell to 8° below zero. What must it be up there, high on the North Face? Could the two men still be alive? Many continued to hope against hope; but no one could know anything of Sedlmayer and Mehringer's desperate fight for life, for the curtain of cloud never parted for a single instant. Their fifth day on the Face was followed by another murderously cold night.

It was now Sunday, the 25th. Who would have dared to believe that the two men from Munich could still be alive? Then, toward noon, the covering of the mists lifted for a little while. A watcher with his eye glued to the telescope could not believe his eyes. But suddenly there could be no more doubt and he shouts:

"I can see them! They are still alive! They are moving! Climbing!"

And so in fact they were. One could see the tiny dots, moving slowly upwards across the sheer, smooth shield of ice which leads to the "Flatiron." So they were really still alive, after five days on this fearful Face, after four bivouacs in spite of the bitter cold, raging storms, avalanches, everything. They were alive and still moving upward.

Hope flickered again; an unnatural optimism surged up. Surely the lads were going to pull it off in spite of everything. Otherwise, they would certainly have turned back!

But the guides and the climbers, who had spent a life in the mountains, remained silent. One doesn't announce publicly that one has written men off as lost. The guides and the climbers knew well enough why they hadn't turned back; it was because the avalanches and the falling stones had caught them in a terrible trap. In addition there were the fearful difficulties of rocks, now plastered with ice and snow, and at the very best swept by cascading waterfalls. The only hope now was to fight a way out to the top. That is what the guides and the climbers knew. They sensed, too, that Sedlmayer and Mehringer, the first two to attempt the North Face, also knew it all too well and were struggling forward simply because one mustn't give in.

The two men climbed on, toward the arête of the "Flatiron."

The curtain of the mists closed down again, to hide the last act of the first tragedy of the Eiger's North Face from the eyes of men.

A gale, whipping the snowflakes horizontally against the rocks, the thunder of avalanches, the plash of waterfalls, in which the staccato rattle of falling stones mingled shrilly—these were the melody of the Eiger's Face, the funeral organ-voluntary for Max Sedlmayer and Karl Mehringer.

On Tuesday, the 27th, friends of the two men reached the mountain from Munich, among them Sedlmayer's brother and that Gramminger who was later to achieve world renown in the field of mountain rescue. They tried everything to effect a rescue, but there was nothing left to save. There was nothing to be seen or heard from the summit, from the towers of the West Ridge, or from below. No human sound interrupted the grim voice of the mountain. It was impossible to climb up onto the Face from below. To bring aid from above was out of the question.

Sedlmayer's brother and his friends—tried and tested climbers all—stood powerless before the fury of unbridled nature.

Swiss military planes tried to fly along the Face during the following days. They discovered no sign of the missing men. Weeks later, on September 19, when the weather at last improved, came Ernst Udet, Germany's ace airman. This was an extraordinary twist of fate. In 1928 Dr. Arnold Fanck had introduced Udet to mountain flying during the filming of the "White Hell of Piz Palü." Then it had been make-believe; Udet had to fly close to an ice slope to try to locate a party that had lost its way, and to lead the rescue operation. This time it was tragic actuality. Only now there was no question of rescuing anyone, only of finding some bodies.

The outstanding Grindelwald guide and ski runner Fritz Steuri accompanied Udet on his daring venture. Flying to within sixty feet of the cliff, they located one of the missing men—which of them was it?—knee-deep in the snow, still upright, frozen to death at the last bivouac at the point of the "Flatiron," at the upper rim of the Third Ice Field, ever since known as the "Death Bivouac."

Two men had perished on the Face.

But courage had not been quenched, nor the eternal yearning for adventure, nor the longing to press forward into the unknown. It was decided to search for the bodies next year and, if possible, to bring them down.

All the same, it was possible to recognise the mistakes—avoidable mistakes—the first pair had been bound to make just because they were the first. And if the youth of the climbing world, itself brimming over with life, felt they were fulfilling their duty towards the dead men by trying to bring down their mortal remains, their enthusiasm and imagination were at the same time fired by their thoughts of the menacing Face and the way up it.

Youth didn't bother its head about the sharp tongues of the wordy warfare that flared up after the first tragedy on the Eiger's face. It only heard in the mountain's threats a siren call, a challenge to its own courage. It even invented the pious untruth that it was its duty to fulfill the bequest of the men who had died. Perhaps it even believed it. But the real spur was that inexplicable longing for the eternal adventure.

Nineteen thirty-six was to be the year marked by the shattering death of the last survivor of two parties; of the man who tried to come back from the beyond into the world of living men—the year of the tragedy of Toni Kurz.

THE TRAGEDY
OF TONI KURZ

As is often the case with mountain folk, whose features have been carved by wind and storm so that they look older in their youth, younger in their old age, Albert von Allmen's face is ageless. He might be in his middle thirties or his middle fifties.

The mountains have been von Allmen's strict teachers and loyal friends, even if his profession leads him more into than onto the peaks. For Albert is a sector guard on the Jungfrau Railway. He is responsible for everything along the line inside the Eiger, and sees to it that nothing goes wrong in that long tunnelled section; but he is equally interested in everything that goes on outside. True, he doesn't quite understand the young people who are trying to climb the terrific Eiger precipice, but, even if he thinks them a little deranged, he has a soft spot for them. Von Allmen's eyes are kindly eyes. They are surrounded by many little creases which record not only cares and the hard life of the mountains, but also the joy of laughter.

At noon on July 21, 1936, Albert was standing outside the gallery entrance at Kilometer 3.8, after opening the heavy wooden door.

It was a Tuesday. Ever since Saturday, the 18th, there had been four climbers on the Face; two Austrians, Edi Rainer and Willy

Angerer, and two Bavarians, Anderl Hinterstoisser and Toni Kurz. Everyone had fallen for the fresh-faced, clean-limbed Toni Kurz, not only because he was himself a professional guide, but because of his laugh. When Toni laughed, it was as if life itself were laughing. All young men, these; Angerer, the eldest, was twenty-seven, Kurz and Hinterstoisser just twenty-three. They had already climbed almost as high on the Face as Sedlmayer and Mehringer the year before, on their ill-fated attempt from which they did not return. But these four would come back safely; what had been seen of them during the last few days gave solid grounds for hope that this time there would be no disaster.

None of those present had seen such magnificent climbing. True, one of the climbers, apparently Angerer, seemed to have been struck by a stone. That was why the party had been moving so slowly for the last two days, and that was probably why they had decided to turn back. The descent over ice fields and rock cliffs swept by falling stones and avalanches looked ghastly enough; but the four men were moving steadily, if very slowly, downwards toward the safety of the easier ground below, in obvious good heart and without a moment's hesitation. The three fit ones were continually attending to the one who had clearly been hurt. They couldn't be bad, these lads who looked after each other so well. They must be fine fellows, even if a bit crackpot.

Albert von Allmen thought of the Sunday tourists and excursionists, the blasé men and the ladies in high heels who went to the tunnel-window at Eigerwand Station and uttered their "ah's" and "oh's" as they gazed at what seemed to them the terrifying gulfs and immeasurable heights of the Eiger's precipice. It was people like those, hungering for sensation, who were now crowding round the telescopes at Grindelwald and Kleine Scheidegg. And then, too, there were the pronunciamentos of the know-it-alls, busy weighing up the chances of another catastrophe or of the safe return of four living men to the valley.

They *must* get back safely, thought Albert. His sympathy lay with youth, youth generally, but particularly these four youngsters on the Face. It would be a good idea to take a look at them and hear for himself how they were getting on. Allmen pushed back the bolts of the heavy wooden doors and stepped out into the open, as he had done a hundred times before. He was used to the grim aspect of the Face; but that day, perhaps because there were people on it, it seemed particularly horrific. A layer of glassy ice overlaid the rock; here and there a stone came clattering down; many of those lethal bullets went humming menacingly down for thousands of feet quite clear of the Face. Then, too, there was the hissing of snow avalanches as they slid down, whole cascades of snow and ice. The very thought that there were living men somewhere up in that vertical hell was oppressive. Could they still be alive?

Von Allmen shouted, listened, shouted again.

Then the answer reached him. A cheery, gay answer. The voices of four young people shouting, yodelling. Albert couldn't see them, but, judging by the sound, they couldn't be more than three or four hundred feet above him. It seemed incredible to him that anyone could climb down those icy, perpendicular or even overhanging rocks, continually swept by falling stones; but these crazy kids had so often shown how possible it is to climb impossible things. And, above all, there was that cheery shout coming down from above:

"We're climbing straight down. All's well!"

All well with all of them. The sector guard's heart beat faster for joy.

"I'll brew you some hot tea," he shouted back.

Smiling with pleasure, Albert von Allmen went back through the gallery door to his shelter inside the mountain and put a huge kettle on for tea. He could already see, in his mind's eye, the arrival of the four lads, exhausted, injured perhaps by stones, maybe seriously frostbitten, but alive and happy. He would meet them with his steaming tea. There was no better drink than hot tea for frostbitten, exhausted men. He was slightly cross at the time it was taking the water to start bubbling; the lads would be here in a minute or two.

But the lads didn't come in a minute or two.

Long after the tea was ready, they hadn't come. Albert set the golden-brown drink on a low flame, just enough to keep it hot without getting stewed.

Still the lads didn't come; and the sector guard, this man whose age it was impossible to guess, had time for second thoughts. . . .

In truth, one could not hold it against a public avid for sensation that it should be throning inquisitively about the telescopes. These climbs on the Eiger's Face had been worked up into a publicity feature. The press and the radio had taken charge of the "Eiger Drama." Some of the reports were sound enough, informed by the heart and mind of true mountain folk behind them; others displayed a woeful lack of knowledge of the subject.

Nineteen thirty-six had started badly. The first to arrive had been the Munich pair, Albert Herbst and Hans Teufel, who were already at Kleine Scheidegg before the end of May. Had they come to look for last year's victims? The thought may have been there, but their secret aim was certainly the ascent of the Face. They were splendid climbers, to be sure, but perhaps lacking in that calm and relaxation that is the hallmark of the accomplished master climber.

They did not come to grief on the Eiger's Face. They knew that to start up that gigantic wall so early in the year, in almost wintry conditions, would be nothing short of suicide; but the waiting about became unbearable. According to the calendar it was summer by now, but storms and snow didn't seem to mind about that. So Teufel and Herbst decided as part of their training to climb the as yet unclimbed North Face of the Schneehorn. This was purely an ice and snow slope. Conditions were far from favorable. The heavy falls of new snow had as yet failed to cohere firmly with the old snow beneath. In spite of this, the pair tackled the ice slope on July 1 and succeeded in reaching the summit cornice, beneath which they were forced to bivouac. They suffered no harm from their night in the open and, next morning, reached and traversed the summit. Everything seemed to be going well; but on the descent, while they were crossing a snow slope, an avalanche broke away, carrying them with it for some six hundred feet. Teufel struck the lip of a crevasse, breaking his neck. Herbst got away with his life.

That was a bad enough beginning. . . .

A few days later two Austrians, Angerer and Rainer, arrived and put up a tent near the Scheidegg, both proven climbers, especially good on rock. As such, they were particularly outstanding at route-finding on vertical cliffs. They remembered how difficult the great rock step below the First Ice Field had proved, and how Sedlmayer and Mehringer had taken it out of themselves on it. They felt sure there must be a direct route over to the right—up what later came to be known as the "First Pillar" and the "Shattered Pillar"—toward the smooth, perpendicular, unclimbable wall of the Rote Fluh (the Red Crag, a long-established feature of the Eiger's base). Below it, there must be some means of traversing across to the First Ice Field. Would such a traverse be possible?

On Monday, July 6, Angerer and Rainer started up the Face by their newly conceived route.

What did the wall look like at that particular moment?

The late Othmar Gurtner, the great Swiss climber and well-known writer on Alpine matters, wrote the following on July 8 in a Zurich paper, *Sport*.

An unusually changeable period of weather has hampered the progress of glaciation during the last few weeks. Heavy falls of snow and cold, raw days have preserved powder-snow down as far as 8,000 feet. . . . If one examines the North Face of the Eiger thoroughly for its conditions, one is led to the fol-lowing possibly deceptive conclusion: on account of the heavy covering of snow the lower parts of the Face, and also the two great shields of ice above Eigerwand Station, invite climbing in the cold hours of early morning, when the snow ruined by the evening sunshine has become crusty again. It is possible to kick safe steps without use of the axe and to move forward very quickly in such snow; at the same time it lacks solid glaciation, i.e. firm consolidation with the old snow beneath. Because of the slight amount of sun on the Eiger's North Face it behaves like typical winter snow. Higher up on the Face and especially on the almost vertical summit structure itself, the powder snow is plastered on the rocks like sweepings from a broom. And, in between, there is the glitter of water ice . . . this ice has its origin in the melting water which runs down from the mighty snow-roof of the mountain. So long as there is water ice hanging from the summit structure, the whole Face is seriously threatened by falls of ice. Then one can actually see whole torrents coming down and craters made by them very closely situated in the snow. The Face is at the moment in the terrifying conditions that persist between winter and summer. . . .

As we write this report, the Rainer–Angerer rope is moving "according to plan" up the death-dealing wall on whose actual conditions we have reported above. . . .

The warning expressed in that report was written by a very great expert.

But Angerer and Rainer were no suicide squad; they, too, were well aware of the great danger, transcending all human strength and courage. They succeeded in opening a new route up the lower part of the Face to just below the Rote Fluh, where they bivouacked; next morning, July 7, they climbed down again, and reached their tent wet through and tired, but safe and sound. "We shall go up again," they said, "as soon as conditions improve."

The papers scented a coming sensation. Now that climbing attempts had been focused in the limelight of public interest, their readers had a right to be kept informed in detail about proceedings on the Face of the Eiger. The reports were almost like communiqués of the General Staff during a war, even down to the constantly repeated titles: "The battle with the Eiger Wall," "The Acrobatic Contest on the Eiger's Face," "New Life on the Face," "Lull in the Eiger Battle," "The all-out Investment," "First Assault Repulsed." And sometimes they even went to the length of puns, such as *Mordwand* for *Nordwand*.[1]

The ill fortune of Herbst and Teufel appeared in many papers under the common headline of "Accidents and Crimes." Many sarcastic comments appeared on the subject of "extreme" climbers and the public, avid for a show. But was it really surprising that people who knew nothing of mountains should make pilgrimages in their thousands to savor a shiver of horror while standing in perfect safety at the eyepiece of a telescope? The Eiger's Face had become a magnificent natural stage.

The newspapers of July 7 and 8 certainly carried widespread expressions of delight at the safe return of Rainer and Angerer. All the same, every word and movement of the two men was recorded, and interpreted however it suited best (for gladiators must needs bow to the wishes of their public); yet the climbers themselves wanted only to be left in peace and, finding they were not, defended themselves after their own fashion. Many high-sounding phrases were uttered and accorded more weight than is normally given to the pronouncements of V.I.P.s. "We are having another go!" they said. What presumption, after the grim bivouac, which many papers had described as a life-and-death battle, while Angerer and Rainer laugh it off scornfully with: "Grim? No, only just a trifle wet!"

And since these were no men of worldly affairs, but just ordinary lads, who did not weigh every word in the balance, and certainly

---

[1] "Murder Face" for "North Face" — Translator's note.

didn't suspect that under the tension of the moment it would be given undue emphasis or be wrongly reported, they gave this answer to the barrage of questions as to why they came here bent on such a venture: "We have to climb your Wall for you, if you won't do it yourselves!" Or, still more in keeping with their pathetic youthfulness and the age in which they lived: "We must have the Wall or it must have us!"

That sparked off a new storm.

In this context, an article in the *Berner Bund*, which read: "Everyone who has come to know these charming, good-natured lads heartily wishes them a successful outcome to their venture," did much to pour balm on wounds.

Yet neither ridicule nor solemnity could influence events. On Saturday, July 18, 1936, the two ropes Angerer–Rainer and Hinterstoisser–Kurz started up the Face. At first they moved independently; at the level of the bivouac previously occupied by the two Austrians they roped up as a foursome. The rope joining them was no longer a dead length of hemp for them but, as it were, a living artery, seeming to say: "for better or for worse, we belong together." This was an uncommonly daring but in no sense featherbrained undertaking.

They climbed the exceptionally severe crack below the Rote Fluh successfully. Above it, Andreas Hinterstoisser was the first to achieve the traverse to the First Ice Field, climbing in textbook fashion with the help of the rope. This technique of the "rope traverse" had already been discovered and developed before the First World War by that master of rock climbing, Hans Dülfer, during his first ascents of the East Face of the Fleischbank and the West Wall of the Totenkirchl in the Kaisergebirge. In this way Dülfer showed how to link climbable pitches by the use of a diagonal "lift" from the rope on unclimbable ones. The current joke about the Dülfer technique ran: "You go as long as it goes, and when it doesn't go anymore, you just do a traverse and go on."

It was this kind of traverse which Hinterstoisser did on the Eiger Face. He had discovered the key to the climb. When they had all completed the traverse, he retrieved the traversing rope. In doing so he threw away the key. If it came to a retreat, the door to the way back was now locked behind them . . . but who was thinking of a retreat?

Many were watching the four men through field glasses. And the spectators forgot their criticisms in admiration, even astonishment, at the speed and assurance with which the two ropes crossed the First Ice Field, climbed up beyond it and reached the barrier between it and the second—the greater—ice slope. Since the Sedlmayer-Mehringer attempt, everyone knew how difficult those rocks must be.

But what had happened? Suddenly the second pair, Rainer and Angerer, were seen to be following the leaders slowly and hesitantly. Hinterstoisser and Kurz were already moving up to the rocks above the Rote Fluh. The other two remained motionless for a long time. Then it could be seen that one was supporting the other. Had there been an accident?

It will never be known exactly what happened, but it seems almost certain that Angerer was struck by a stone and Rainer was busy tending him. Presently Hinterstoisser and Kurz could be seen letting a rope down from their stance, which was plainly safe from bombardment by stones. Their joint efforts succeeded in bringing Angerer up to them. Then Rainer followed quickly, without making use of the emergency rope.

The tiny nest in the rocks above the Rote Fluh thus became the first bivouac place for this party of four. They had reached an incredibly high level on their first day—more than halfway up the Face.

On the morning of Sunday, the 19th, there were more crowds around the telescopes. They saw the four men leave the bivouac at about seven o'clock. And how was the injured man? Obviously better, for instead of retreating, they were climbing on, across the huge slope of the Second Ice Field. All the same, they were moving more slowly than on the first day. Were they all tired, then, or was it all because of the injured man? Why didn't they turn back?

One fact stands out for certain; the four men were a united, indissoluble party. Kurz and Hinterstoisser, climbing in the lead again, never thought of leaving Rainer behind with the injured man. The Austrians didn't want to rob the other two of their chance of reaching the top. And so they all stayed together, though the leaders had frequently to wait for quite a time.

The weather was neither fine nor definitely bad. In the context of the Eiger, conditions were bearable. By the end of this Sunday the party had reached the Third Ice Field; a little below the bivouac which had proved fatal to Sedlmayer and Mehringer, the four men made ready to spend their second night in the open. It had been a good day's work, but they had not gained enough height to make sure of a successful push forward to the top on the following day. What kind of a night would it be? In what condition is Angerer and how are the other three? The spectators down in the valley don't know any of the answers. They withdraw for the night, rubbernecks, reporters, guides, and mountaineers. Tomorrow will show. . . .

The next day was Monday, July 20. Once again no movement could be seen in the bivouac till seven o'clock. It was a tiny place, with hardly room to sit down. Once again Kurz and Hinterstoisser began to climb the steep ice slope leading to the "Death Bivouac." After about half an hour they stopped. The others were not following them. Nobody knows what the four men said to each other. Whatever it was, the decision taken was crucial and bitter for the leaders, a matter of life and death for the other two. It was clear that Angerer was no longer in a condition to climb any farther.

All of a sudden the Hinterstoisser party could be seen climbing down to the bivouac, where they remained for some time; then they all began the descent together. A human being was more important than the mere ascent of a mountain face. Perhaps the united strength of the whole party would succeed in bringing the injured man down?

They crossed the great slope of the Second Ice Field comparatively quickly; but the descent of the rock step, on the doubled rope, to the First took several hours to accomplish. Once again the watchers were amazed at the care and assurance with which the ropes were handled. But night fell just as the men reached the lower ice field. Close to where Sedlmayer and Mehringer's second bivouac had been, they camped for their third night on the Face. There could not be a stitch of dry clothing on their bodies and this third bivouac must needs sap their strength; yet three must now have enough strength for the fourth. They had only managed to come down about 1,000 feet during the whole day; fully another 3,000 of the Face still gaped below them. Still, once the Traverse and the Difficult Crack were behind them, the safety of the valley would not be so far away. They knew that part of the Wall from having climbed down it once already.

Yes, but that Traverse. . . .

It would be the crux of this new day, Tuesday, July 21. All four seemed to have stood the bivouac quite well, for they came down the ice slope to the start of the Traverse at a good pace; but at that point those watching could suddenly only see three men at work. Had one of them fallen off?

Mists wreathed about the Face, the wind rose, the rattle of falling stones grew sharper, avalanches of powder snow swept the track of yesterday's descent. The worst danger from falling stones would be over as soon as the four men were safely across the Traverse. But where had the fourth got to?

When the cloud curtain parted again, the men at the telescopes could see all four climbers again, but Angerer, apparently *hors de combat*, was taking no part in the attempts to master the Traverse. One man seemed to be taking the lead in these efforts—surely it must be Hinterstoisser, the man who first dealt with this key point on the way up. But now there is no traversing rope fixed to the rock. And the rock doesn't seem to be climbable without artificial aids.

The weather was worsening; it had in fact already broken. The water which had all along been pouring down the rocks must have hardened into ice. All the experts with field glasses could sense the fearsome tragedy to come. Retreat was cut off; nobody could move over the glassy film overlying the rock, not even an Andreas Hinterstoisser. The precious hours of the entire morning were consumed by vain, frustrating, incredibly exhausting, and dangerous attempts. And then came the last desperate decision: to climb straight down the vertical rock face, some 600 or 700 feet high, which at some points bulges far out even beyond the vertical.

The only way led through the line of fire from stones and avalanches. Sedlmayer and Mehringer had taken a whole day to climb that pitch, and that in fine weather on dry rock. Now all hell had broken loose on the mountain. But it was the only chance.

They began to get the ropes ready for the descent through thin air.

It was at this moment that they heard Albert von Allmen's shouts coming up from below.

Someone shouting, so close at hand? Then things could not go wrong! A man's voice, giving strength and courage and the certainty that the bridge back to the living world was still there. And in spite of the dangers and their awareness of the seriousness of their situation, they all joined in yodelling back: "All's well!" Not a single cry for help, not even an admission of their terrifying peril.

All well. . . .

Albert von Allmen was getting cross. How long was he expected to keep their tea warm? Presently his irritation changed to apprehension. Two whole hours had gone by since he spoke to the climbers, and still no movement at the entrance to the gallery. Could they have climbed down past it? Could they have missed the ledge, which runs across to the window?

The sector guard went back to the door. The Face was looking grim and ghastly now; visibility was very restricted; mists were steaming up everywhere. Stones and avalanches were singing their pitiless song. Albert shouted.

And back came an answer.

This time no cheery yodel, but a shocking answer coming now from one man, the last lone survivor, crying for help. . . . Toni Kurz.

The voice of a brave, unbelievably tough, young guide, cradled in Bavaria in the shadow of the Watzmann; a man who had rescued many in distress on the mountains, but who had never yet shouted for help. But now he was shouting, shouting desperately for his very life.

"Help! Help! The others are all dead. I am the only one alive. Help!"

The wind, the avalanches, and the whistling stones forbade a more exact exchange of information. In any case, Albert von Allmen by himself could bring no aid. He shouted, "We'll be coming," and hurried back into the gallery to telephone.

Eigergletscher Station, down below, answered his call.

"Allmen speaking. There's been a fearful disaster on the Face. There's only one survivor. We must fetch him in. Have you any guides with you?"

Yes, there were guides down there—Hans Schlunegger, with Christian and Adolf Rubi, all from Wengen. Yes, they would come up, of their own accord, even in face of instructions. It was a case of humanity triumphing over the regulations.

For Bohren, the chief guide of Grindelwald, in his concern for the guides under him, had issued a communication to the Guides' Commission in Berne, and to the Central Committee of the Swiss Alpine Club, which had also been repeated in the *Grindelwald Echo*.

One cannot help regarding the contemplated climbing attempts on the North Face of the Eiger with serious misgivings. They are a plain indication of the great change which has taken place in the conception of the sport of mountaineering. We must accept that the visitors who take part in such attempts are aware of the dangers they are themselves risking; but no one can expect the dispatch of guides, in unfavourable conditions, on a rescue operation, in case of any further accidents on the Eiger's North Face. . . . We should find it impossible to force our guides to take a compulsory part in the kind of acrobatics which others are undertaking voluntarily.

That was the chief guide's stated position. Nobody could have held it against the guides at Eigergletscher Station if they had refused to take a single step onto the Face when they heard of the accident. But there was one man still alive. They were all determined to rescue him, to snatch him, if possible, from the clutches of that fatal wall.

The railway provided a train, which immediately took them to the gallery window at Kilometre 3.8; through it they stepped onto the Face, glistening under its coat of ice. Clouds of snow dust blew into their faces, as they quietly traversed diagonally upwards on the slippery, treacherous ledges, till they reached a point about 300 feet below where Toni Kurz was hanging from the rope in a sling.

There was mixed despair and relief in his voice—still astonishingly strong—as he heard his rescuers and answered them.

"I'm the only one alive. Hinterstoisser came off and fell the whole way down. The rope pulled Rainer up against a snap link. He froze to death there. And Angerer's dead, too, hanging below me, strangled by the rope when he fell. . . ."

"All right, pal. We've come to help you."

"I know," shouted Toni. "But you've got to come from above, to the right, up through the crack where we left some pitons on the way up. Then you could reach me by three descents on the doubled rope."

"That's impossible, pal. Nobody could climb it with this ice about."

"You can't rescue me from below," Kurz shouted back.

Day was drawing to its close. The guides would have to hurry if they were to get back safely to the gallery window before dark. They shouted up the wall: "Can you stick it for one more night, pal?"

"No! No! No!"

The words cut the guides to the quick. They were never to forget them. But any aid was out of the question in the dark, on this Face, in this weather.

"Stick it, pal!" they shouted. "We'll be back first thing in the morning!"

They could hear Toni's shouts for a long time, as they climbed down.

The young Berchtesgaden guide must have despaired of seeing the night through. But life had a strong hold on him; in spite of the gale, the volleys of stones, the fearsome cold, he survived the night, swinging backwards and forwards in his rope sling. It was so cold that the water thawed by the warmth of his body froze again immediately. Icicles eight inches long formed on the points of the crampons strapped to his boots. Toni lost the mitten from his left hand; his fingers, his hand, then his arm, froze into shapeless immovable lumps. But when dawn came, life was still awake in his agonised body. His voice, too, was strong and clear, when the guides got in touch with him again.

Arnold Glatthard had by now joined Schlunegger and the Rubi brothers. The four guides together were ready to fight this merciless wall for the life of their young colleague from Bavaria. The rocks were covered with an appalling glaze of ice. It seemed almost impossible to climb at all. And there was Toni pleading again: "You can only rescue me from above. You must climb the crack. . . ."

It was impossible. Even Kurz and Hinterstoisser in their full and unimpaired strength could not have climbed the crack in such conditions. It was a pitch that even in fine weather would have seriously tested these four men, first-class guides, brought up in a great tradition, master climbers all, but little versed in the technique of modern, artificial climbing. It would have called for just that kind of "acrobatics" against which chief guide Bohren had taken such a strong stand.

However, the four guides succeeded in reaching a point only about 130 feet below where Toni Kurz was hanging on the rope. So far did the overhang beetle out over the abyss that they could no longer see him from there. If Kurz had another rope on which to rope himself down, he would be saved. But how to get one to him? Attempts with rockets failed. The rope went shooting past Kurz, far out from the Face. There was only one thing left.

"Can you let a line down," they asked him, "so that we can attach a rope, rock pitons and anything else you need?"

"I have no line," came the reply.

"Climb down as far as you can, then, and cut away Angerer's body. Then climb up again and cut the rope above you. Then untwist the strands of the piece of rope you have gained, join them, and let the resulting line down."

The answer was a groan: "I'll try."

A little while later they heard the strokes of an axe. It seemed incredible that Kurz could hold on with one frozen hand and swing the axe with the other. Yet he managed to cut the rope away; only, Angerer's body didn't fall, for it was frozen solid to the rock. Almost in a trance, answering the last dictates of the will to live, Kurz climbed up again, cut away the rope there. The maneuver had won him twenty-five feet of rope, frozen stiff. And then began the unbelievable work of untwisting the strands. Every climber knows how difficult that is, even on firm ground, with two sound hands. But Toni Kurz was suspended between heaven and earth, on an ice-glazed cliff, threatened by falling stones, sometimes swept by snowslides. He worked with one hand and his teeth . . . for five hours. . . .

A great avalanche fell, narrowly missing the guides. A huge block whizzed close by Schlunegger's head. And then a body came hurtling past. Toni's? No it wasn't Toni's, but Angerer's, freed from the imprisoning ice. Those were hours of agony for Toni, fighting for his life, agonising too for the guides, who could do nothing to help, and could only wait for the moment when Kurz might still achieve the incredible.

Presently the fabricated line came swinging down to the rescue party. They fastened a rope to it, with pitons, snap links, a hammer. Slowly those objects disappeared from the view of the guides. Toni Kurz's strength was ebbing fast; he could hardly draw up the line, but somehow he managed it. Even now the rope wasn't long enough. The guides attached a second to it. The knot where the two ropes were spliced swung visible but unreachable out there under the great overhang.

Another hour passed. Then, at last, Toni Kurz was able to start roping down, sitting in a sling attached to the rope by a snap link. Inch by inch he worked his way downwards. Thirty, forty, fifty feet down . . . a hundred feet, a hundred and twenty. Now his legs could be seen dangling below the overhang.

At that moment the junction knot jammed in the snap link of the sling in which Toni was sitting as he roped down. The knot was too thick and Toni could not force it through the link. They could hear him groaning.

"Try, lad, try!" the frustrated rescuers cried to encourage the exhausted man. Toni, mumbling to himself, made one more effort with all his remaining strength, but he had little left; his incredible efforts had used it almost all up. His will to live had been keyed to the extreme so long as he was active; now, the downward journey in the safety of the rope sling had eased the tension. He was nearing his rescuers now; now the battle was nearly over, now there were others close at hand to help. . . .

And now this knot . . . just a single knot . . . but it won't go through. . . . "Just one more try, pal. It'll go!"

There was a note of desperation in the guides' appeal. One last revolt against fate; one last call on the last reserves of strength against this last and only obstacle. Toni bent forwards, trying to use his teeth just once more. His frozen left arm with its useless hand stuck out still and helpless from his body. His last reserves were gone.

Toni mumbled unintelligibly, his handsome young face dyed purple with frostbite and exhaustion, his lips just moving. Was he still trying to say something, or had his spirit already passed over to the beyond?

Then he spoke again, quite clearly. "I'm finished," he said.

His body tipped forward. The sling, almost within reaching distance of the rescuing guides, hung swinging gently far out over the gulf. The man sitting in it was dead.

It will never be known exactly how the whole disaster built up or what precisely happened while sector guard and humanitarian Albert von Allmen was getting his tea ready. The very fact that Andreas Hinterstoisser was off the rope at the moment of his fall leads to the conclusion that he—probably the best technician of the four—was trying to find a specially safe place for pitons to secure the descent on the rope. It was impossible to establish from Toni Kurz's fragmentary and incoherent sentences whether Hinterstoisser was hit by a stone, or whether they all fell owing to a fall of stone, or whether the others were trying to catch Andreas as he fell and so were all pulled off their holds. The guide from Berchtesgaden needed all his strength for his own preservation, nor could he spare thoughts or words for reports. It is quite clear that all three were on the same rope, and that it ran through a snap link attached to a piton. The fall jammed Rainer against the piton so that he could not move. Tatters of bandage found on Angerer's skull, when his body was recovered much later, proved that he had been the injured member of the party, seen on the Face by those who watched.

It was one of the grimmest tricks of fate which left Toni Kurz uninjured at the outset, so that he was forced to endure his agony to its uttermost end. He was like some messenger from the beyond, finding his way back to earth simply because he loved life so well.

The tragedy of Sedlmayer and Mehringer had been enacted behind the curtains of the mountain mists. Men could only guess at it. But Toni Kurz ended his brave and vigorous life before the eyes of his rescuers. It was this that made the tragedy of 1936 so impressive and so shattering that it will never be forgotten.

Arnold Glatthard, that reserved and silent guide, said: "It was the saddest moment of my life."

Unfortunately, not everybody showed that respect and reserve which death—and particularly death in such a manner—commands.

One newspaper wrote of Toni Kurz's death: "Kurz spent his fourth night complaining. When the search for notoriety and obstinate willpower conspire to bring a man to grief, one cannot really register regret. . . ."

Another, dated July 24, 1936, produced the following remarkable description of the men who climb the Eiger's Face and the motives that impel them:

Perhaps these young men have nothing more to lose . . . what is to become of a generation to which Society offers no social existence and which has only one thing left to look to, a single day's glory, the swiftly tarnishing highlight of a single hour? To be a bit of a hero, a bit of a soldier, sportsman or record-breaker, a gladiator, victorious one day, defeated the next. . . . The four recent victims of the Eiger's North Face were poor creatures. When some kindly folk in Grindelwald invited them to dinner, they tucked in to the proffered meal like true warriors; afterward, they said they hadn't had such a good meal for three years. When asked what was the purpose of their risky venture, they replied that its main object was to improve their positions. They believed that such an exceptional feat would bring them honor and glory, and make people take notice of them. . . .

Another article bearing the same date and headlined "Climbing under Orders" gives the matter a bizarre twist in the opposite direction.

Kleine Scheidegg, July 24. A report is current here that the four climbers had been ordered to make the ascent. It has been said that they were very excited on Friday evening; that they would never have taken such a grave risk as free agents. Perhaps their records will reveal this or that secret which did not pass their lips, now numbed and frozen into silence.

This was, of course, the direct reverse of the truth. Kurz and Hinterstoisser were at this time on the strength of the Mountain Ranger (Jäger) Regiment No. 100 and on leave from Bad Reichenhall. When their commanding officer Colonel R. Konrad, who had experience of climbing in the Bernese Oberland, learned of their plans he telephoned Grindelwald and, in the strictest terms, vetoed any attempt on the Eiger. That was on the Friday evening. The message reached the tents on the Kleine Scheidegg too late. Kurz and Hinterstoisser had started up the Face a few hours earlier. . . .

In the context of previous tragedies on the Eiger's North Face a great many things were invented and written up at various desks, which served to poison the atmosphere and made mutual understanding more difficult. Genuine mountaineers in Germany, Austria, or Switzerland wrote on common lines, irrespective of whether they were for or against "Operation Eigerwand." They used the language of understanding, humanity, and respect for the dead. While various papers were trying to drive a permanent wedge between German climbers and Swiss guides, Gunther Langes was writing in *Bergsteiger*, the official organ of the German and Austrian Alpine Club: "I know the Swiss guides, who have shown typical mountaineering qualities in such an outstanding manner. I spent several weeks last year with Arnold Glatthard on difficult rock; a man carved from the best and hardest wood, with enough pluck for three. The Eigerwand guides deserve the recognition and gratitude of all climbers for what they did!" And as a postscript, Gunther Langes published a letter from Glatthard, which summarised the judgment of all the guides on the four men who died on the Face in 1936: "I watched them climbing and can only praise the lads. The North Face dealt harshly with our comrades. . . ."

It is safe to say that guides, of whatever nationality, are fine men. It is nothing against them that they often exhibit a rugged exterior and don't speak in the smooth phraseology of diplomats.

On the flyleaf of his guide's record book Toni Kurz, when only nineteen, had written a little poem; the fruit of his fine, serious nature. It told of his love for the mountains, of the sober approach to every climb, and of the sacred obligation—

never to give one's life away to death.

To round off my report on the tragedy of 1936 I propose to quote the words of Sir Arnold Lunn, an enemy of unhealthy pathos and all forms of false heroics. This is what he wrote about Toni Kurz's death in his book *A Century of Mountaineering*.[1]

His valiant heart had resisted the terrors of storm and solitude and misery such as mountaineers have seldom been called on to endure. He had hung in his rope sling buffeted by the storm, but determined not to surrender. And he did not surrender. He died. In the annals of mountaineering there is no record of a more heroic endurance.

---

[1]Arnold Lunn, *A Century of Mountaineering* (London: George Allen and Unwin Ltd., 1957).

1937:

ON THE

EIGER

The Eiger's Face is still covered in sheets of snow. It is snowing as if here were winter's last defence bastion, against which spring and summer are launching their attacks in vain. But the new Eiger teams have already moved into the huts and inns of Alpiglen and the Kleine Scheidegg. Tents are springing up on the Alp. The German dialects of Bavarians and Austrians, to a lesser degree Italian and *Schwyzerdütch*, are to be heard everywhere.

Samuel Brawand, himself once a guide, later a lecturer and now a member of parliament, has raised his warning voice, a voice well respected among mountaineers. Brawand has special knowledge of the Eiger, for in 1921 he and his brother guides Fritz Amatter and Fritz Steuri led the young Japanese climber Yuko Maki up the Mittellegi Ridge to achieve the first ascent of that exacting route.

In an interview given to the *Neue Zürcher Zeitung*, Brawand said:

It is a fact that several ropes are again interested in attempts on the North Face of the Eiger. Here in Grindelwald, we have so far heard of four parties.

Your paper has asked me to state the position of the Rescue

Service in the event of a new attempt on the Face. To date, neither the local corps of guides nor the Section of the Swiss Alpine Club have made a serious pronouncement on the subject. In my view it is unnecessary to take any decisions. Even if the corps of guides were to decide not to fetch down the body of anyone who started to climb the Face—which the administration in Berne might empower them to do—what would be achieved by such a ruling? Would it act as a deterrent? I do not believe it would. To the men who climb the Face of the Eiger it is all one whether their bodies are left up there or brought down. It would be ludicrous indeed to threaten not to fetch down even those in distress on the Face. If people up there shout for help and the guides are in a position to bring them that help, then of course they will always do so. The only time when they won't do it is when the dangers are so great as to make it obvious that no rescue attempt could stand a possible chance of success.

Last autumn, the administration in Berne issued a ban on all climbing on the North Face. It has since been withdrawn, and rightly so. To start with, it could never be effective because the fine imposed by the law is so small; and, in the second place, you cannot really put a veto on any given method of committing suicide.

In this fight against "North Face Fever" the Press has a very important duty. It should set its face against pandering to the public's insatiable greed for sensation. Unfortunately, pictures have already been published that border on the irreverent. Finally, it should be remembered that there are more important tasks in this world than the ascent of the Eiger's North Face. I have myself taken part in first ascents and know how uncommonly satisfying such successes are; but one knows, too, that they are only steps in human development. . . .

These are good, sensible words, well spoken by Herr Brawand. They bridge the gap between different kinds of men; they warn without condemning. But even this experienced Alpine climber regards an attempt to climb the North Face as a complicated and expensive form of suicide. He speaks of the great sense of well-being brought by a successful first ascent; but he keeps silence about the impalpable and imponderable mainspring that moves men to accomplish the extraordinary. Perhaps his diagnosis of "North Face Fever" is not so far out. Brawand's object, like that of any scientific, traditional doctor, is to keep the fever down. But surely the fever is itself a sign that a body is fighting for its own health. Let us stick to the unpleasant comparison. The Eiger bacillus has arrived and has attacked the human race. It is—as we have premised from the very start—the bacillus of the everlasting adventure, that lure that always assails the younger generation, and endows the young with a terrifying impetus and strength.

The fever will, in the end, master the bacillus; but by that time the North Face of the Eiger will have lost its claim to inaccessibility. The gigantic precipice will have lost none of its beauty, its might or its perilous nature, for it is so fashioned that every new party which comes to grips with it has to put forward the very best of which men on a mountain are capable. In this sense every climb of the North Face will always be a first ascent. But the fever will have subsided and nobody will talk of a bacillus anymore. The conception of the Eiger's North Face will by then have become part of man's spiritual heritage. Note carefully: his spiritual heritage. One cannot defeat or conquer mountains; one can only climb them. "Defeat" and "conquest" have already become hackneyed expressions, senselessly repeated hundreds of times, false and arrogant descriptions of mountaineering successes. In any case, one cannot "defeat" one of nature's superb defences such as the Eiger's Face; it sounds as if one had built a cable ropeway from Alpiglen to the summit of the Eiger. But even that would not be a "defeat"; it would simply be the annihilation of the North Face, its eradication from the climber's vocabulary.

These reflections are not meant in any way as criticisms designed to belittle that excellent man Samuel Brawand. On the contrary. He held out a hand in reconciliation; his views already foreshadowed the coming turn of events, when good sense and understanding would triumph over mere passion. For alongside the "North Face Fever" there has burned an "Anti-Eiger Fever" which disrupted peace and quiet just as much as did those plucky, unaffected boys who failed to return from the Face. The argument was no longer one of principle; it had become one of men and of human life. . . .

Seen from this angle of a spiritual change, 1937 was a remarkably interesting year, even if it did not bring final success.

To start with, there was the decree about the North Face that the Government in Berne issued at the beginning of July:

The following is supplementary to Paragraph 25 of the Regulations for Guides and Porters in the Canton of Berne issued on July 30, 1914.

1. It is in the discretion of the Chiefs of the Rescue Section to undertake rescue attempts following accidents on the North Face of the Eiger.

2. Parties intending to climb the North Face must be duly warned by the Rescue stations and by the Guides before they start on the ascent. In particular their attention must be drawn to the fact that, in the event of an accident, no rescue operations will be laid on. [Author's comment: not only Herr Brawand's words already quoted, but the actual assistance offered and given, were to prove that, in spite of all pronouncements, guides would continue to serve the cause of humanity by doing any- and everything in their power to save climbers in peril of their lives.]

3. The Governor of Interlaken is to promulgate this deci-

sion to the Chief Guides of the District, for communication to the Rescue-stations and the Guides.

In the name of the Judiciary, President: Jos. County Clerk:

I. V. Hubert

During these early days of July 1937 there were already several parties ready to brave the ascent or at least an attempt on it. Two very good climbers from the Grisons had already gone away because of the bad conditions. An Italian party was still there, consisting of Giuseppe Piravano, heralded as one of Italy's best ice men, and Bruno Detassis, the best-known climber in the savage Brenta Dolomites, who came from Trento. Both men were professional guides. Another party training in the neighbourhood was that of Wollenweber, Zimmermann, and Lohner, of whom the first two had been among those active on the Face the year before. According to a report in the *Neue Zürcher Zeitung*, "two Munich men have also pitched their tent near Alpiglen, a little to one side and without much fuss. So far they have refused to give their names." Actually the two "men from Munich" came from Bayrisch-Zell. One of them was no less a personality than Andreas Heckmair, also a guide by profession.

It was a considerable gathering, linked only by a common target. Each party worked on its own, keeping its own counsel, following its own plans and methods of training.

There was naturally an unspoken rivalry between the separate parties, an element of personal and national competition—though this played quite an important part in the efforts to climb the North Face. The Italians, even Italian guides, have always been accused of an unusual degree of chauvinism, but it should never be forgotten that Italy is a young nation with a burning love of glory and blazing sense of patriotism, which occasionally burst her bounds. Her mountaineering activities began mainly in the years and decades during which her people were achieving political unity in a single State, during the second half of the last century. The dramatic race on the

Matterhorn was not only regarded as a contest between Whymper and Carrel, but as an event of national importance. The question was really—"Il Cervino" or "das Matterhorn"? And Carrel, ex-trooper of the Bersaglieri, was determined to climb the Cervino from Breuil in his native valley, with and for his own countrymen. Less thought was given to the mountain than to the flag on its summit. Let us recall Whymper's moment of triumph when he beat the Italians to the summit and unfurled his flag—the sweat-soaked shirt of Michel Croz, his Chamonix guide; remembering how the victorious Englishman begged Croz "for heaven's sake" to help him roll stones down the Tyndall Arête, so that Carrel and his Italians climbing up it might learn for certain that they were too late, that they had been defeated in the race. . . .

What about such rivalries and races to achieve first ascents? They are as old as mountaineering itself. Even the tremendous opening fanfare to Alpine climbing—the first ascent of Mont Blanc in 1786—was accompanied by the strident trumpet tones of human discord. Jacques Balmat had no wish to share his fame with Dr. Paccard, who accompanied him on the climb. There has always been keen competition between the guides of different nationalities, indeed even of different valleys, a competition that remains as keen as ever today.

We have only to turn back the pages of the Eiger's own history. In 1859 Leslie Stephen and the Mathews brothers, English climbers all, made the first traverse of the Eigerjoch with their guides. Leslie Stephen, one of the most distinguished characters in the "Golden Age" of mountaineering, who invariably gave pride of place to the feats of his guides, keeping his own in the background, describes this "Rivalry of the Guides" in his charmingly humorous book *The Playground of Europe.*

The Mathews [he writes] were accompanied by two Chamouni men, Jean-Baptiste Croz and Charlet, whilst I had secured the gigantic Ulrich Lauener, the most picturesque of guides. Tall, spare, blue-eyed, long-limbed, and square-shouldered, with a jovial laugh and a not ungraceful swagger, he is the very model of a true mountaineer; and, except that his rule is apt to be rather autocratic, I would not wish for a pleasanter companion. He has, however, certain views as to the superiority of the Teutonic over the Celtic races. . . .

While they were reconnoitering the best way through the ice falls there was sharp competition between Lauener and the Chamonix men. Stephen writes:

We had already had one or two little races and disputations in consequence, and Lauener was disposed to take a disparaging view of the merits of these foreign competitors on his own peculiar ground. As, however, he could not speak a word of French, nor they of German, he was obliged to convey this sentiment in pantomime, which perhaps did not soften its vigour.

That was written in 1859.

So it will be seen that various kinds of rivalries are no degenerate phenomena of the new generation. It is impossible to speak of a profanation of the mountains. The great prototypes, whom it is usual to present to the eyes of youth as examples of ice-graybearded distinction, the Pioneers above all, the men of action, did not make the milk of a pious mentality their favourite drink. They were neither supermen nor knights in shining armour, but simply men, like those of today.

During the thirties the Italians achieved a leading place in international mountaineering, especially on rock. And be it only mentioned in passing that, around the turn of the century, the Himalayan and other expeditions of Luigi Amedeo di Savoia, duke of the

Abruzzi, outclassed all similar enterprises sponsored by other nations for their daring and brilliant organisation.

To RETURN TO OUR Italian party on the Eiger, that first Wednesday of July 1937. They started up the so-called Lauper Route on the Northeast Face of the Eiger, a glorious and exposed climb in the old classical style. It is a route for masters, not virtuosos. Dr. Hans Lauper and Alfred Zürcher discovered it and in 1932 they climbed it with those fine Valais guides Alexander Graven and Josef Knubel. The Lauper Route certainly offers a training climb on the way to the North Face, but only for the best-trained and the most accomplished of climbers. Others would not be good enough to tackle it. Let no one dream of starting on the Lauper Route as a "practice climb" unless he can wield his ice axe with the same skill and assurance as the peasant of the valley swings his scythe on the precipitous slope, so that he strikes the ice in the right rhythm and at the right angle accurately to a fraction of an inch. Even in this era of the ice piton and the ice hammer the true criterion of the climber on ice is his axe. It is as wrong as it is useless to try to reverse the current of development, but it is the duty of every mountaineer to learn to cut steps as efficiently as did the guides of yesterday, even with their clumsy ice axes, whose master craft in providing ladders of steps was such that they were for a long time able to dispense with the use of the modern crampon. When people begin to use on moderately difficult ground equipment and methods suitable for the unusually severe, it is not just a sign of extraordinary prudence, but an indication that another step in the development of technique has been surmounted. It is, of course, possible to escape from a difficult situation with inadequate and unsuitable equipment; but it is not to be recommended.

Our two Italian guides Piravano and Detassis embarked on the Lauper Route, which looms up above the small ice field of the "Hoyisch," or "Hohen Eis," a sharp-crested, steep route, armored with glassy rock slabs and towering ice cliffs. Their object was to get to know the mountain from every side. At first they had no intention of climbing the whole Lauper Route, but only meant to reconnoiter part of it. This was an entirely new conception in the history of the North Face. It was a notion ahead of its times, a true guide's notion. Giuseppe and Bruno intended not only to climb the North Face, but eventually to guide tourists up it. If that proved to be too difficult, dangerous and impracticable, they meant to withdraw from the whole enterprise. Even if their attempts and experiences finally proved negative, it was a notion worth bearing in mind; for it was not merely new, it was revolutionary. It must be recalled that the company of Swiss guides was still clinging to its old tradition, admittedly a grand and fine tradition. Their attitude towards the North Face was hardly a whit different from that of the old Berchtesgaden guide—the first man to climb the East Face of the Watzmann—Johann Grill-Kederbacher, who had come to the Eiger as long ago as 1883(!) with the intention of climbing its North Face. Kederbacher's verdict had then been: "Impossible!" Now, in 1937, the Swiss guides were still saying "Impossible!" At a time when the two Italians, Bruno and Giuseppe, had arrived to climb the North Face—with a view to guiding tourists up it. . . .

It was on a Wednesday that they started up the Lauper Route. On the Thursday they could not be seen, the weather was too bad. Snowslides and heavier avalanches could be seen sweeping the route. That was enough to authorise a reporter to send off a telegram in a great hurry to the *Neue Zürcher Zeitung:* "The two Italians have probably fallen." The report went the rounds in many papers. Many know-it-alls and ignoramuses added the opinion that Piravano and Detassis had entered upon their venture without sufficient thought and inadequately equipped. Yes, they were ready to denigrate even Italy's best ice expert.

But what had actually been happening?

The slabs and ledges on the lower half of the route were treacherous and slippery with fresh snow. The two Italians moved slowly upwards, using every known precaution. Above the first cliff they bivouacked, at a point reached by Lauper's extraordinarily strong and thrustful party, in unusually favourable conditions, before midday. On the Thursday the pair climbed on up the mighty roof of the mountain.

That was when the accident happened. A snowslide swept Piravano, who was leading, from his footholds. Bruno, belaying his companion on an ice piton, managed to hold him; but he could not prevent Giuseppe from seriously injuring a leg. So that superb ice climber, unfit now to lead or even to move without support, was completely out of action. Pride and the guides' code forbade them to call for help. A descent was impossible, for avalanche threats and snow-covered slabs forbade a retreat. A traverse across to the Mittellegi Hut was equally out of the question. Piravano had to be continually belayed from above, so that traverses were unthinkable. Yet the rocky upper pitches of the Lauper Route would be equally impossible, because a man with such leg injuries would be unable to stand the pain. So Bruno Detassis decided to climb straight up the fearsome ice slope, steeper than the roof of a Gothic cathedral, and bring his injured friend up onto the top part of the Mittellegi Ridge, belaying him vertically from above.

And he succeeded. It was a memorable and altruistic effort on the part of the guide from Trento. It was evening by the time they reached the Mittellegi Hut, perched like an eagle's eyrie on the stormswept ridge. And on Friday, July 8 the two men who had fought their way so gamely to shelter and safety, without calling for aid, were brought back safely to the valley by their Swiss colleagues, Inäbnit and Peter Kaufmann. Both expressed the greatest admiration for Bruno and Giuseppe.

Needless to say, the reaction of part of the Italian Press to the prematurely sensational reports from the Job's comforters, already quoted, and the actual safe return of their compatriots was not exactly amiable. The national trumpet was blown fortissimo—without the assistance, or indeed the wish, of the two first-class guides from

Trento and Bergamo—and a great triumph celebrated, when it was really only the sort of victory of courage and endurance one would expect of guides of that quality.

Unhappily, there were still many papers which had not sensed the great change of 1937 and were still pandering to their readers with sensational reports in the style of the previous year. And there were even professed mountaineers, shunned and despised by the fraternity, who either through a desire to show off or as mere parasites wished to cook their own little brew on the flame of public interest.

Andreas Heckmair, waiting at the foot of the Face with his friend Theo Lösch, withholding his name from all the inquisitive reporters, quietly studying the wall and its tricks—he even discovered a new line of ascent under the Rote Fluh and up by the right to the Northwest Ridge, but did not publicize the variant because he thought it unimportant—this same Heckmair reported as follows on those strange lads who would have done so great a disservice to the cause of mountaineering had they not been shown up as the charlatans they were.

> They told everyone, who wanted or didn't want to know, about their Eiger intentions, climbed about on the approaches to the North Face in such an obvious way as to be an invitation to those interested to watch them, let themselves be entertained in Grindelwald, and generally gathered advance commendation wherever it was to be found. Not only we ourselves, but the Grindelwald guides were rightly infuriated by them. These Alpine crooks were attracted by the Eiger as a moth is drawn to a light. It is a relief to report that at the end of their ill-doing they received the punishment they had invited and finished up by getting the push out of Switzerland.

It can be imagined how delighted the real climbers, the quiet, serious men genuinely at work on the problem of the North Face, were when these parasitic impostors were ejected. Besides the Italians, besides the three Munich men, Wollenweber, Zimmermann, and Lohner, besides Heckmair and Lösch, a number of others were either occupying the tents and hayricks or were just moving in. There was Rudi Fraissl, who had earned a great name in Viennese climbing circles by his first ascent of the North Face of the Peternschartenkopf in the Gesäuse. His rope mate and close compatriot was Leo Brankowsky, a pleasant, helpful lad, whom all his friends called Brankerl. Leo was certainly no "Brankerl" in the Viennese sense, no "softy," but a tower of strength when an overhang had to be climbed or a companion held on the rope. Fraissl was a fanatical lover of freedom and an individualist who found it difficult to subordinate himself. The mountains could devise no way of encompassing his end. His craggy skull and his courageous tongue, never a respecter of authority, signalled him out for a harder death than any the mountains could have handed out to him. He died in Russia in February 1942, in the company of a number of the best climbers of the Army Mountaineering School, during an attack on which it was senseless to employ such handpicked specialists. Rudi Fraissl protested beforehand—as if he were engaged in a trade-union meeting. He protested with all the inflexible strength of his Viennese tongue, with that very unViennese firmness he adopted on anything he had rightly made up his mind about. As an N.C.O. in the German army he dared to protest against his senior officer on behalf of his comrades and himself; he died, not as an N.C.O., but as a private soldier, reduced to the ranks as punishment for his crime. And he died as the leader of a roped party should.

At that time in July 1937, Fraissl and "Brankerl" were in their tent near Alpiglen; so were Liebl and Rieger; and Primas and Gollackner too, two men from Salzburg.

Just when Andreas Heckmair had pronounced it as unlikely that the weather conditions would improve sufficiently to warrant an attempt on the Face and turned his back on it on July 15, Ludwig

Vörg and Hias Rebitsch arrived, followed a little later by Otto Eidenschink, the first to climb the West Wall of the Totenkirchl direct, and his fellow member of the Munich Section, Möller. It was an elite of the climbing fraternity who were together at the bottom of the wall or succeeding one another down there during the summer of 1937. Heckmair left and Vörg arrived without actually meeting one another, or ever suspecting that they might be going to form a single rope resulting in a common success the following year.

And besides the "Storm Troops," one kept on meeting members of the Voluntary Rescue Service, particularly of the Munich Section, ready to try the Face and, above all, to climb to the rescue if there was an accident. The guides of Grindelwald, too, were holding themselves in readiness, without orders or obligation—just as they had in 1936.

The large body of newspaper readers demanded to be kept continually informed of what was happening on the Eiger. "Every stroke of an axe, every tug on a rope is recorded," remarked the Zürich paper *Sport* sarcastically.

Yes, the much sought-after sensation was on the way again. Not really a sensation but a tragedy; and yet not a sheer tragedy like those of recent years, but a very sad chapter in the long history of the Eiger. It started on Thursday, July 15, that same Thursday on which Ludwig Vörg, waiting for Hias Rebitsch down in Grindelwald, stood staring doubtfully up at the rain, which set in towards evening; the same Thursday, when Andreas Heckmair and Lösch went down to Grindelwald without knowing that a certain Ludwig Vörg was standing moodily at a nearby window. The Thursday on which Franz Primas and Bertl Gollackner started up the Lauper Route.

Primas was a well-known, extremely competent climber from Salzburg. He belonged to the climbing club "Die Bergler," formed by a number of the best Salzburg climbers. On a ski tour in the Tennengebirge, close to their home, Primas had come to know Gollackner, hardly nineteen years old, but a good rock climber and a plucky ski runner full of the spirit of adventure. Secretly, without a word to anyone, these two decided to go and "have a look" at the North Face of the Eiger. It would be quite wrong to smile in a superior fashion at the mountain enthusiasm of men like these who, with empty pockets, mount their bicycles on the long pilgrimage, just to have a look at the peak of their dreams.

Primas was cautious and he also felt responsible for his youthful companion—he was perhaps lacking in that deep knowledge of the Western Alps that would have warned him to explore a mountain from every angle before tackling its most difficult side. But he was certainly not charging blindly up the North Face that, by a hideous pun, the masses had rechristened the Murder Face.[1] He wanted to take a sideways look into the North Face from its eastern rim, approaching it by the Lauper Route. True, only a few days ago, the two Italians, Piravano and Detassis, had only just escaped with their lives from a similar reconnaissance. But Primas and Gollackner only wanted to try the Lauper Route, that great climb thought out by the brains of the best Swiss climbers and opened by the ice axes of the best Swiss guides. Just the Lauper Route. . . .

No, they had no intention of climbing the Eiger's Northeast Face; only a part of it, so that they could get their sideways look at the North Face. Just as they were starting to climb, Gollackner remembered that he had left his bag of provisions in the tent. Very annoying, but they would be back by evening, and Franz had enough along with him for both on a single day's climb: a crust of bread and a hunk of sausage.

They started up and climbed on. Once again the mountain chose to be unkind. The conditions were even worse than those met by the Italians—avalanches, showers of stones, rushing torrents. Every foot of the climb was treacherous, slippery. Primas realised that there was no going back; a bivouac was unavoidable. A bivouac without a

[1] See p. 44.

tent sack—hadn't they meant to be back by nightfall?—and without food. No, there was still some food: a smaller crust and a shorter sausage, to last till tomorrow. No, not till tomorrow, but till they got back to civilization. . . .

They endured a cold, wet, perilous bivouac on the precipice, and it robbed nineteen-year-old Bertl of much of his strength. But throughout the next day, another day of bad weather, Primas showed his great skill as a climber. He led up through the steep and dangerous wall; by evening both had safely reached the cornice of the Mittellegi Ridge. There they dug themselves a rough and ready cave in the snow for their second bivouac. In the night the storm rose to a blizzard. Their food ran out. The bitter cold numbed their muscles and their willpower; but next morning, Primas tried to force himself and his exhausted partner to move on again. And then something absolutely incredible happened: Primas led on upwards towards the summit of the Eiger. Surely he knew that down below, on the crest of the Ridge, there stood a hut, the Mittellegi Hut? Had he formed the opinion that a traverse of the summit was possible, a descent of the ridge impracticable?

Just below the steep step, where the fixed rope was hanging, now thickly encased in ice, Gollackner's strength gave out. Yet another bivouac in the snow, in the storm. Primas shouted for help; Gollackner was past all shouting. But Primas did not seek his own personal safety, alone; he remained loyally by his friend's side. His feet lost all sensation and were soon frostbitten. His sacrifice was, however, in vain. On Sunday, July 18, their fourth day on the mountain, Bertl Gollackner, nineteen years old, died on the Mittellegi Ridge. The blizzard muffled his friend's calls for help. . . .

All the same, people were thinking hard about the two Salzburg climbers, even if their S.O.S. remained unheard. Though nothing could be seen of them, there were many who thought they had seen something when the cloud curtain lifted for a moment either on Saturday, or was it Friday? Somebody spread the rumour that Primas and Gollackner were climbing down. Then again, the latest news at the tents near Alpiglen was that a rescue party had left Grindelwald to search the Mittellegi Ridge and the upper part of the precipice. But suppose they were lower down?

Matthias Rebitsch and Ludwig Vörg—whom we shall be getting to know more intimately later on—had erected their tent near Alpiglen on Sunday, the 18th; but their worries about the two Salzburg climbers gave them no respite. If the guides were searching higher up, they would start a search lower down. They left their tent at about 4 A.M. on Monday, the 19th, accompanied at first by two friends anxious to help, Liebl and Rieger. A search of the avalanche cones at the foot of the Lauper Wall revealed no trace of the missing men. Rebitsch and Vörg climbed on; but there was nothing to be seen on the rock ledges farther up. They then made rapid progress till brought to a halt by an overhanging step. The only way through it was up a chimney. At the moment there was a waterfall pouring down it, and there was no other way; so Rebitsch and Vörg went up it. Soaked to the skin, they searched the network of ledges in the central section of the cliff thoroughly. Here, too, they found no signs of Primas and Gollackner. So long as they had not fallen off, there was always hope for their survival.

Rebitsch and Vörg were the third party that July to find the Wall had sprung to dangerous life, cutting off their retreat. The warmth of the day had loosened parts of the cornice that came shooting down, endangering all below. There were avalanches, waterfalls, stones into the bargain. No, for Rebitsch and Vörg there would once again be no hope of a return to their tent at Alpiglen. For them, too, the only way of escape lay upwards.

They wanted to make a diagonal ascent across to the Mittellegi Ridge, in the neighbourhood of the Hut; but they were halted by an overhanging belt of rock such as even a Rebitsch and Vörg could not climb in such conditions. It forced them to make a traverse, the like of which had not been seen on this face.

It was a roped traverse to the left, underneath the rock step. A rope traverse on rock doused with running water, on ice-glazed rock, on ice itself. A rope traverse, did I say? A dozen rope traverses. The ice crackled and creaked under the pressure of their crampons, when they leaned outwards and hauled on the rope, pushing off with their feet from the rock, trusting to the pitons they had banged in. It was nearly the end of the day. The pair had reached a steep ice slope about 1,000 feet below the Mittellegi Hut. They could even see its roof, high up above, but where they were, there was no sheltering roof.

The two men took to their axes and hacked seats out of the ice and steps for footrests. They hadn't a dry stitch on them, when they perched themselves on their tiny places for the bivouac. A single piton and the rope attached to it were their only protection against falling off the mountain, if one or the other fell asleep.

To a layman, or even to the average climber, such a bivouac may sound appalling and it may seem incredible that anyone could survive such an ordeal. But Matthias Rebitsch, one of the best, most experienced, and toughest climbers of his day, and Ludwig Vörg, the first to climb the 7,000-foot West Face of Ushba in the Caucasus, nicknamed "the Bivouac King" by his friends, spent that night resting with a stoical calm. Next morning they climbed the steep slope to the Mittellegi Hut.

Right glad they were to reach its shelter. They found wood there and soon a fire was crackling in the tiny hearth. They were able to dry their drenched things. They took a brief rest. . . .

But early in the afternoon some guides came in from above, bringing the utterly exhausted Franz Primas with them. They also brought the bitter news that Gollackner lay dead up there, 500 feet below the summit.

Without hesitating an instant, Rebitsch and Vörg volunteered to bring the boy's body down next day.

Early next day they raced towards the top. There they found

Gollackner. The pathetic young face looked relaxed, at peace with the world, as so often happens when death comes by freezing, for the last dreams of those who die that way are magical ones of succour, warmth, and life.

Vörg said afterwards: "It was just as if he were sleeping and one had only to awaken him." With every care not to disturb the last sleep of their young climbing companion, they carried him down. They said nothing of the tremendous labor involved in bringing a body down the endless razor blade of the Mittellegi Ridge.

Down below, it was not yet known that Gollackner was dead. Nor had the news filtered through of the magnificent feat of Vörg and Rebitsch, nor of the Grindelwald guides, in the service of rescue and recovery; nevertheless, the Eiger was, at the moment, a red-hot source of public interest and controversy.

The following is from the Zurich paper *Sport* on July 19:

What measure of psychical greatness would not the Eiger register if it were personified and given a soul. Year after year, a few ludicrous earthworms camp at the foot of its North Face, planning to force a passage with ropes and pitons. It is only necessary for a tiny icicle on the giant's hat rim to sneeze in order to annihilate the intruders. When one is lying in complete peace among the pasturing cattle, the sky seems stretched very high overhead and beautifully blue above the world. The Eiger's Face glitters under its shields of ice, the echo of the falling stones rattles from wall to wall and one can enjoy the rush and rustle of the snowslides.

Is it either good or necessary that this realm of nature's tremendous forces should be invaded by beings which were not created as carefree mountain eagles or climbing plants, but as human beings? The urge to achieve things cannot be used as an excuse for self-annihilation. It is easy enough to push the sporting aspect into the foreground, but sport does not necessarily mean the ultimate in achievement. To clear one's mind it is only necessary to recall the *mens sana in corpore sano* of the ancients. The ascent of the Eiger North Face is forbidden. It is not the administration in Berne which has pronounced the veto. It is the Eiger itself speaking with a dumb-show language no one can fail to understand. If anyone fails to comprehend its message, he must be deaf and deserves to be hauled away from the danger area exactly as one would lead a blind man off the tramlines onto the pavement. . . .

This article might have been controversial, though still off the target, in earlier years. In 1937 it had a reactionary air and to find it then, especially in so respected and serious a newspaper as *Sport*, was in some ways quite astonishing. A passive observation of nature and the passionless bliss that can be won from it is known to mountaineers as well as others; but it does not constitute their whole nature. An idyllic poem might be born of inactive observation of nature's forces and it might bring pleasure to the reader. Among mountaineers, too, there have been and still are many sensitive, artistic men, who are as familiar with the howling of the tempest, the hammer tattoo of the stones, as they are with cold, with steep ice slopes and with overhanging rocks. They absorbed their awe-inspiring experiences irrespective of whether they were going to clothe them later in literary form or not. But while they were on the mountains, in difficulty and in danger, they behaved simply like ordinary men. The men who discovered the Poles or ventured into unexplored deserts and jungles or mastered the air space high above the clouds were certainly not of the type which observes nature passively. Yet, one might just as well have said to those pioneers: "Don't go into the Arctic or Antarctic, for you are neither polar bears nor penguins. Don't go into the jungle or the desert, for you are neither monkeys nor lions. Don't venture up into the air, for you will be upsetting the rhythmic balance of the silvery clouds in their silent march!"

Admittedly, man is small and insignificant in nature's scheme; but he is part of it. And are we to think less of the man who exposes himself to nature's forces than of him who just delights in looking at her, safe from dangers and tempests? Even those ridiculous earthworms know that an icicle can "sneeze"; but they have learned by observation when and where it happens, and will do their best to avoid the danger with that clear-eyed alertness which they owe to their own daring. They are not deaf; they too hear the mighty voice of the mountains, but they understand and interpret it in a different way from those who enjoy it so passively and with such self-satisfaction.

Now let us go back and follow the steps of the two men who, on a brilliant day, had made that sad journey with the boy's body. For the weather turned fine on the day of the recovery and remained so for days.

It was the 25th before they felt sufficiently recovered to go up again from Grindelwald to their tent at Alpiglen. They studied the Face quietly, drawing their own conclusions. They recalled how Hinterstoisser's party had shown its greatest impetus on the first day, after which its strength faded badly. There was obviously something wrong about that. It was essential to preserve enough strength to push on just as quickly in the unexplored, but obviously very difficult, upper part of the Face, below the summit. That meant siting the first camp as high as possible and stocking it lavishly.

Liebl and Rieger proved to be real friends of the kind indispensable on attempts to climb high peaks. Although themselves fit and anxious to tackle the climb of the North Face, they offered to help Rebitsch and Vörg carry their loads up to the first camp and so to forgo their own attempt. At about 6 A.M. on July 27, they started up the lower part of the Face with the two protagonists. Once again the weather was glorious.

About 1,000 feet above the Bergschrund, Liebl saw a body lying about 150 feet diagonally below him at the edge of a patch of snow. He attracted the attention of the others.

"That can only be Hinterstoisser," he said. "Anderl is still missing. . . ."

Liebl had taken part in the previous year's recovery attempts. He knew that Hinterstoisser and Mehringer had not yet been found. "Still missing." Tragic words, embodying all the sadness which can be felt for a lost comrade, even when matter-of-factly uttered, without a touch of sentimentality. The weather was fine and would almost certainly remain so for the next few days. But Rebitsch, who always kept a silent tongue when most moved, knew that there would be no attempt on the Face for him and Vörg in the morning. The body of Andreas Hinterstoisser had been lying down there ever since last year. . . .

So they spent that day, the 27th, in carrying up bivouac equipment and provisions to a knob of rock at the top of the so-called "Second Pillar," and then came down again. On the 28th it was as fine as ever, just as on the day when they brought Gollackner down. Once again the four men spent it in bringing down a body. And once again the brilliance of the sun seemed a ghastly mockery of their tragic work.

No doubt many will say: "What cold, unfeeling young men Rebitsch and Vörg must have been! How could they bring themselves to recover two dead bodies, in the space of a week, on the eve of their own attempt on that dread Face? Couldn't even that fearful omen shake them? And isn't it a sign of sheer brutal insensitivity?"

Nobody knows what Rebitsch and his companions thought during those recovery operations. They didn't advertise their feelings. The fact remains that they put off their supreme effort, which might quite probably have ended in success, because they found Hinterstoisser's body on the way up. They brought it down in spite of the stones whistling about their ears. They carried out what to them was an essential, final act of piety. In so doing they proved themselves true pupils of the mountain school, in which they had learned to do what was right and necessary. Did that mean that they ought to abandon their plans? They had already made up their minds to attempt the climb. They followed their own law.

They started up the Face again on July 30. Dawn was a many-coloured splendor—a sure sign of bad weather. They met the first storm at the Bergschrund below the cliffs.

So it was decided only to carry more supplies and equipment up to the top of the Pillar. They reached it at about noon. The weather had moderated by then. Curiosity lured them on; they would reconnoiter a part of the route. The rock became difficult, very difficult indeed. This was no place for nailed boots or crampons. Rope-soled slippers were the thing . . . but they were down below there. This wasn't meant to be the start of the attempt on the Face; they were only exploring the way and carrying gear up. So both men took to "Nature's climbing boots"—bare feet.

In order to save time and speed things up Rebitsch, that master of rock climbing, climbed the super-severe "Difficult Crack" without threading a rope through the pitons he found in position there. Vörg followed him equally quickly. And so they reached the vital traverse and, marvelling at the razor-keen solution of the problem how best to reach the First Ice Field, christened it the Hinterstoisser Traverse.

They immediately furnished it with two rope handrails, to ensure a safe retreat in all circumstances. After the traverse, they climbed another difficult crack and there found a small stance, protected from falling stones by an overhang, on which one could even sit in an emergency—in terms of this particular Face, an ideal bivouac. There they dumped everything they could spare and started down again. The second thunderstorm of the day caught them on the far side of the traverse. Dripping wet, and climbing down through vertical waterfalls, they disposed of the 2,700 feet of the lower part of the Face and got back to their tent at Alpiglen before dark.

The rain led to a fresh period of bad weather. Days lengthened into weeks. On August 6, during a temporary improvement, Vörg and Rebitsch teaming up with their friends Eidenschink and Möller climbed the North Face of the Great Fiescherhorn. This magnificent wall of snow and ice, first climbed by Willo Welzenbach in 1930, had also been chosen for a final climb, before they turned their backs on the Bernese Oberland for this year, by Fraissl and Brankowsky. Many others, too, had grown tired of waiting.

Rebitsch and Vörg, however, stayed on. It was now the start of the fourth week since they had withdrawn from the Eiger's Face. Still they never lost patience, made no careless, irresponsible move. The Press had also quieted down a good deal about the Eiger. There was one article in the *Frankfurter Zeitung* that caused great amusement in well-informed circles. In it a Mr. M. gave all and sundry what was intended for well-meaning advice. For instance, he suggested that the traversing ropes ought to be fixed at the Hinterstoisser Traverse during a period of Föhn, that is to say during warm weather, when the ice had melted, the following period of bad weather should be spent waiting in the valley and a fresh start made on the Face as soon as the barometer began to rise again. The Zurich paper *Sport* expressed its opposition to such "cookery book recipes" in witty, ironical terms.

The traversing ropes were already there. They had been fixed, not during a spell of Föhn, but during a spell of thundery bad weather. But it looked as if they were going to remain unused till the following summer.

On August 9 Berne at last forecast fine weather. On the 10th the hot sun cleared masses of fresh snow from the Face. And early on the 11th Rebitsch and Vörg started out on their second attempt.

It was only 10:30 when they reached their depot on top of the Pillar. They moved on across the roped traverse to their bivouac place very heavily laden. They were in such splendid form that they were back at the top of the Pillar by one in the afternoon to fetch up the rest of their gear. And by 5 P.M., everything was safely lodged at the bivouac place. They had even managed to drag fleece-lined sleeping bags and air mattresses up to it. They improved their sleeping quarters by building a low wall of stones, then they stretched their tent sack from a projection overhead, to keep the heavier drips off them, and enjoyed a precious night's sleep in the

"Swallow's Nest" they had built for themselves high up on the precipice.

Next day they climbed on, over ice-covered rock and ice, and achieved the difficult ascent of the overhanging cliff between the First and Second Ice Fields. Then came five hours of upward traversing—twenty rope lengths diagonally upwards—across the Second Ice Field. Then the ice-plastered rocky step leading from the Second to the Third Ice Field. Then the Ice Field itself. . . .

The watchers at the telescopes down in Grindelwald, up at the Kleine Scheidegg, were amazed. They had already seen much wonderful climbing on the Eiger's Face. All the men who had come and had died on it had climbed wonderfully. But nobody had yet seen anything like the assurance and care of this pair, Rebitsch from the Tirol and Vörg, the Munich man. Would these two succeed, at last, or would bad weather come, once again, to rob them?

It wasn't a question of coming; it was already there. Above the arête of the "Flatiron," the men were swallowed up by the mists. Up above that, there still loomed more than 2,000 feet of the summit wall, a precipice about which nobody knew anything, for no living being had yet reported on it.

The pair climbed on up the steep ice, penetrated by rock ledges, to where Sedlmayer and Mehringer had spent their last bivouac. There they were half expecting to find Mehringer's body, which Udet had seen from his plane the previous September, frozen rigid in its steps. They seemed fated always to be meeting dead men.

But there was no body . . . nothing but a couple of pitons in the rock.

It was 7 P.M. They had reached a height of 11,000 feet, and it was starting to hail. They had come to climb the Face if they could, or at least to reconnoitre its upper precipices. A little lower down there on the left was the start of the great "Ramp"; Vörg and Rebitsch started to traverse across towards it on steep ice. Then, suddenly, hail and rain began to pour down in such absolute torrents that their curiosity about the rest of the route was completely quenched. Their only desire was to crawl under their tent sack and find some shelter from the deluge.

Nowhere could they find a good spot for a bivouac; nor, for that matter, a bad one either. Finally, they were forced to hack a tiny place out of the ice, on which to pass the night. The cold became so intense that a film of ice formed inside the tent sack owing to the condensation. For the first time the two men suffered intensely from the cold. All night long icy sleet drummed on the tent. Every now and then they heard the crashing of stones unpleasantly close at hand.

Towards dawn the sleet ceased. As daylight came, the mists parted, but not to reveal a fine morning. A great black bank of cloud was approaching, full of menace, from the west. There was only one possible decision: to retreat.

It was a painful thought, to have to retrace that long dangerous way; but it was the thought of self-preservation.

Bitter cold as the night had been, it had failed to numb or weaken either of the climbers. Down they climbed, rope length on rope length. They reached the place where the cliff down to the Second Ice Field has to be descended on the two 100-foot ropes joined together. They roped down; then they tried to pull the ropes down after them; they refused to come down. It was still the day of hemp ropes which, when wet, became as stiff as cables. They both tugged on one end of the rope; still it refused to budge. So Rebitsch just climbed, free and unbelayed, up to the top again and cleared the knot by which the ropes had jammed. Assuredly, the North Face had not robbed these two either of their strength or of their ability to make decisions. Both were as strong and courageous as on the first day.

The descent of the Second Ice Field seemed endless. All the time, little snowslides were coming down it, forcing their bodies away from the steep slope, but they both stood firm. They climbed steadily downwards, safeguarding one another with ice pitons. The surface of the ice had gone soft and slushy from so much water pouring down. It had become necessary to hack away quite a foot before a piton could be banged into the firm ice below. This all took a long time, but Rebitsch and Vörg continued to descend astonishingly quickly.

The next task was to climb and rope down the overhanging rock cliff to the First Ice Field. At times they had to knock in four pitons before they could fix the sling for the *abseil* securely. In spite of the bad weather and the pressure of time, they did not risk a single hasty handhold. This was an orderly retreat, rigidly controlled; no flight from the mountain.

They descended the First Ice Field; then Rebitsch was already traversing to their first bivouac—that luxury bivouac, the "Swallow's Nest." Soon he reached it and Vörg, following him, was still on ice. At that moment a horrible clatter and whining set in; stones went whizzing past his head. Lumps landed close around him, cutting holes in his rucksack; but when the fall of stones was over, Ludwig's skull was undamaged. At five o'clock he joined Rebitsch at the bivouac.

Both were soaked to the skin. Nothing could be more inviting than to use the three or four remaining hours of daylight to continue the descent. The traverse was no problem; it was ready roped. Nothing would have been more natural than for these two to have been mastered by their longing for the safety of the valley. But neither of them was exhausted, nor were their senses in any way dulled, so as to allow longings to get the better of them. So they stayed at the bivouac.

There they got out of every stitch of wet clothing, wrung it all out, got dry underwear out of their rucksacks, put it on, then their damp things over it, and crawled into the fleecy sleeping bags they had cached there. And there they perched themselves, huddled together and went to sleep.

Their fourth morning on the Face dawned, and the weather was if anything still more miserable. A final descent was inevitable; but now it had to be done carrying all their gear, whose weight had been doubled by the wetting it had sustained. Both were in the habit of humping rucksacks of such vast proportions that even on ordinary expeditions to Huts their wearers groaned and sweated under them. A descent with such ballast seemed quite impossible.

All the same, Rebitsch and Vörg climbed down safely with all their luggage. First along the traverse, then down the overhanging pitches—a bitter struggle made far harder by the stiffness of the ropes—to the top of the Pillar, then down and down for hour upon hour.

It was late afternoon before they reached the foot of the Face.

There they met a solitary figure coming up the debris slopes. Was he a member of the rescue service? Were people searching for them already then, already talking of new Eiger victims?

No, it was only their devoted friend Eidenschink coming up. It is a good thing to be welcomed home by a true and understanding friend when you come back to earth.

The Face had not claimed Rebitsch and Vörg. They were tired, but not exhausted; they were able to laugh and to tell their story. All the same their tent near Alpiglen seemed like a palace to them.

BY THEIR SAFE RETURN and by the manner of it Matthias Rebitsch[1] and Ludwig Vörg brought about the change in the attitude of conservative climbers, of the guides, of the publicity media towards the problem of the North Face. The Face had given nothing away to them; yet they had been higher on it than anyone else and had still come back safely, relaxed and calm. This spiritual superiority, the fruit of bodies incomparably well trained, was the decisive factor. The

---

[1]In the following year Rebitsch was appointed Deputy Leader of the German Nanga Parbat Expedition, which prevented his taking part in the first successful climb of the Face. Nonetheless, his name stands high indeed in its history.

two men had learned from the tragic errors of their predecessors and had themselves made no new mistakes. They had maintained their strength and their courage alike from start to finish of their venture. From now on, nobody talked of ridiculous, presumptuous earthworms. Instead, they spoke of men.

THE FIRST ASCENT

OF THE FACE

The summer of 1938 began sadly enough, with the death of two young Italian climbers. Bartolo Sandri and Mario Menti, employees in a wool factory at Valdagno in the Province of Vicenza, were both respected members of the Italian Alpine Club, though only twenty-three years old. Sandri, especially, was known to be an unusually fine rock climber, who had done a number of super-severe climbs ranking as "Grade VI," among them some first ascents. True, they had hardly any experience of ice climbing in the Western Alps. Like all true mountaineers, they came to Alpiglen and the Scheidegg quietly, without any fuss, indeed almost secretly. They studied the Face, tried themselves out by a reconnaissance of its lower structure, and came down again. They decided that the direct route, followed three years before by Sedlmayer and Mehringer, was easier than that discovered by Hinterstoisser. But it wasn't any easier. The fact is that the Face was not yet fit for climbing at all.

Nonetheless Bartolo and Mario started up it early on June 21. They reached a greater height than Sedlmayer and Mehringer had on their first day. Their courage and enthusiasm ran high, and they were driven on by a burning urge to succeed. They just couldn't wait. Nature, however, followed her own laws, heedless of courage, enthusiasm, or ambition. Late in the evening one of the Eiger's notorious thunderstorms set in. . . .

The very next day a search party of Grindelwald guides, led by Fritz Steuri Senior, found Sandri lying dead on a patch of snow at the foot of the Face. Menti's body was only recovered with some difficulty a few days later from a deep crevasse.

That was a bad enough start to operations on the Eiger in the summer of 1938, but it could not hold up the developments that were due. The memory of the successful retreat of Rebitsch and Vörg, which had been the turning point in men's minds, was still vivid. So was the lesson that it was impossible to capture the Face by surprise. *Veni, vidi, vici* wouldn't work on the Eiger. Endless patience was required and long waiting . . . for days, even weeks.

Meanwhile, Fritz Kasparek was waiting impatiently for my arrival. That tremendous climber from Vienna, bursting with life, blessed with an optimism nothing could destroy, had already been in Grindelwald for some time, skiing around the Bernese Oberland, keeping a constant watch on the Eiger's mighty Face. Though, so far, there hadn't been much to watch except continual avalanches, sufficient in themselves to nip in the bud even the thought of an attempt. All the same, Fritz would have liked by now to have had with him his partner on the big climb they had planned to do together; for one never knows what may happen to interrupt one's plans. Sepp Brunnhuber, too, with whom Fritz had done the first winter ascent of the North Face of the Grosse Zinne as long ago as February—to some extent as a training climb for the Eiger project—could still not get away. I had promised Fritz to arrive at Grindelwald by July 10; but at the bottom of his heart he had good grounds for mistrusting students' promises.

Actually I was no longer a student by the time I got to Grindelwald. My tutors at the University of Graz were greatly astonished at the speed with which I suddenly attacked my finals. I could hardly explain to them that I wanted my studies out of the way before I climbed the North Face of the Eiger. They would certainly have shaken their heads and—not without some justification—reminded me that it was quite in order to "come off" that climb without having graduated first. I told nobody of our plan, not a fellow student, not a mountaineering or sporting acquaintance. The only person I let into the secret was that wise, practical, and plucky woman, my future mother-in-law, Frau Else Wegener. In 1930 her husband Professor Alfred Wegener had given his life for his companions on Greenland's inscrutable inland ice, when he perished in a blizzard; so she might well have had strong grounds for being fiercely opposed to ventures involving a risk to life. She, however, uttered no warning word; on the contrary, she encouraged me, though well acquainted with the reputation of the Eiger's North Face.

My last paper was on the morning of July 9. At lunchtime I mounted my heavily laden motor bicycle; and I arrived at Grindelwald punctually on July 10, as promised. Fritz Kasparek, burnt brown by the glacier sun, his fair mop almost bleached white, greeted me in unmistakable Viennese.

He was blessed with the gift of the gab. His was a positively original gift for inventing expletives when faced with apparently insurmountable difficulties of the kind he was never in the habit of giving in to—both in the mountains and in ordinary life. However, he never used to parade his feelings; nor did he waffle about companionship and friendship. But his nature was such that, at times of crisis, he would not only share his last crust of bread or crumb of chocolate with his companions, but would give the whole of it away to them. And then not as a pathetic gesture, but to the accompaniment of some good nervous Viennese expression or other.

With friends of that kind one could go horse rustling, invite the devil to a picnic, or—attempt the North Face of the Eiger.

Fraissl and Brankowski, those two old Eiger hands, were also in Grindelwald. We strolled up to a pasture above Alpiglen together and there set up house. It was our firm intention to avoid the errors which had proved fatal to previous parties. The most important thing was to get to know our mountain as a whole, before attempting its most interesting and difficult face. So we first of all climbed from the "Hoheneis" diagonally across the (northeast) flank to the Mittellegi Ridge, then up it to the summit and down again by the normal route. In addition, we climbed the Mönch by the "Nollen."

Meanwhile, cows had been driven up onto our idyllic pasture. Fritz and I decided to move our abode, and pitched our little tent in a small meadow close under the Face. Fraissl and Brankowski stayed on the pasture. It was a fine day when Fritz and I started up the lower part of the Face and after climbing about 2,300 feet, to the so-called "Bivouac Cave" above the "Shattered Pillar," parked a rucksack full of provisions and equipment there. We attached a label to it, which read: "The property of Kasparek and Harrer. Don't move."

This notice did not indicate any particular mistrust of other North Face climbers. It was simply that, thanks to the many attempts and frequent rescue and recovery operations, the Face was littered with pieces of equipment, ropes and pitons, which served as very welcome aids and additions to the equipment of subsequent parties. This made it absolutely necessary to mark clearly any rucksack intentionally parked on the Face like this one of ours.

We climbed down again to our tent. Conditions would not yet allow of an attempt with the slightest prospect of success. We had taken a firm stand not to let ourselves be pushed, driven, or goaded. Past tragedies and particularly the deaths of the two Italians earlier in the summer had taught us that unseemly haste can ruin every sober consideration and lead to the direst results. We could wait and we meant to wait.

Days of fine weather set in; and still we waited, watching how the snow which had fallen during storms and been whipped against the rocks altered in consistency, melted away, settled, and bound firmly with the old underlying layer. It now seemed reasonable to hope that conditions up on the higher, unknown sector of the Face too would be bearable.

By July 21 we decided that everything was in order. At about 2 A.M. on that day we started up the Face, crossing the edge crevasse in the dark, climbing independently, unroped, up towards the "Shattered Pillar." We moved in silence, each of us picking his own line, each of us thinking his own thoughts.

Those hours between night and day are always a keen challenge to one's courage. One's body goes mechanically through the correct movements essential to gaining height; but the spirit is not yet awake nor full of the joy of climbing, the heart is shrouded in a cloak of doubt and diffidence. My friend Kurt Maix once described this diffidence as Fear's friendly sister, the right and necessary counterweight to that courage that urges men skyward, and protects them from self-destruction. It is certainly not fear that besets the climber; but doubts and questionings and "butterflies" are human failings. And climbers are after all only human beings.

They have to reconcile themselves with their own shortcomings and with constraining feelings; they have to subject themselves to the willpower already geared to the enterprise in hand. And so the first hour, the hour of the grey, shapeless, colourless dusk before dawn, is an hour of silence.

Sheer thrustfulness is false, indeed fallacious, at times when a man is struggling to achieve a balance and is busy trying to reconcile subtle nuances of feeling with his willpower. And the glorious thing about mountains is that they will endure no lies. Among them, we must be true to ourselves, too.

Fritz and I climbed on up, in the darkness before dawn, to the right of the "Shattered Pillar." From time to time we heard voices behind us, could distinguish individual words. It was Fraissl and Brankowski, who like ourselves had waited for the fine weather, and had started up the Face behind us. We would get on well enough with them. Two parties on that great precipice are no hindrance to one another; indeed, they can help each other in a variety of ways.

The rocks looked grey, even the snow looked grey in the first livid light of dawn. And there was something else grey moving in front of us. Not rocks this time, but people, peeling out of their tent sacks in front of the bivouac cave.

In an instant all thought, doubts, and self-questionings that had risen up out of the secret depths of our ego had sunk back again. We did not talk about them, least of all in front of strange fellow climbers who were at one and the same time comrades and competitors.

Strangers? Climbers are never really strangers, least of all on this Face. We introduced ourselves to these two who had only just woken up from their night's sleep. Then they told us who they were: Andreas Heckmair and Ludwig Vörg. It was a unique place for such an introduction. The light of an unborn day was strong enough for each of us to be able to see the faces of our opposite numbers clearly, to sample their features, to assess their characteristics.

So this was the famous Andreas Heckmair. At thirty-two he was the oldest of us four. His face was limned by the hills themselves, spare, deeply lined, with a sharp, jutting nose. It was a stern, bold face, the face of a fighter, of a man who would demand much of his companions and the last ounce of himself.

The other man, Ludwig Vörg, seemed to be exactly the opposite type: a well-rounded, athletic type, not in the least sinewy or spare, nor were his features as prominent as Heckmair's. They radiated amiable relaxation; his whole being personified latent strength and an inner peace. His friends with whom he had been to the Caucasus two years before had nicknamed him the "Bivouac King." Even those nights in the open on the 7,000-foot ice face of Ushba, the "Terrible Mountain," had failed to rob him of his sleep. On a snap judgment one would attribute the dynamic force to Heckmair, the stamina to Vörg. In any case two such diverse and complementary characters couldn't help making up a rope of quite extraordinary climbing ability and strength.

We couldn't tell if the two men were disappointed at our all being on the Face at the same time. If they were, they certainly didn't show it. Heckmair said: "We knew you were trying the Face, too. We saw your rucksack and read the label." We couldn't quite grasp why we had been in the dark about the presence of these two men, who hadn't been living in a tent either at Alpiglen or Kleine Scheidegg, nor in the hay on any of the pastures. We only found out later that this time they had completely covered their traces. They had come to Grindelwald with luggage and taken a room in one of the hotels at Kleine Scheidegg. Who ever heard of a candidate for the North Face of the Eiger sleeping in a hotel bedroom? The ruse had worked perfectly.

Heckmair and Vörg had with them the best, most up-to-date equipment. They were in fact just as poor as we were, but had raised a sponsor for their climb in advance and had therefore found themselves for the first time in their lives in a position to buy to their hearts' desire at Munich's best sports shop, and even to order gear which had to be specially manufactured. Of course, they both had the twelve-pointer crampons that had just become fashionable. Fritz had ten-pointers, but I hadn't any at all. Admittedly this was a mistake, but it wasn't the result of carelessness, but rather of overcareful consideration. We had taken the view that the North Face was a rock wall with aprons of snow and ice embedded in it. A pair of crampons weighs a good deal, and we felt that if we did without it, we could take more equipment or provisions along. My boots were nailed with the well-known claw system popular in Graz, a layout providing an equally good grip on rock and ice. Our plan was for Fritz to lead on the ice pitches and me to take over on the rocks. We also hoped to avoid the irksome and time-wasting necessity of strapping crampons on and taking them off again all the time. We were quite wrong, and it was a mistake; but it did not prove disastrous, for all it did was to lose us time and provide me with extra exertion. But we hadn't yet discovered that as we stood talking to Heckmair and Vörg outside the bivouac cave.

Vörg, used to bivouacking in all sorts of conditions and places, was grousing about the night they had just spent. "It was cold and uncomfortable," he complained. "Falling stones wouldn't allow us to stay outside the cave, and the cave itself was narrow and wet. It dripped steadily on our tent sack all night long."

Heckmair studied his altimeter and shook his head dubiously. "It has risen about sixty meters," he announced, "which means the barometer has fallen about three points. I don't like the look of the weather."

Just at that moment Fraissl and Brankowski came up with us. Introductions and friendly greetings followed, but by now there was a note of real concern detectable in Heckmair's voice. Like a good trouper he concealed his disappointment. He just pointed to a fish-shaped cloud on the horizon and said: "I'm sure the weather's breaking. We're not climbing any further."

We ourselves felt certain that the weather would hold, and Fritz put forward that viewpoint in his optimistic way: "Oh, sure, the weather'll hold all right. And someone's got to climb the Face sometime, after all!"

Heckmair and Vörg were getting ready to go down, as we moved on up. I kept on thinking about the retreat of those two superb climbers and remembering the look of utter disappointment on Vörg's face. And what about Heckmair? I soon realised that his fishy cloud and the "rise in the altimeter" were only excuses. He knew that the presence of three ropes on the Face could mean serious delays, but he was too good a sport to stand on his rights of "first come, first served" and ask one of our parties to turn back. So he turned back himself: instead of saying "you're in the wrong," he remarked that he didn't like the look of the weather. It was a decision dictated by a true sense of mountaineering responsibility.

Time and again climbers on the North Face had got into difficulties, through allowing themselves to be hurried not only by the state of the Face or by weather conditions, but by the competition of others. Vörg, one of the finest climbers ever to attempt the climb, was not going to let himself be hurried.

At the moment there was little time for psychological studies or similar problems. The Face itself was providing our immediate problems, as we reached the "Difficult Crack." Twilight had at last been forced to yield to the first full light of morning. We roped up, and Fritz tackled the first severe pitch with his own personal craftsmanship. The heavy Eiger pack on his shoulders brought his first swift upward drive to a halt. Down he had to come and leave his rucksack at my feet. Then he began his second assault. It was a pleasure to watch him. Higher and higher he went, stylishly, using every projecting wrinkle, never breaking his rhythm, never struggling. And in a staggeringly short time he had mastered this first great defence work on the Face.

The job of roping Fritz's rucksack up after him was difficult and time-wasting; it kept on jamming under overhangs. However, the first one got up there in the end; the second, weighing fifty-five pounds, followed, but on my shoulders. We just hadn't time to indulge in another bout of roping up. Fritz hauled on my rope; his assistance at least offset the weight of my pack, and I, too, was soon at the top of the crack. The pitch gave me a gentle foretaste of what the Face had in store; but the fact that I hadn't lost my breath coming up the crack strengthened my confidence that I was up to the work in hand. There is, of course, a huge difference between balancing upwards like a gymnast totally unencumbered on even the hardest Dolomite wall and climbing heavily laden up the Face of the Eiger. But then isn't the ability to hump heavy loads a requisite for every successful major climb?

Many climbers still to come will use rope slings on the "Difficult Crack." We preferred to climb it free. A rock climber of Kasparek's supreme skill only resorts to slings where they are absolutely unavoidable.

By now we were just below the Rote Fluh, that sheer wall, hundreds of feet high, which goes winging up to the sky in a sweep of incomparable smoothness. According to the book of the rules, based on man's experience, the mountain walls sleep quietly in the early morning, blanketed by the night frost. Even the stones are supposed to be frozen into inactivity. But the Eiger's Face doesn't go by any Queensberry rules; this was just another instance of the way it tips human experience overboard. Down came the stones. We could see them taking off over the top edge of the Rote Fluh and whizzing out through empty space in a wide arc. The Face was raking us with defensive fire. We hurried on upwards, for the nearer we got to the foot of the Rote Fluh, the safer we should be.

We could hear another heavy block coming. It landed below us, splintering into a thousand pieces.

Then we heard Fraissl's voice. Not a call for help or an S.O.S., just a communication; one of them had been hit on the head and hurt.

"How bad is it? Do you need help?" we asked.

"No, but I'm pretty giddy. I think we've had it. We'll have to turn back."

"Can you manage it alone?"

"Yes, we can."

We were sorry that our two Viennese friends couldn't keep us company, but we didn't try to dissuade them. So Fraissl and Brankowski started to climb down again.

Now, before sunrise, we two were alone on the Face again. Only a little while ago there had been six of us; now Fritz and I had only each other to rely on. We didn't discuss it, but subconsciously it strengthened our feeling of mutual dependence and comradeship. We made rapid progress over easier ground; and then, suddenly, we were at the passage that Rebitsch and Vörg had christened the "Hinterstoisser Traverse" the year before.

The rocks across which we now had to traverse to the left were almost vertical, plunging away beneath into thin air. We were full of admiration for Hinterstoisser's brave achievement when he opened up this rope-assisted traverse across to the First Ice Field for the first time, feeling his perilous way from hold to hold. We were full of gratitude too to Vörg and Rebitsch for having left a traversing rope—shouting a welcome to us, it seemed—in place here. We tested it and found it firmly anchored and secure against any strain, although it had been exposed for twelve months to storms and showers, to the wet and the cold.

We knew from reports, descriptions, and photographs how to effect the traverse. Nobody, however, had described the pitch when heavily iced over. The rock was absolutely glazed, offering no hold whatever to a frictioning foot. Nonetheless, Fritz led off into the traverse with that tremendous skill of his, fighting for his balance on smooth holdless film, winning his way, inch by inch, yard by yard, across that difficult and treacherous cliff. In places he had to knock away snow or a crust of ice from the rock with his ice hammer; the ice splinters swept down the slabs with a high whirring sound, to disappear into the abyss. But Fritz held on, pushing, feeling his way over to the left, climbing, hanging right away from the rock on the rope, from hold to hold, till he reached the far end of the traverse. Then I followed, shoving Fritz's rucksack along ahead of me on a snap link in the traversing rope, and soon joined him at the other end.

Soon after the traverse we came to the "Swallow's Nest," the bivouac place already made famous by Rebitsch and Vörg, and there we halted for a rest and some breakfast. The weather was holding, and a fine dawn had turned into a lovely day. The light was so good that it had already been possible to take pictures down on the traverse, a traverse that is certainly one of the most photogenic pitches in all the Alps. That one prosaic epithet tells the whole story—the extreme difficulty, the exposure, the daring of the traverse. And I should at once like to take the opportunity of correcting a misapprehension: the Hinterstoisser Traverse is one of the key pitches to the climb, not the only one. There are numerous critical places on this incredibly huge Face, which—thanks to the safe return of Rebitsch and Vörg—had by now been reconnoitered as far as Sedlmayer and Mehringer's "Death Bivouac." As yet we didn't know what key pitches lurked up there on the final precipice. All we knew was that, wherever it might rise in the Alps, it would by itself have been an object of wonder to the beholder and a highly prized objective for the best rock climbers alive.

We were going splendidly, the weather was fine, and we had no doubt that we stood a good chance of success; but we also knew that the very best of climbers had had to beat a retreat. So we equipped the "Swallow's Nest" as a strong point in case of a withdrawal. The old rope left by the 1937 party on the traverse was not enough. We proposed to ensure the direct line of descent, which in 1936 had proved fatal to the party of four, a tragedy which only reached its appalling end with the ghastly death of Toni Kurz. At the "Swallow's Nest," we left behind us 330 feet of rope, pitons, snap links, rope slings, and provisions.

It was July 21, 1938. Exactly two years ago to a day Hinterstoisser had spent hour upon hour in desperate attempts to climb back along the traverse he himself had been the first to discover. All in vain. He, and with him Angerer and Rainer, died on that same day. We were tremendously impressed by that memory. If those four men had only left their traversing rope in place at the Traverse, if they had only had a long enough rope at the "Swallow's Nest," if only . . . We had to thank the dead for our knowledge. The memory made us both proud and sad, but it did not scare us. Life has its laws, which we unconsciously obey. They pointed to the way up.

Fritz had strapped on his crampons; soon he was on his way up the First Ice Field. Here was no névé, but hard, brittle somewhat watery ice. I assessed the angle at from 50 to 55 degrees, that is, somewhat steeper than the average slope of the Grossglockner's

Pallavicini Couloir. After the first rope-length, Fritz cut a big stance and drove in an ice piton, to protect me on my ascent. We were already beginning to realise that our calculations had gone astray when we decided to leave my crampons behind. I now had to make up for lack of equipment by a considerable increase in muscular energy. Never mind, my training in several forms of sport would be a great asset. . . .

We were aiming for a vertical cliff, which leads from the First to the Second Ice Field. The only possible way seemed to be through an icy groove, later to be known as the "Ice Hose." This barrier between the two shields of ice is one of the many snares and delusions on this Face. Optically, a wall in the Dolomites is far more impressive than any single pitch on the Eiger's Face. When I recall the great Dolomite faces, there is much which seems more difficult, steeper, more inaccessible than it really is. But when you lay your hand on the Dolomite rock, you immediately delight in the rough surface, the horizontal stratification, the resulting proliferation of holds, and of the never-failing crannies and cracks into which pitons may safely be driven.

But here? The first illusion—the ice-covered rock barrier doesn't look particularly difficult. All you have to do is to hammer in a belaying piton below it . . . but it doesn't offer a belay. In fact there isn't a cranny anywhere for a reliable piton, and there aren't any natural holds. Moreover, the rock is scoured smooth by falling stones, bread-crumbed with snow, ice, and rubble. It isn't an invitation to cheerful climbing, it offers no spur to one's courage; it simply threatens hard work and danger. All the same, it is a part of the Eiger's North Face, which we are trying to climb. . . .

The "Ice Hose" does justice to its name. The rock was thickly plastered with the stuff; but even the hose part couldn't have been more accurate. Water was pouring down under the frozen layer, between the ice and the rock. The only way was up through it. The water poured into our sleeves, flowing right down our bodies, building

up for a short time above the gaiters, which were supposed to separate our trousers from our boots, before finding its way out. There
were practically no holds in this crack consisting of ice, rock, and water. It is severe, calls for the best climbing technique and demands the
most ingenious balancing maneuvers. Here, too, Fritz showed his
supreme skill; but it took hours to reach the Second Ice Field. We
were wet to the skin when we got there.

It was still early in the afternoon. High and wide above us loomed
the Second Ice Field. Our way led diagonally up to the left towards
the arête of the "Flatiron," in the direction of the last bivouac of
Sedlmayer and Mehringer. The huge ice apron was greatly fore-
shortened from where we stood; but even allowing for the optical illusion and remembering that it had taken first-class ice exponents like
Rebitsch and Vörg five hours—twenty rope lengths—to reach its
upper rim, we still had plenty of time to do it and probably even to
reach the "Death Bivouac." For there would still be at least six hours
of daylight.

In spite of all that, we decided to climb not to the left but to the
right, to a little knob of rock sticking out of the snow above the upper edge of the Rote Fluh. The fine afternoon was letting the sun beat
diagonally down on the upper part of the Face—up there where the
"little icicles blow their noses." That was what started the avalanches;
and stones, once released from the imprisoning ice up there, were in
the habit of following the laws of gravity.

And farther over to the west—for one has to traverse diagonally
across the Face for hundreds of feet on those ice shields—
snowslides, stone falls, and cascades of water were coming down in
their vertical, unhampered course from the "Spider."

Admittedly, every stone doesn't find a target. But we hadn't carefully built a strong point for a retreat down at the "Swallow's Nest"
in order to be knocked out by stones or wiped off the Face by
avalanches up here. Falling stones are numbered among the "objective" dangers of climbing or in other words as circumstances over

which man has no control; but to venture with one's eyes open into the line of fire of falling stones is no longer an objective but a subjective exposure to danger, the outcome of sheer carelessness or stupidity. This huge ice apron was a place to be climbed during the morning. Even then the danger from stones wouldn't be entirely eliminated, but it would be considerably less.

We reached our knob and were able to fix two belaying pitons; then we spent hours in digging a small seat out of the ice below it. It was still daylight when we began to make the final preparations for our bivouac. We tied ourselves and our belongings to the pitons for security's sake, furnished our seat with coils of rope, and started to cook our meal. The knob of rock afforded us complete protection from stones; the view from our perch was magnificent. All the conditions for a happy bivouac were present; but we hadn't a dry stitch on us. Yet, although we had warm clothing and a change of underwear in our rucksacks, we dared not risk getting it, too, damp by putting it on under soaking clothes. We didn't know what the weather might do, or how often, where and under what conditions we should have to bivouac. So we would have to keep our spares dry against nights yet to come; but it needed some strength of mind not to fetch them out of the packs and put them on, even though we knew better.

The night was long, cold, and uncomfortable. The bivouac was not a good one. We were only to know later on that it was the worst on the whole Face, in spite of its comparatively good sitting space. Our wet clothes made us doubly susceptible to the cold; our minds and spirits were as busy as our bodies trying to cope with the discomfort. No training in the world is proof against that.

Every night has to come to an end sometime. In the grey light of dawn we got up with chattering teeth and prepared the ropes for the day's climbing. The weather was still good and the frost had anchored all the stones, as we started on the diagonal climb across the Second Ice Field. It was only now that we realised to the full what a mistake we had made in leaving my crampons behind. Fritz counteracted the error by a tremendous output of energy, as he built a positive ladder of steps. It was amazing to see how expert with his ice axe was this best of all Vienna's rock climbers. For hours on end he swung it rhythmically to cut step upon step, resting only when he stopped to safeguard me up them. And the steps were so good that my claw nails gave me excellent holds in them.

From down below, the Ice Field looks like a smooth surface; but that is pure illusion. Huge waves in the ice constantly gave the impression that we were quite close to the safety of the rocks above; but we soon realised that we had only reached another bulge in the ice and that there was yet another ice valley to be crossed. It was the phenomenon the climber so often experiences in the Western Alps, when he mistakes one of many subsidiary excrescences for the main summit.

The fully equipped modern mountaineer handles his ice axe like a guide of the classical Alpine era. Speed is the essence of modern climbing; steady, slow progress that of the classic past. We were naturally taking longer because we were using the technique of the past. Even Rebitsch and Vörg had taken five hours the year before to cross this huge patch of ice. We took exactly the same time.

Just before the rocks separating the Second from the Third Ice Field, I looked back, down our endless ladder of steps. Up it I saw the New Era coming at express speed; there were two men running—and I mean running, not climbing—up it. Admittedly, practised climbers can move quickly in good steps; but for these two to have reached this point quite early in the morning was positively amazing. They must have bivouacked last night on the lower part of the wall; it hardly seemed possible that they had only started up it today. But it was, in fact, the case.

These two were the best of all the "Eiger Candidates"— Heckmair and Vörg—wearing their twelve-pointer crampons. I felt quite outmoded in my old claws. We exchanged a brief greeting; then they went on up to Fritz. I knew my friend and his highly developed set of Alpine etiquette pretty well; I knew he preferred to find his own way, and that, though he wore the honourable badge of the Mountain Rescue Service, he himself didn't like assistance. Even Heckmair's obviously joking inquiry whether he wouldn't prefer to turn back only brought a good strong Viennese reply from Fritz.

But Anderl didn't mean to start a squabble. His is a character with no touch of malice in it; moreover, Kasparek and Heckmair had far too great a respect for one another, and so the result of the encounter was neither discord nor rivalry, but a teaming up such as has rarely been seen on this mighty Face. We naturally continued to climb as two separate ropes, with Heckmair and Vörg now taking over the lead. They told us later how they had seen Fraissl and Brankowski turn back; after that there had been no holding them. They had started up the Face early in the morning and now they had already caught us up. And now, too, we would be staying together. . . .

We moved on up the steep ridge towards the "Death Bivouac" at a uniform pace. During our extended midday rest at that point we felt completely united. Not a word was spoken indicative of any sense of disappointment. It was just as if we had always intended to climb together and now we were glad to have joined up at long last.

There could be no difference of opinion as to the continuation of the route. It led from our resting place diagonally downwards across the Third Ice Field towards the foot of the "Ramp," the rock feature rising steeply towards the ridge up which lies the Lauper Route; then from the "Ramp" a right-hand traverse to the "Spider"; across the "Spider" and then up the adjacent exit cracks to the summit névé, crowning the final wall. It all sounds so easy. Yet each of the pitches named has its own big question mark. But when I looked at my companions, Fritz, Anderl, and Wiggerl, I felt quite certain that any pitch that offered the faintest possibility of a route up it would be climbed by our party of four.

It might perhaps have been possible to climb straight up the cliff from the "Death Bivouac" to the "Spider," but we could not see very far as we looked up the precipice. Mists were closing in on the mountain, and beginning to drift gently down to us. These were the mists that are known "out there" as the Eiger's "Wad of cotton wool" and hug every contour of its ice and rock. That didn't upset us very much. It is one of the Eiger's regular features to put on a skullcap for its after-lunch nap, much to the fury of the inquisitive people milling around the telescopes. We, of course, couldn't know the intensity of that fury, stemming from the fact that queue tickets were being issued and that their purchasers had to pay for three minutes' viewing, whether they saw anything or not. Meanwhile, unobserved by the great world outside, we were traversing across an ice slope, whose inclination exceeds 60 degrees, to the start of the "Ramp."

The "Ramp"—well, it fits that Face, on which everything is more difficult than it looks. You cannot run up it, for there are no rough slabs, no good footholds or handholds. Here too the rock-strata slope outwards and downwards and the crannies into which a piton can be driven can be counted on one hand. At all events, I had a good belaying piton at the foot of the "Ramp." I stood watching Fritz as he moved upward with even, rhythmic movements, to a point some 80 feet above me.

Suddenly he slipped. I couldn't tell whether a hold had come away in his hand or whether he had failed to find a foothold. Everything went so quickly—he was already out of sight. I took in as much slack as I could and stood there waiting for the shock. I knew the piton was firmly in and would hold. And the rope, cushioned by the belay around my shoulders, ought with any luck to take the strain. Anybody coming off unbelayed at this point would go winging straight down to the outcrops at the bottom of the Face. . . .

Luck was with us. The rope ran out over a little ridge of snow, cutting into the surface névé. This checked the velocity of Fritz's fall to such an extent that the shock I had to withstand was perfectly bearable. But was Fritz hurt?

My mind was soon at rest. Up from below came a couple of words intelligible only to one who knows Viennese slang inside out—a good aggressive oath. Then Fritz was climbing again. Soon he was at the top of the "Ramp," moving on above it, just as if nothing had happened, till presently I shouted up to him that there was no more rope. On my way up, I took a look at the place where he had come off. Fritz had fallen 60 feet through thin air straight down from the diagonal "Ramp" and had then calmly climbed back again by a difficult crack. We didn't mention the mishap again. Fritz carried it off as quietly as a player whom the dice condemn to go back to the start in Snakes and Ladders. We weren't in the least upset; we just laughed because we were enjoying life. No sentimental handshakes either. Back to the start—and then six forward up the next waterfall—that was the way we looked at it. It was quite natural for Fritz to have climbed straight up again after his fall, for he hadn't hurt himself. And it was quite natural for me to have held the rope because that was what I was there for. Fritz was just the right companion for this great Face. He treated irrelevancies as such, never burdening his friends with "if" and "suppose," nor with the thought "what might have happened," or the question "why did it happen?" What really mattered was that nothing *had* happened.

Late in the afternoon the four of us were all together again. Above us the "Ramp" had contracted to a narrow gulley with a crack blasted out of it. Water was running down the crack. None of us wanted to bivouac in wet clothes—our own had dried out during the morning, while we were traversing the Second Ice Field; moreover, we were beginning to find the day's labours sufficient. The crack would be a good prelude to the next day's work; so we prepared to bivouac.

That sounds easy enough. And we had thought it would be easy enough when we were looking at the "Ramp" in photographs or through a telescope. We even thought we could pick our seats. Actually there were no seats, in fact not a single seat. Indeed, good stances were a rarity.

We arranged our bivouac about 8 feet below that of Heckmair and Vörg. We managed to drive a single piton into a tiny crevice in the rock. It was a thin square-shafted piton. It held after only a centimeter, but it was just jammed. Obviously, once we hung our whole weight on it, it would very likely work loose with the leverage. So we bent it downwards in a hoop, till the ring was touching the rock. In this way we did away with any question of leverage and knew we could rely on our little grey steely friend. First we hung all our belongings onto it and, after that, ourselves.

There was no room to sit down. The "Ramp" was very narrow and very steep at this point; but we managed to manufacture a sort of seat with the aid of rope slings, and hung out some more to prevent our legs from dangling over the gulf. Next to me there was a tiny level spot, just big enough for our cooker, so we were able to brew tea, coffee, and cocoa. We were all very much in need of liquids.

Heckmair and Vörg were no more comfortably lodged. The relaxed attitude of Vörg, the "Bivouac King," was quite remarkable; even in a place like this he had no intention of doing without every possible comfort. He even put on his soft fleece-lined bivouac slippers, and the expression on his face was that of a genuine connoisseur of such matters. It is absolutely no exaggeration to say that we all felt quite well and indeed comfortable. Experienced climbers will understand that statement, and laymen must simply believe it. A famous philosopher, when asked what true happiness was, replied: "If you have some broth, a place to sleep in, and no bodily pains, you are well on the way." We can improve on that definition. "Dry clothes, a reliable piton, and precious revivifying drinks—that is true happiness where the North Face of the Eiger is concerned."

Yes, we were quite happy. This huge mountain face had brought our lives down to the lowest common denominator. After cooking for hours we pulled the Zdarsky sack over us and tried to find as comfortable a position as possible, so that we could at least doze off occasionally. It was great to be able to look forward to a night in dry clothes. Our perch was about 4,000 feet above the snowfields at the base of the precipice; if one of us fell off now, that was where he would certainly finish up. But who was thinking about falling off?

It was a good bivouac. Bodily aches and discomfort made no disturbing intrusion on the train of our thoughts. As I fell asleep, I saw a picture, a happy, sunny picture of something that happened when I was very young; no mirage of a sheltering roof over my head or a warm bed, but a memory of one of my first experiences in the mountains.

It happened when I was only fifteen. I had climbed all alone to the top of the Mangart, that proud summit in the Julian Alps, and was coming down, very impressed by my great experience. I reached a huge scree slope, of the kind one so often finds in the Julians, miles long. Down it I went, through the bleak hanging valley, taking long bounding strides. The sun was scorching and my tongue was sticking to my gums. There in the middle of the rubble, I saw two eagles tearing huge lumps of flesh from the carcass of a chamois. The birds of prey only flew away reluctantly as I came by. I was so fascinated by the sight that I momentarily forgot my thirst. Young as I was, the knowledge that the death of one thing can mean the life of another was borne in on me ineradicably. Was that an immutable law of Nature? I wondered. Was it true for people as well as for animals? Every fibre of my being protested against the notion.

I came down to the shore of the Weissenfelser See. There, by the lake, stood a shepherd's hut, next to a spring, from which fell a glittering column of water. I bent down and let the water run down over my wrists. Then I drank and drank and drank. . . .

Suddenly I felt a sharp box on my ears. The tall, white-haired herdsman was standing there, his sharp-etched face burnt mahogany by the sun.

"Boy, why are you drinking water?" he asked. "There in my hut

I have cool milk and sour cream. You can quench your thirst and drink your fill indoors."

I shall never forget that old man, who allowed his tongue to grow sharp in order to do me a good turn. I remained for days as his guest, eating and drinking everything the little farm produced, milk, and cream and cream cheese. He was a proud, hospitable man and, what is more, educated and much travelled, who could speak eight languages fluently. For many years he had been a ship's cook over the face of the seven seas; and all his life's experiences added up to kindness toward his fellow men. I remembered the horrible picture of the eagles and the dead chamois. And instantly I realised, with the receptive idealism of early youth, that Nature's cruelty didn't hold among men. Men must be kindly. . . .

With that memory of the old man by the Weissenfelser See I nodded off, into a deep and dreamless sleep. I don't know how long I slept like that. Suddenly, dreaming now, I saw the old man there again in front of me. His face was no longer kind; he was angry as he tugged at my breast. I tried to shake him off, wanting to go on sleeping, but I could not, he was so strong. He tugged at me and shook me harder still.

I only half woke up, but could still feel the fierce pressure on my chest. It was the rope. I had slid off my perch as I slept, and was hanging on it with my full weight. I knew then that I was on the "Ramp," on the Eiger's North Face, and that I really ought to straighten myself out, raise myself, and resume a proper sitting posture; but I was too lethargic and only wanted to go on sleeping. Vaguely I recognised that one shouldn't for a moment longer than necessary weigh down a piton that is only a centimeter deep into the rock; but it was so pleasant to snatch just a few more minutes before straightening everything out. So I fell asleep again.

The moment I nodded off, there was the dream, back again. This time the old man shook me properly awake. I stood up in the slings, resumed my sedentary posture on that vertiginous little stance. Fritz mumbled something in his sleep.

Then I heard Andreas and Ludwig talking overhead. Vörg's voice sounded worried, so I asked what was the matter.

"Anderl feels sick," came the answer. "The sardines he ate last night have upset his tummy."

I was wide-awake by now and fully restored. I could hardly feel the cold anymore. There, close by me, on its little level spot, stood the cooker.

"I'll brew you some tea, Anderl," I said. "It always helps."

Tea is surely the king of all drinks. It helps against cold, it helps against the heat, against discomfort and sickness, against weariness and weakness. And it helped on this occasion too. The sardines quietened down in Anderl's tummy. We dozed and slept till the stars began to pale and the light of a new day crept through the twilight before dawn. Night was over; it had not been a bad one.

Vörg began cooking at about four o'clock. Like everything else, he did it thoughtfully, unhurriedly, and thoroughly. He cooked porridge and coffee in large quantities. That cheered us up and drove away the cold. It was seven o'clock before we finally started to climb again. To have to cope with the crack in the gully as early-morning physical training was quite a big demand on bodies still stiff from a bivouac. It didn't look any easier this morning than it had yesterday evening, except that the waterfall had stopped. In its place there was a thin armoring of ice on the rocks. Even Anderl, leading up it, looked a little doubtful.

He seemed to think straight on up was the best way and took the gully direct, knocking in a piton wherever he could. One of them actually held safe. He worked his way higher and higher with supreme technical skill, trying to get off the ice by climbing into the overhanging cliffs on the Face. He was nearly up the overhang, trying out a hold from which to get a final pull-up; but it wasn't a hold, it was a loose block, and it broke away bringing him down with it. A second or two later our friend was hanging safely from the good piton below the overhang. That wouldn't do at all for Andreas Heckmair: overhangs can't behave like that. He was very cross indeed. If it wouldn't go on the ice-free stuff, then it had better go right up the middle of the ice itself. So he put on his famous twelve-pointer crampons.

Then he treated us to an acrobatic *tour de force,* an exhibition exercise, such as we had rarely witnessed before. It was half superb rock-technique, half a toe dance on the ice—a toe dance above a perpendicular drop. He got a hold on the rock, a hold on the ice, bent himself double, uncoiled himself, the front points of his crampons moving ever upwards, boring into the ice. They got only a few millimeters' purchase, but that was enough. Heckmair defeated that difficult pitch, cut footholds, and banged pitons into the ice slope that began above it, then safeguarded Vörg up it after him.

We were still climbing as two separate ropes. It was now Kasparek's turn to tackle the crack in the gully. Not only had he no twelve-pointer crampons, he had a completely different conception of the pitch. He took it direct, avoiding entanglements with the icy and the ice-free containing walls alike. By a masterly piece of climbing he got up the crack as if climbing in the Gesäuse[1] at home rather than on the great Face of the Eiger.

I came up last. Then we were all four together again on the ice, looking up in incredulous astonishment at the menacing bulge of ice that here threatens finally to bar all progress up the "Ramp." Could anybody climb that?

The cliff was more than 30 feet high. I had never seen anything to match it; even the others at first seemed flabbergasted. Would it go on the left? No. On the right? No. Straight up seemed to be the best bet: but was this "best" a possible one? Hekmair had a go. He began by banging pitons into the ice below the bulge. One

[1] The famous Austrian rock-climbing area in Upper Styria, with limestone faces of more than 3,000 feet.—Translator's note.

of them went in and held like a vice. Then he balanced his way delicately upwards. There were icicles hanging from the bulge; to one of these he fastened a sling and pushed himself up a bit in it. It looked terrifying, but he didn't seem in the least impressed by the danger; inch by inch he moved upwards, but as soon as he trusted his weight to the icicle, the pretty glittering thing broke away and off he came. . . .

The piton held.

Once again we saw the same reaction as before. A rebuff as thoroughgoing as a fall rouses Heckmair to a cold fury. He immediately tackled the bulge again. This time he didn't trust to the icicles with which the architect of our mighty prison had decorated it. Was it really a prison? Was this where we were going to have to give in and turn back?

No, our Andreas climbed up and out of our prison, having found an "ice handle." An icicle hanging down had coagulated with an ice stump pushing upward—a stalagmite and a stalactite, both of ice, had grown into one. And this object, carpentered by some freak of nature, proved to be the key to our prison door. Heckmair threaded another sling through the handle, leaned outwards almost horizontally, banged some notches with his ice hammer in the ice above the bulge, felt around with one hand, took a firm hold.

I had never seen a pitch that looked so hazardous, dangerous, and utterly extraordinary. Fritz, who knows many of the famous key pitches in the Alps, thought that the famous overhanging roof on the Pillar of the Marmolata looked like child's play in comparison with this bulge. We were all pretty tense. Vörg had a tight hold on the rope, ready at any moment to hold Heckmair if he came off again.

But he didn't come off. We couldn't imagine how, but in some masterly fashion or other he had managed to drive an ice piton deep into the ice above the bulge and thread the rope through a snap link. Then he gave the order: "Pull!"

Vörg pulled him up on the rope, over the bulge, up to the piton.

Heckmair used his axe a few more times. Then "Let her go!" he said.

Vörg let the rope go loose, so that Heckmair could stand up; at the same time he was still keeping a careful watch in case of another fall. But Heckmair was soon in firm holds; he hurried a few feet up onto the ice slope above the bulge, cut a roomy stance in the ice, and drove a belaying piton deep into firm ice. Then as the curtain cue to an unusually dramatic scene we heard the welcome words: "Up you come!"

Our prison gate was open. Vörg followed through it. The North Face of the Eiger is so vast, so difficult, and so serious that any display of human vanity would be out of place. No doubt Fritz and I could have climbed the bulge without any assistance from above, but it would have taken precious hours we would later have begrudged. So Fritz didn't hesitate a moment to take the rope Vörg let down to us. We who followed were robbed of the thrill and the adventure of this, the hardest pitch till now on the Face; we only tasted the toil it involves. And I, as last on the rope, had to knock out and retrieve all the pitons. I was decorated with them like a Christmas tree and the clank of the ironmongery drowned my gasps as I struggled up over the bulge.

The ice slope above was easy compared with what we had just done. We went straight up the ice for a short way only, then traversed out to the right at once.

It is of course easy enough for anyone who has made a successful first ascent to shake his head about the mistakes of those who follow. I do not propose to do it. But I am surprised that so many parties which climbed the Face after us went straight on up the ice slope toward the Mittellegi Ridge and only tried to traverse across to the "Spider" much too high up. This was the cause of many delays and also brought about the disaster of 1957. It was perfectly clear to the four of us that the right-hand traverse must be attempted as soon as possible.

So we were traversing out to the right from the ice slope, all four roped together, along a brittle belt of rock below an overhanging cliff. It was midday by now, and we could hear the hissing of the avalanches and the tattoo of the stones, but we were protected from both by the overhang.

While we were traversing these broken rocks—Heckmair was about 200 feet ahead of me at the time—we suddenly heard a fearful humming and whining sound. It was neither a stone fall nor an avalanche, but an airplane flying past quite close to us. We could see the faces of its passengers quite plainly. They waved and we waved back. Hans Steiner, the Bernese photographer, managed to take some photographs of unique documentary value at that moment. His pictures showed three of us on the traverse while Heckmair had already started up a crack beyond it.

That crack is the only possible line of ascent from where the brittle belt peters out to a level on which the traverse to the "Spider" can be completed. Heckmair thought he could climb it by the usual methods; but every pitch on the Eiger's Face is harder than it looks and tricky with ledges on which the snow is only pressed against the rocks, with hand- and footholds that let you down. So he had to leave his rucksack behind to have a second go at the pitch, unencumbered. For this he kept his crampons on, in view of the icing one continually meets on the Face. It was an entirely new type of rock climbing, this ascent of severe, often super-severe rock, overhanging in places—on crampons. Heckmair frequently stood in imminent danger of a fall, but somehow his fingers held him when he thought his strength was used up. The scrape of his climbing irons on the hard rock sounded like a furious gritting of teeth, which only stopped when he disappeared from sight overhead.

We three followed without crampons.

It took ages before we had all got up that 100-foot vertical rock pitch. But surely not so long that it was dusk already? It had suddenly grown very dark; but a glance at the watch showed that, in spite of the darkness, it was still early afternoon. Heavy clouds bulked up into the sky; and this time the thundering roar caught up by the rocks and thrown back in a hundred reverberations was not the sound of an airplane, flying past dangerously near. This was genuine thunder.

By the time I reached Fritz's stance, the other two had gone ahead. They had untied from the communal rope again, so as to reach the "Spider" before the storm broke.

The thunderstorm provided a gloomy, menacing, but magnificent setting. A few minutes before, the sun had been shining, at least for the people down in Grindelwald. This sudden change was typical of the North Face; but we were already so familiar with its caprices that the oncoming storm caused us no alarm. Indeed, I was even sorry that there was no time to linger on the stance where Fritz had been waiting for me. That stance had all the elements of the miraculous; it was the first place, indeed the only one, in the whole 6,000-foot Face where you could make yourself comfortable. It would have been grand to sit and rest there, looking down the great wall, into the valley, out over the surrounding hills. But the weather was hunting us on, and we followed the others.

The rock traverse to the "Spider" is no promenade. But at least the rocks at this point are horizontal and the stratification consequently favourable. And the patches of ice which link them were firm enough to allow us to bite deeply into them with our ice pitons. Not only is the traverse indescribably fine from the scenic angle, but it is so exciting and technically safe that we almost forgot the approaching storm. I cannot remember who first gave it the name of "the Traverse of the Gods," but it is comprehensively descriptive.

We reached the "Spider," the great sheet of ice set in the Face, quickly and without encountering any great difficulties. We hadn't time to examine the scene and the terrain more closely, and now even the possibility of so doing was withdrawn, for the sky had meanwhile taken on a blue-black tinge; then it disappeared altogether, as tattered mists chased across the Face, closing in on us, then lifting again to give a glimpse of things, then settling into a thick blanket of cloud. As the storm set in it began to sleet, mixed with snow; lightning began to flash and thunder to grumble and roar.

We could still see Heckmair and Vörg, already on the way up the ice slope of the "Spider," about a rope's length and a half ahead of us; so we followed them up.

As I have already explained, the name "Spider" has been given to this steep patch of névé or ice high up in the almost vertical Face because of the white streaks spreading out from it in every direction like legs and clutching arms. These run more especially upwards—in cracks and gullies up towards the summit snowcap—and down towards the "Death Bivouac." But nobody had discovered how apt the appellation was before we got there; nor had we, as yet, while we went up the first rope's length. We hadn't yet discovered that this "Spider" of snow, ice, and rock can become a fearful trap; that when hail or snow falls, ice particles and snow, coming sliding down from the steep summit névé, get canalised in the cracks and gullies, shoot out onto the "Spider" under pressure, there join up in a flood of annihilating fury and then sweep across the "Spider's" body, finally to fling themselves outwards and downwards, obliterating and taking with them everything that isn't part of the living rock. Nor is there any escape from the "Spider" for anyone caught on it by bad weather and avalanches.

We didn't know it then, but we very soon found out. Very soon. Immediately. . . .

I was already on the "Spider's" ice and had hacked out a reasonable stance in which I was able to stand quite well without crampons. I felt very safe on account of a deeply embedded ice piton. The rope ran through a snap link hung on the piton ring to Fritz, working his way up about 60 feet above me. I could see him vaguely through the mist and the driven snow.

Presently he disappeared from my sight, swallowed up in the mist. The screaming of the storm, the rattle of the hail were alarming. I tried to penetrate the grey veils to catch a glimpse of him, but in vain. Only a greyness within a greyness. . . .

The howling of the wind increased, gathering a very strange note—a banging and swishing, a whistling hiss. This wasn't the voice of the storm any more coming down out of wild dance of ice particles and snowflakes, but something quite different. It was an avalanche, and as its harbingers, rocks and fragmented ice!

I snatched my rucksack up over my head, holding it firmly with one hand, while the other gripped the rope which ran up to my companion. I jammed myself against the ice cliff, just as the whole weight of the avalanche struck me. The rattle and hammering of stones on my pack was swallowed up by the clatter and roar of the avalanche. It snatched and clutched at me with fearful strength. Could I possibly survive such pressure? Hardly. . . . I was fighting for air, trying above all to prevent my rucksack from being torn away and also to stop the endless stream of rushing snow from building up between me and the ice slope and forcing me out of my footholds.

I hardly knew whether I was still standing, or was sliding down with it. Had the ice piton come adrift? No, I was still standing, and the peg was still firm; but the pressure was growing unbearable. And Fritz must be coming off any moment. Standing out there in the open he couldn't possibly withstand the fury of the avalanche . . . it must sweep him away. . . .

My thoughts were quite clear and logical, although I felt certain that this avalanche must hurl us all off the "Spider" and down to the bottom of the mighty wall. I was only resisting because one tries to resist so long as there is life in one. I was still gripping the rope with one hand, determined to do all I could to hold Fritz. At the same time I began to wonder whether we were already so high on the "Spider" that he wouldn't hit the rocks below, but would remain hanging on the ice slope if he came off, slid past me, and fetched up on the full run of the rope 60 feet below? And could I stand the shock if he hit me in passing?

All these thoughts were calm, without any sense of fear or desperation. I had no time for things like that. When would Fritz come off? I seemed to have been standing in this crushing, sliding Hell for endless ages. Had stones cut the rope and Fritz fallen alone, deprived of its protection? No, if that had happened the loose rope would have come sliding down to me. It was still stretching upwards, so Fritz must somehow or other still be holding on. . . .

The pressure decreased, but I got no time to draw new breath or to shout before the next avalanche arrived. Its fury exceeded that of the first; it must bring the end for us. Even that realisation was almost objective. It was odd that no important thoughts moved me, such as one might expect on reaching the very frontier of existence itself. Nor did scenes from my whole life go chasing past in front of my eyes. My thoughts were almost banal, ridiculous, unimportant. I felt a little cross that the critics and wiseacres, and also the Grindelwald gravedigger, who had already numbered us, like all those who try the North Face, as belonging to his parish had been justified. Then I remembered my accident on the West Face of the Sturzhahn in the Totengebirge, years ago. I was trying to climb that difficult wall in the winter and fell 150 feet. On that occasion, too, I hadn't lived all my life over again, nor had I felt any great sense of despair, much as I loved life. Is everything different when one really crosses that border, then?

And now, I was still alive; my rucksack was still protecting my head; the rope was still threaded through the snap link; and Fritz had still not fallen.

Then a new, unbelievable, and this time shattering realisation came over me. The pressure of the avalanche had ceased. The snow and the ice granules were tinkling away into the gulf. Even the raging of the storm seemed gentle to me, now that the crashing of the avalanche was stilled.

Then, tremulously, through the grey mists, came the first shouts, to be caught up by the cliffs framing the "Spider" and thrown back to the human beings, scarcely able to grasp the incredible truth. Names were being called, voices were answering: "Fritz! Heini! Anderl! Wiggerl!" I told myself that we were all alive. The others were all alive, and so was I. The greatest Eiger miracle had happened. The "White Spider" had not claimed a victim.

But was it really a miracle? Had the mountain been kind? Would it be true to say that the "Spider" had spared the lives of her victims?

Climbers are not only men of action, they are also matter-of-fact people. Such reflections are only to be explained by the first upsurge of joy at one's recaptured life; they won't stand up to sober judgment. The miracle and the mercy were none of nature's fashioning nor the mountain's, but were the result of man's will to do the right thing even in moments of direst peril. Who can say we were merely lucky?

A famous man once said: "In the long run only the efficient man has luck." I am not so presumptuous as to claim that we mountaineers are always efficient. It seems to me that one of Alfred Wegener's remarks fits our situation on the Eiger's "Spider" better. He said: "Luck is the output of one's last reserves."

We had put out our last reserves.

Kasparek was standing 60 feet above me on the ice slope. When he heard the avalanche coming, he tried, with an instantaneous reaction, to drive in an ice piton. He had no time to be frightened even for a split second. The piton was only a few centimeters into the ice, and quite loose, when the first avalanche arrived. In spite of the danger, even while the avalanche was roaring down on him in all its fury, he thought of the loose piton. It would have to stay firm, it simply mustn't be torn out by the shock of the cascading masses of snow and ice, nor by a falling stone; so Kasparek kept one protecting arm over the piton. Stones hit him on the hand, tearing the skin away. He was in great pain, but his will to keep the piton firm was greater. And during the short respite between the first and second avalanche, he drove the piton into the ice up to its ring, hooked a snap link in, and attached himself to it. And that is why Fritz didn't come off. . . .[1]

It was only afterwards, when the tension of the moment had passed, that I remembered having fastened myself by a rope sling to my own piton for greater protection during that same interval.

The avalanche took Heckmair and Vörg by surprise, on a projection about 60 feet below the rock rim above the "Spider." Owing to the configuration of the Face, it divided close above them into two separate streams; but the snow and ice granules pouring down over each of them were quite strong enough to sweep even men of their build away. Neither of them could obtain protection by driving in a piton, not only because there was no time, but because they hadn't one between them. I had the whole collection by then: owing to being last on the rope, I was carrying about twenty pounds of ironmongery that I had retrieved.

Heckmair had only his axe to hold him. The river of ice came up to his hips and threatened to whirl him away like a dead leaf; but he managed to resist the apparently irresistible pressure. At the same time he proved himself as an outstanding climbing partner as well as an outstanding leader of a climb. In spite of his own terrible distress, he had time to think of his number two, standing below him and still more exposed on the top of the knob. Holding his axe with one hand as an anchorage, he grabbed Vörg by the collar and held him tight. And so they both survived the assaults of the avalanches.

It was only now, when the danger was over, that Fritz felt the burning pain in his "scalped" hand. Only then did he shout up to Heckmair and Vörg. "Send a rope down, I'm hurt."

It took a long time to splice the ropes and send them down towards where Fritz was standing. And then they were still 30 feet short, so that Kasparek had to climb that distance unprotected.

---

[1] Fritz Kasparek, "Vom Peilstein zur Eiger-Nordwand," *Das Bergland Buch* (Salzburg: 1951).

How right Wegener is! Luck is certainly the output of one's last reserves.

This is how Heckmair described the end of the avalanche and his joy at finding that we were all still alive:

Slowly it grew lighter and the pressure eased. We knew then, but still could hardly believe, that we had come through safely. And how had the others fared? The mists were thinning now—and there—

"Wiggerl," I cried. "They're still on!"

It seemed impossible, an outright miracle. We started to shout, and there they were, actually answering. An indescribable joy swept over us. One only discovers how strong a thing team spirit can be when one sees the friends again whom one has counted for dead. . . .

We all joined up again at the upper rim of the "Spider." Our feeling of delight at seeing the faces of our comrades again was overwhelming. As the outward sign of our friendship we decided to tie up again in a single rope of four—all the way to the top. And our leader should be Anderl. The "Spider's" avalanches hadn't been able to wipe us off the Face, but they had succeeded in sweeping away with them the last petty remnants of personal niggardliness and selfish ambition. The only answer to this mighty wall was the enduring bond of friendship, the will and the knowledge that each of us would give of his very best. Each of us was responsible for the lives of the others, and we refused to be separated anymore. We were all filled with a great joy. From it stemmed the certainty that we would climb out of the Face onto the summit and find our way back to the valley where men live. It was in a mood of almost cheerful relaxation that we resumed the climb.

Our climb was in the full glare of public interest, though we neither knew nor cared about that; but it is interesting to note how the doings on the North Face were being interpreted by the watching eyes below. This is how Ulrich Link, the well-known Munich journalist, reported it from his observation post on the Kleine Scheidegg:

On Saturday at about 12:30 P.M., a break in the weather announced itself on the Eiger. A slate grey menacingly dark cloud covered the Lauterbrunnen Valley. At that time the four climbers had, after five hours of tremendous labour, scaled the "Diagonal Gully," perhaps the hardest sector on the whole Face. . . . At one o'clock all four were one behind the other at the left-hand edge of the snowfield. Heckmair, himself a guide and probably the hardest trained and most proficient on ice, was leading.

For half an hour a cloud hid the climbers from our view. At about 1:30 the Face was clear again. By then they had traversed the snow ledge and the leader had already reached the crossing to the snowfield called the "Spider." Heckmair led in splendid style—he had been in the lead all day—across to the "Spider." Kasparek and Harrer had meanwhile rested at the end of the snow ledge. From 3 to 3:30 P.M. the Face was once again enveloped in cloud. Then it cleared again and everyone rushed to the telescopes. The leader of the second rope was just traversing from the rocks onto the "Spider." At the same moment Heckmair reached the rock outcrop in the upper snow couloir. The second party was moving more slowly, but with the same steadiness and caution as the first. Heckmair and Vörg had now reached a height of 11,800 feet and it was ten minutes past four. Mist came down on the Face again, and we were left cut off with our fears and our hopes. The summit was still more than a thousand feet above the four men.

And now the weather was looking very bad again. Hour by hour it was impossible to tell whether it was going to finish up better or worse. The Lauterbrunnen Valley lay under a dirty gray pall; the Jungfrau and the Mönch were wrapped in cloud. The ice falls glimmered pale blue and bluish green in the lurid light. There was a patch of blue sky between the rain clouds. The Grosse Scheidegg over yonder was still quite clear, but the weather was making up relentlessly. Meanwhile the second party must be in the Funnel on the "Spider."

At 4:25 it began to rain gently, and exactly five minutes later a violent, noisy downpour set in, as if the clouds had been torn apart. It must be hitting the Face and the four climbers on it like a tidal wave. One could hear many voices raised in a confused gasp of alarm. The whole breadth of the North Face had become one fearsome waterfall. Water was pouring down the cliffs in ten, twelve, fifteen wide columns of white foam. A marvellous rainbow stood arched widely over Alpiglen; but who had any eyes for its miraculous play of colour? Up there, two of the men must be on the snow slope, exposed to the full force of the flood pouring down on them. Would they be able to hang on?

At last the cloud lifted. The telescope was clear at last. There lay the great snow slope . . . and there were the climbers, both moving up quietly and calmly. They had survived the deluge, then. Vörg and Heckmair had probably had a much easier passage, for they had managed to escape into the rocks at the edge of the couloir. Then the clouds closed down again. . . .

At 6:45 all four men were reunited and moving towards the upper end of the belt of snow. At 7 o'clock they reached it; at 8 they were still moving on up, either because they had not yet found a bivouac site or else, having decided to go ahead as long as daylight allowed, to get as near the summit as possible. They had now reached 12,150 feet, high above the "Spider," a wonderful performance in fourteen hours. At 8:20 it began to rain again. During short intervals when the clouds permitted, we could see them climbing on and on. At 9 o'clock they were still moving, probably preparing their perch for the night; Kasparek and Harrer's third, Vörg and Heckmair's second bivouac. It will certainly be an ordeal, in wet clothes on an inadequate resting place most likely. But all four are tough as steel. . . .

Ten o'clock and pitch dark now. From now on the four men have to endure the long hours of darkness; they have enough food for six days. They will probably find little sleep during the night and will probably crouch over their cooker making hot tea and warming food. There can be no retreat now. . . .

That report from a knowledgeable and experienced journalist makes pleasant reading even for a climber; for it is written in a manner which would also grip a layman, but without any uncalled-for dramatisation, and without cheap sensations thought up at a writer's desk. The mere facts, the keen observation of nature, the bare description of the Face are quite sensational enough by themselves.

But Ulrich Link was wrong about one thing. We couldn't crouch over our cooker. There was no room for that, though cooking still played its important part.

As to our bivouac site, with the exception of the site above the crack leading to the "Traverse of the Gods," there is no single tiny spot where one can sit or where one can bivouac without thorough preparation.

After we had climbed an ice bulge, we came upon a rock ledge protected by overhangs from falling stones and avalanches. When I say a ledge, I do not mean a smooth comfortable feature on which it is possible to sit; it was far too narrow and precipitous for that. Heckmair found a place where he could drive in a rock piton firmly, and with great patience fixed enough hooks on which to hang all the stuff, as well as securing himself and Vörg. There was no room there for us. Fritz and I arranged our overnight abode about 10 feet away. The ledge was scarcely as broad as a boot, and only just allowed us to stand erect, pressed close against the rock; but we contrived to knock in a piton to which we could tie ourselves. Even then we still couldn't sit, not even on the outer rim of the ledge.

However, we found a solution. We emptied our rucksacks and tried fastening them, too, to the piton, in such a way that we could put our feet in them and so find a hold. We were sure it would work all right, and so it did.

Between us and our friends we had fixed a traversing rope, along which a cookery pot went shuttling back and forth hanging from a snap link. Vörg had taken on the important post of expedition cook. So, even if we couldn't crouch over it, as Link had imagined us doing, the bubbling of Vörg's cookery pot produced a comfortable feeling. None of us wanted any solid food; all we needed was drink. So Ludwig brewed coffee, for hours on end. As soon as a bowl was ready, he would have a taste and then pass it to us others in turn. Fritz, being Viennese, is a coffee connoisseur, and praised Ludwig's concoction.

But good coffee calls for a cigarette, if one is a smoker; and Fritz was the only real addict amongst us four. Unfortunately, his cigarettes hadn't stood the deluge of rain, hail, snow, and avalanches at all well; they were soaked and pulpy. Fritz, who hadn't uttered a word of complaint about the considerable pain in his damaged hand, grew feeble at the thought of his cigarettes: "If only I could light a dry cigarette with a dry match. . . ."

I don't know what I would not have given to be able to fulfill Fritz's wish, but I hadn't any cigarettes.

Then I remembered how I had come to know Fritz Kasparek in the first place. It was at the beginning of the thirties, when I was a young student with a great enthusiasm for climbing but precious little money. Those were the days when one somehow contrived the miracle of spending weeks on end in the Dolomites with but thirty shillings in one's pocket. A bicycle was one's only means of transport and as one needed a licence for it in Italy at that time, and since that cost money, we used to tramp the roads for endless hours on foot, in order to reach one mountain group from another.

One day I left my bike at the frontier at Sillian and walked across into Italy, on my way to Innichen in the South Tyrol. There is an old wayfarers' song of Hermann Löns's that goes: "I never, never get my fill of dust." I was hungry, and thirstier still, but I was compelled by the thought of my slender purse to pass by inns and shops displaying the most glorious fruit and delicacies.

Then I saw another wayfarer coming towards me. He too had a huge pack, a typical climber's rucksack; he also had a mop of fair hair, two amused-looking eyes and a suntanned face. We summed each other up, mutually recognised a kindred soul in one another, nodded. Then the fair-haired one, marching towards the Austrian frontier, called out: "Hi, who are you? Where from? Where to?"

"I'm Heini Harrer from Graz," I told him, "on my way to the Sexten Dolomites."

"I'm Fritz Kasparek from Vienna."

Fritz Kasparek. . . . I knew that name already. He was one of Vienna's most daring and experienced climbers. This young Viennese had done the Pillar of the Marmolata, the North Face of the Western Zinne, the North Buttress of the Admonter Reichenstein, innumerable other super-severes and new routes. He was only a year or two older than I was, but I addressed him as "Sir" out of respect for his great reputation. "Nonsense," said he, shaking his head. "I'm Fritzl and you're Heini and that's that." And then straight out: "Hungry? Thirsty? No money, eh?"

I nodded.

Kasparek disencumbered his shoulders of his rucksack, waved invitingly towards the bank of grass at the edge of the road, sat down, and produced a huge bag of glorious pears and peaches out of his pack.

"Eat!" he commanded.

I didn't wait for a second order. We ate all the fruit, lock, stock, and barrel, and I must admit that Fritz only consumed half the amount I did. He laughed, got up, shook my hand. "So long," he said. "I'll be seeing you."

Then he strolled off towards the Austrian frontier, and I stood watching him for a long time. I didn't know then—it wouldn't have been Fritz Kasparek if he had breathed a word of it—that he had bought that fruit as his provisions for the journey to Vienna with his last penny. As a result he had to pedal his pushbike 300 miles from Sillian to Vienna without a coin in his pocket and no food to eat. Maybe he used his unblushing Viennese charm to cadge an invitation from one or two farmers to a glass of milk; I couldn't say. But the reader will understand how sorry I was up there on the North Face not to be able to hand Fritz a dry packet of fags and say: "Smoke!"— just as he had once held out a bag of fruit to me on a red-hot high road and said: "Eat!"

It was now 11 P.M. Ludwig had given over cookery and "retired to rest." Even here, on this tiny perch 12,300 feet up, and 5,000 feet sheer above the nearest level ground, he hadn't forgone the comfort of those bivouac slippers. Andreas had to keep his crampons on, so as to get some kind of a stance in the ice for him to maintain a hold; but his head rested on Vörg's broad back. Next morning we discovered that Vörg had sat motionless, without a single movement of a muscle, so that Heckmair's sleep might be undisturbed. Fritz and I had pulled the Zdarsky sack over us; our rucksack architecture served splendidly as support for our legs, and very soon I could hear the deep, regular breathing of my friend as he slept by my side. Through the little window in the tent sack I could see that there were no stars in the sky and the weather was still bad; it looked as if it were snowing. There was an occasional small snowslide from above, but they only slid over the skin of the tent, with a gentle swishing sound, like a hand stroking it. . . . I wasn't worried about the weather. I was possessed by a great feeling of peace; not the resignation to our fate, but a certainty that, whatever the weather might be, we would reach the summit tomorrow and after that regain the safety of the valley. This sense of peace increased to a conscious glow of happiness. We humans often experience happiness without recognising it; later we realise that at such and such a moment we were happy. But here, in that bivouac of ours, I was not only genuinely happy; I knew I was.

This, the third bivouac for Fritz and me on the North Face, was the smallest in terms of room; in spite of that it was the best. And if you ask why, the reason was the rest, the peace, the joy, the great satisfaction we all four enjoyed there.

If, during the hours just past, while we were being tried to the utmost, one of us had given in or lost his nerve for a second; if, driven by the instinct of self-preservation, one of us had thought of trying to save his own life by leaving the party—no one would have blamed him. His companions would not have cut him, even if they might perhaps have greeted him a little less warmly ever after. If, down in the valley, people had honored and cheered him, his friends would not have said a word. But that particular happiness which is born of absorption in a common endeavour would have passed him by and he would not have tasted its joy. We four in that bivouac on the Face of the Eiger were all happy. It might snow, and the little slides might come swishing over our covering tent sack; but our sense of happiness was deeply rooted in us. It allowed us to think pleasant thoughts; and we were able to sleep. . . .

Putting oneself to the supreme test—the expression is in itself an exaggerated description of a healthy, honest experience, and a contradiction of the quiet account one renders to oneself. But a far greater mistake is to suggest that this extreme testing of oneself is the mainspring of mountaineering. It is a suggestion initiated by the incurable complex-fiends, because no better explanation of what was to them inexplicable has occurred to them. I really cannot help smiling when I imagine Fritz Kasparek's face if one of these know-it-alls asked him whether he climbed in order to prove himself. The questioner would no doubt retire discomfited, routed by a caustic reply couched in those well-known Viennese terms that are so hard to translate into good classical German.

Of course, no climber embarks on a difficult climb in order to test himself. If during moments of extreme danger on the mountain he thinks first of his rope mates, if he subordinates personal well-being to the common weal, then he has automatically passed the test; and so he probably would in any of the everyday disasters, flood, or fire. Nor would such a man go whizzing past injured people on the Autobahn; but he would bring aid where he could. For him the knowledge that he has done his best is enough. A passion to prove his mettle can never be the mainspring which makes him tick.

It makes me very angry to think of the many critics who categorise climbers of the "extreme" school as mentally abnormal. I can think of no more normal men than my three Eiger companions. True, the position in which we were situated was quite out of the ordinary; but my friends' reaction to that element of extraordinariness was perfectly normal. Fritz longed for dry cigarettes; Ludwig changed into cosy, lined boots for the bivouac; and Andreas, anchored upright in the ice by his crampons, protected by Ludwig's broad back, slept the sleep of the just.

The peace and harmony of that night in the open allowed me to drift off into a twilight state between waking and sleeping. My body, almost bereft of being, was at rest. The cold did not plague; it only served to remind me that I was on a great mountain face, as indeed did the somewhat cramped posture imposed by our rucksack bivouac. But that didn't plague me either. Here, as elsewhere in life, bliss was born of contrast. For, after the drubbing we had gone through a few hours before at the hands of the avalanches on the "Spider," our bivouac perch seemed a very heaven.

I was awakened by a considerable snowslide over our tent. Dawn was glimmering through the little window; a new morning was at hand. Unfortunately it was not heralded by the gorgeous play of colour of sunrise, nor by a clear pale blue sky in which the stars were being dimmed by the new light of day; its approach was a greyness coming out of a grey fog. When we pulled the tent sack away, we looked out on a winter landscape. It was still snowing; everything sharp or edgy had been fined away by the snow. Even our ledge had disappeared. Our friends, a few yards from us, appeared to be stuck onto the vertical rocks. The very idea that in this landscape, savage beyond the wildest dreams of imagination, people were alive, and actually planning to escape, this very day, from this prison of perpendicular rock, glassy with ice and plastered with snow, was ludicrous. But we were indeed alive; and we were not only planning to climb up out of it, we felt certain that we would manage to do so.

We could hear the gale shrieking across the ridges overhead. Where we were not a breath was stirring. Only the avalanches coming down and sweeping out over us generated a wind. We studied their timetable and planned how to use the knowledge. It was somber to reflect in what poor case we would have been had we been farther down the Face, with the ice slope of the "Spider" still to be climbed. The little slides that came down upon us from the gully were only a fraction of the great avalanches which get fed by the many diverse channels above to sweep over the slope of the "Spider." We were lucky indeed to be as high up as we were. But we soon realised that our cramped bivouac would seem a light trial compared with what we would still have to cope with today.

We were in good shape. The pain in Kasparek's hand seemed to have diminished. Thanks to Vörg's broad back, Heckmair had enjoyed a splendid sleep. Vörg was already busy in his capacity as chef. He brewed pots full of coffee, melted chocolate in condensed milk, and altogether prepared a fine and plentiful breakfast. And while we consumed it, we held a council of war. The weather had done all the changing it was likely to do—for the worse. It was as bad as it always was when men had to stay on the Face for days on end. We had enough food and fuel to bivouac there for several more days. What good would that do us? Even if it cleared up tomorrow or the day after or in three days' time, the conditions on the Face could not improve, nor the rocks be fit to climb, for several days after that. Were we to let ourselves be worn down by sitting and waiting?

"It is better to fall off than to freeze." This remark came from Michel Innerkofler, the oldest of a famous dynasty of Dolomite guides. We were not thinking of falling off, but still less of surrendering just because the Face had put on its winter raiment. We decided to move on.

As soon as the decision had been taken, I lightened our rucksacks by throwing down the precipice that part of the equipment and provisions which had become superfluous. Among it was a whole loaf of bread, which disappeared at a great pace in the mists below us. I had grown up in hard circumstances and had never before thrown away a piece of bread; but now the act almost seemed symbolic to me— we were moving on. "Forward" was the only way now; no more turning back. The past was wiped out, all that mattered was the future; and the future lay over the snow-plastered, ice-glazed summit wall. I believe no man can be completely able to summon all his strength, all his will, all his energy, for the last desperate move, till he is convinced that the last bridge is down behind him and that there is nowhere to go but on.

We moved on. Anderl would lead us out at the top of the Face; this was to be Heckmair's great day.

It is my considered opinion today, as I sit writing these lines, that we would all have escaped safely from the Face, even without his protection from in front; Fritz too would have done it solo, in spite of his injured hand. But we would never have done it so well, without Anderl's leadership; and we might in all probability have had to bivouac again. That probably wouldn't have killed us either; I think we were all good enough, strong enough, and in high enough spirits to survive even that. But are we one whit the worse, do we lose one jewel out of our crown, by recognising with all due admiration that one of us was the best of us all?

We roped up again as a single, united rope of four. The order was now: Heckmair, Vörg, myself, and Kasparek, who was coming up last today so as not to have to haul on the rope with his damaged hand.

Heckmair ran into problems from the very start. The first decision to be made was which of two routes to take? The icy overhanging, cracklike chimney which looked damnably difficult, but seemed safe from snowslides; or up the steep, icy gully to its left, down which little avalanches seemed to descend from time to time? He chose the chimney and Vörg belayed him; but it proved necessary to drive a piton straightaway. The chimney proved so difficult that even Heckmair's skill was of no avail.

So back he had to come and try the gully, having first studied the timetable of the avalanches. It kept on snowing, and now that day had come, it was damp snow, the kind that slides and adds to the fury of avalanches. But even without an avalanche the couloir was so difficult that even Heckmair slipped down it twice, and it was only at the third attempt that his well-known powers of attack succeeded in taking him up to a small rock crest to the left of the gully. There he knocked the snow and ice away with his axe and so managed to fashion usable footholds.

"Up you come," he said.

Vörg went up, and we two followed. Then Heckmair went on climbing on stuff that made the utmost demands on us all. He could not afford to waste time, for he had to reach the next safe stance in the pauses between avalanches, before the next snowslide arrived. Not that there were any safe stances; a step in the ice, a piton, onto which to belay oneself, were the best we could hope for up here. But the higher we got, the thinner grew the film of ice in the gully; so thin that it would not bear the strokes of an axe, nor offer a reliable hold for a piton. The steel shafts went clean through the ice, impinged on the rock beneath, and simply bent over.

We were all on a single rope. If the leader came off and number two couldn't hold him, it would be up to me to try to arrest the fall. And if I should be pulled off, the whole force would come on Fritz. We knew that one man could not hold three on this terrain. No one knew it better than Heckmair, who was often moving, and was forced to move, at the very limit of safety, if he was to force a way up to freedom for us. And once we were very close to annihilation. I was standing on a small knob, seeing Fritz up to me. One hundred feet above me stood Vörg, safeguarding Heckmair, as he grappled with icy rock, treacherous ice gullies, and snowslides high above us in the mists and driving snow. We couldn't see either of them.

Fritz joined me on my stance.

Still no order from Vörg to come up. We could hear voices and short, muffled cries. What could have gone wrong up there?

Then we could only hear a murmur of voices. At the same time a snowslide came down on us. That was nothing unusual and we were quite used to it by now; but this wasn't white snow. It was stained red with blood. Definitely blood, because the next thing to come down was an empty bandage cover and this was followed by a small empty medicine bottle.

"Hallo!" we yelled. "What's happened?"

No reply. We waited for what seemed an age, racked with doubt and anxiety. Then, according to schedule, another avalanche came down with savage force. Not till it had passed did we obtain relief in the shape of an invitation to move on up.

Vörg was hauling on the rope so hard that it took my breath away. But I understood what this manhandling meant. No longer was there time to climb pitches neatly according to the rules. Time was now the watchword, if we were to escape from the Face. And evidently something had happened up there to cause great delay. What could it be?

When I reached Vörg's stance, a great weight fell from me. They were both alive and not even seriously hurt. Vörg had a blood-soaked bandage on one hand, but Heckmair was already a whole rope higher up, on a tiny, exposed, rickety stance.

Later on, he reported in his dry but lively way how Vörg came by his injury:[1]

Wet snow was coming down heavily. There hadn't been an avalanche for a long time. So—quick, up the overhang! Curse it . . . the ice on the rock had thinned out, and the pitons wouldn't hold anymore. At the second stroke they went clean through and bent themselves on the rock. On the overhang itself I could only cross my crampons, because there was only a narrow strip of old ice in the gully and the new ice overlying the rock was too hard, smooth and thin. The point of the ice piton onto which I was clinging for dear life only went a little way in and so did the pick of my ice axe. Suddenly the piton came out, and at the same moment my axe gave way. If I could only have straddled, I could have kept my balance. But with my legs crossed, there wasn't a hope.

I shouted, "Look out, Wiggerl!"

Then I came off.

Wiggerl was looking out all right. He took in as much rope as he could, but I bore straight down on him—not through thin air, for the gully was inclined, but in a lightning-swift slide. Just as I fell, I turned face outwards so as not to go head over heels.

Wiggerl let the rope drop and caught me with his hands, and one of the points of my crampons went through his palm. I did turn head over heels, but in a split second I grabbed the rope piton, which gave me such a jerk that I came up feet first again. I dug all twelve points of my irons into the ice—and found myself standing.

[1] Andreas Heckmair, *Die drei letzten Probleme der Alpen* (Munich: Bruckmann Verlag, 1949).

The force with which I had come down on Wiggerl had knocked him out of his holds but he, too, had been able to save himself and there we were, standing about 4 feet below our stance on steep ice without any footholds. One stride and we were back on it again. Naturally, the pitons had come out and I immediately knocked new ones in.

All this took only a matter of seconds. It was a purely reflex action that saved us; our friends, standing a rope length below and linked to us by the same rope, hadn't even noticed that anything had happened. If we hadn't checked our fall we would have hurled them out from the face with us in a wide arc.

Meanwhile Wiggerl had taken his gauntlet off. Though blood spurted out, it was quite dark in color, so it couldn't be a severed artery.

I looked quickly up the wall; thank goodness, there was as yet no avalanche on its way down. Off with my pack, out with the bandage, and I had Wiggerl's hand tied up. He was very pale; in fact, if he had any colour at all, it was green.

"Do you feel bad?" I asked.

"I'm not very sure," he answered.

I placed myself in such a way that he could in no circumstances fall, and urged him to pull himself together, because it was now or never.

Just then a little vial of heart drops came to hand in the first-aid bag. That devoted woman Dr. Belart of Grindelwald had made me take it along in case of emergency, remarking: "If Toni Kurz had only had them along, he might even have survived *his* ordeal."

We were only supposed to use them in the direst need, though.

On the bottle it said . . . "ten drops." I simply poured half of it into Wiggerl's mouth and drank the rest, as I happened to be thirsty. We followed it up with a couple of glucose lozenges, and were soon in proper order again.

An avalanche was due, but I couldn't see any signs of it.

"Look, I'm going to have another whack at the overhang," I told him.

"All right," he said, "but please"—and his voice was still quite weak—"no more using me as a mattress."

I braced myself, and managed the difficult pitch absolutely safely this time, doing entirely without pitons so as to get as quickly as I possibly could across the really tricky bit it turned out to be. I went up nearly 100 feet—almost the whole run of the rope—without finding a stance; but I was at least able to put in one of the small rock-pitons up there.

And just at that spot and at that moment, when Heckmair had anchored himself to that kindly little piton, down came the avalanche which shook us so severely down below, as already described.

It failed to carry away Heckmair or Vörg, or either of us; but it was many hours after our start before I was up alongside Vörg and in a position to see Fritz safely up. Vörg, freely assisted by the rope, hurried on to join Heckmair. I too hauled Fritz up. In fact we all pulled on the rope, for time was racing away and the sector still to be climbed was high, steep, and difficult; nor had we any idea what it would be like. I had never been on a face climb where there was so much chasing and racing with time as on this Eiger thing. And yet this final cliff, in its ice-armoured snowed-up state, called for an inch-by-inch struggle on the leader's part.

On we went. It snowed without respite. Visibility was hardly more than a rope's length upwards or sideways. Then through the cloud and the whirling flakes we heard shouts coming down to us, though we couldn't say exactly where from. They might come from the summit, or again from the West Ridge. Anyway they were reaching us. We agreed, on the spot, not to answer. Whoever was calling to us was too far from us to understand exactly what we might say in reply. Our answer might well launch a rescue operation which, once in motion, could not be called off; there might be a long descent for someone from the summit to the valley, a drumming up of the rescuers, a renewed ascent . . . one shout from us might well precipitate all that, if they misunderstood us . . . even if we only yodelled up a greeting. . . .

So we climbed on with Anderl in the lead. Minutes passed into hours. Up we went, yard by yard, rope by rope.

Then we heard more shouts, this time clearer and nearer. We could even recognise that these were different voices from the earlier ones. Once again we refused to answer. We learned later that the first voices were those of Fraissl and Brankowski, shouting down the Face, deep in their concern for our fate. The second time it was Hans Schlunegger, that great Oberland guide, shouting down to ask if we wanted help. True, he and the two Vienna boys were equally convinced that at the moment the foul conditions on the snow-laden Face made it quite impossible to lend us any aid; but he and our friends were equally ready to help us, or rescue us, as soon as the weather improved. At this point I must stress again the self-sacrificing readiness of the local guides. The two parties had reached the summit independently by the relatively easy normal route up the Northwest Face, but had turned back immediately on receiving no answer from us. Obviously, after the hopeless reports brought back by those who had climbed to the summit to search for us, nobody rated the value of our lives very highly.

All the same, we were still alive, and still climbing. The steepness of the gully eased off. The avalanches were harmless now, too; up here they had as yet no strength. And then we emerged from the gully onto an ice slope.

It was the Summit Ice Field. If we hadn't just come off the Eiger's Face we would have said it was steep; now it seemed flat. The final gully was behind us; we had escaped from the clutch of the "Spider's" last arm. It was noon when Heckmair reached the lower rim of the ice slope. An hour later the last of us four was safely up.

Only the ice slope now separated us from the summit ridge. We didn't traverse to the left towards the Mittellegi Ridge, but climbed diagonally to the right, somewhere in the direction of the summit.

Only the summit ice slope. Only . . .

Even this last rampart of the Eiger is no joke. The wet snow had not cohered firmly with the névé and ice beneath; it kept on sliding away. This is the very source of the Eiger's avalanches. We couldn't hasten our assault. We all had it firmly anchored in our minds that the Face had not yet given us leave to feel indifferent and stroll away in a carefree manner. Anderl was still leading, as coolly and carefully as ever. He knew that a change of the lead would mean maneuvering with the rope and the loss of time; added to which he could get his breath back while seeing us up on the rope, while we arrived completely out of breath. These explanations, too, sprang from the modesty of his nature.

At this point I was particularly conscious of the absence of my crampons. Even though Heckmair was cutting huge steps for me where necessary, even though Vörg was carefully watching the rope which ran down to me, I couldn't and wouldn't risk any sign of weakness. I dared not slip; but it called for a great output of strength to hang on with nothing but the claw nails in my boots.

It was snowing harder than ever now. Nor were the flakes falling vertically any more but almost horizontally, whipped by the wind. The ice slope seemed interminable. Two more hours had slipped away.

Then something happened that would have been amusing, if it had not meant a moment of extreme danger. Heckmair was climbing up the slope in the mist and the wild pother of snow. The slope was less steep now but, fighting his way against the wind and unable to see anything, he had not noticed it. Vörg, following him, suddenly saw dark patches in front of him. No—not in front—*below* him. Far, far below him. . . .

They were the rocks on the South Side of the Eiger, which was not so thickly veiled in cloud and driven snow. The first two men ever to climb out of the North Face had almost fallen straight over the summit cornice down the South Face. If they had, I doubt whether we would have been able to hold them. As it was, they stepped back from the cornice in the nick of time.

We followed, gained a lodging on the wind-battered ridge, plodded our way over it to the summit of the Eiger. It was 3:30 P.M. on July 24, 1938. We were the first people to climb the North Face of the Eiger from its base to its top.

Joy, relief, tumultuous triumph? Not a bit of it. Our release had come too suddenly, our minds and nerves were too dulled, our bodies too utterly weary to permit of any violent emotion. Fritz and I had been on the Face eighty-five hours, Heckmair and Vörg, sixty-one. We had not had a hair's-breadth escape from disaster; on the contrary, our bond of friendship had throughout given us a firm sense of mutual reliance. And hard as the climb had been, we had never doubted its successful outcome.

The storm was raging so fiercely on the summit that we had to bend double. Thick crusts of ice had formed around our eyes, noses, and mouths; we had to scratch them away before we could see each other, speak, or even breathe. We probably looked like legendary monsters of the Arctic, but we felt in no mood for the humour of such a reflection. Indeed, this was no place in which to turn handsprings or shriek with joy and happiness. We just shook hands without a word.

Then we started down at once. I remember another remark of Innerkofler's: "Downhill's easy! You've got all the little angels with you. . . ."

But it wasn't easy. The descent was full of spite and malice. The wind hadn't blown the snow away here; it had fallen wet and heavy on the western slope, covering the icy slabs to a depth of nearly three feet. We kept on slipping and recovering ourselves. We suddenly felt tired, terribly tired. I had been given the job of finding and leading the way down because I already knew the route; but when I had traversed the Eiger on that previous occasion, visibility had been good. Now I didn't always find the correct route immediately; then, my companions hauled me over the coals. I didn't argue, for they were quite right. Particularly Anderl, who had led like an absolute hero all the way up the climb—a real hero, quietly doing the job and serving his friends. He wasn't the sort who needed drums and bugles or the cheers of the crowd to spur him on to a great performance. The urge sprang from within him, from his nature, from his true character as a man.

But now we could see how he was collapsing, not in a physical but in a spiritual sense. Uncomplainingly, mechanically, he moved forward; but by now he had given up the leadership. The fantastic nervous tension under which he had lived for days and nights on that mighty Face just had to induce a reaction. During those endless hours of danger he had excelled himself; now he could afford to be an ordinary man again, with all an ordinary man's weakness, susceptible and exposed to all the caprices of normal life.

For instance, take the matter of Anderl's trousers. The elastic band of his overalls had broken. Anderl kept on pulling his trousers up and they kept on falling down again. This man, who had reacted with the speed of lightning when he fell in the icy gully and so saved us all from disaster, the man who had so often withstood the pressure of the deadly avalanches, who had climbed ice bulges in a blizzard and, with unexampled endurance, fought a way to freedom for himself and his three teammates—this same man was almost driven to desperation by a broken elastic.

So Andreas had given up the lead. He had every right to expect to be led down on the descent just as surely and safely as he had led up that appalling Face; and he had every right to swear now when, racked by the exhaustion of a body exerted to the uttermost, he was asked to climb up a few hundred feet again because, in the mirk and the blown snow, I had led the wrong way down. I could see nothing amusing in this internal collapse of Anderl's. On the contrary, the very human nature of his reaction endeared him all the more to me.

We found the right route again and climbed on down it. We slipped, slid, stumbled, all securing one another. Gradually we lost height, and at last we were below the clouds. The snow turned into rain. But close down there now was the safe world of people.

For that multitude of dark dots down there, moving about on the glacier, were people. They were coming slowly up to meet us. We wondered what they were looking for on the glacier. Once we had seen people, we suddenly craved for the comforts of human civilisation, about which we had not even dared to think during our bivouac nights. You mustn't long for a bed when you are hanging from a piton on a snowed-up precipice.

But now as we saw people coming up towards us we were gripped by an overwhelming desire for a hot bath, for a bed, for comfort. True, down there at the bottom of the wall stood our tent, a luxury home compared with our bivouac above the "Spider"; but we hadn't a dry stitch of clothing on us, and oh how we wanted to sleep in a bed! Would a hotel on the Kleine Scheidegg give us credit? How much money had we got left? Anderl was the richest; he still had a franc and a half, but that wouldn't go very far. Yet we still hankered after a bath and a bed.

Suddenly there was a young boy in front of us, staring at us as if we were ghosts. His face expressed embarrassed, incredulous astonishment. Then he summoned up his courage to ask:

"Have you come off the Face?"

"Yes," we admitted. "Off the Face."

Then the lad turned downhill again and ran away, screeching in a high treble: "They're coming! Here they are! They are coming!"

Soon we were encircled by people. Guides, our Viennese friends, the men from Munich, members of the Rescue Service, journalists, rubbernecks—all united in their great joy at seeing alive four men they had believed dead.

They took our rucksacks off for us, they wanted to carry us, and they would have, if we hadn't suddenly felt as fresh and gay as if we were back from a walk and not from the North Face of the Eiger. Someone gave Fritz his first dry cigarette. Rudi Fraissl held out a small flask of cognac to Andreas.

"Drink some," he said. "It'll warm you up."

Anderl emptied the flask at one pull. It didn't make him drunk. We were all drunk with the general joy around us. And then, for the first time, we felt the intense satisfaction, the relaxation, the relief from every care, and the indescribable delight at having climbed the North Face. Suddenly, too, all our problems were solved. Beds, baths? Everyone was showering invitations on us, simply everyone, just because they were human beings and we had come back safely to humanity.

Yes, we had made an excursion into another world and we had come back, but we had brought the joy of life and of humanity back with us. In the rush and whirl of everyday things, we so often live alongside one another without making any mutual contact. We had learned on the North Face of the Eiger that men are good and the earth on which we were born is good.

And now that earth was welcoming us home. . . .

It is twenty years since that first climb of the North Face. I have never lost my great love for the Hills, and I have never lost the memory of that climb, clear and undistorted by any rose-colored spectacles.

I am therefore in a position to correct various mistakes which were given circulation, either through ignorance or by mischievous intent. We climbed the Eiger's North Face because the very aspect of it proved an irresistible challenge to our courage and to our love of adventure. Of course there was an element of competitive spirit and bravado in it. We were able to climb the Face because we had subjected ourselves to a period of critical testing before we ever laid a hand on its rock. We brought our venture to a successful conclusion because it was carried through by the perfect harmony of an ideal team. We all loved life and our actions were at times governed by the instinct for self-preservation; but it was a common instinct, which forbade any escape into personal self-preservation. The well-being of all of us was the aim and endeavour of each of us.

To ascribe material motives and similar external rewards of success to our climb would be a lie and a slander. Not one of us improved his social position one whit thanks to a mountaineering feat which excited such general admiration. Nobody dangled Olympic or other medals before our eyes, nor did we receive any. As to the report that we climbed on the orders, or even at the wish, of some personage or other, it is absolutely off the mark. We followed the dictates of our own will solely.

I am perhaps the only one who had, even indirectly, to thank the North Face of the Eiger for the shaping of my further progress in life. It may be that my having climbed that Face resulted in my being asked to join the German Nanga Parbat Expedition of 1939. But who could claim for me foreknowledge that the further results would be my internment in India, my subsequent escape from the internment camp, and the years of my escape journey to Tibet ending with my safe arrival in Lhasa? I didn't climb the Face to earn "publicity." I didn't consciously choose that particular act to start my adventurous life's journey, which was later to be crowned by my Tibetan experiences and my personal friendship with the Dalai Lama. But I do believe that Fate lies very much in the character, the natural faculties of a man. I have the lucky faculty always to meet good, reliable, and loyal men. My companions on the North Face of the Eiger were just another proof of that claim.

And, at the end of this chapter, it is of those friends that I would like to think, though it is with sadness that I think of them. Wiggerl Vörg, that strong, calm, magnificent climber, fell in the war. Fritz

Kasparek, a true child of the sunshine, who believed so firmly in life that his very presence cheered his fellowmen, fell to his death in 1954 when the summit cornice of Salcantay in Peru gave way.

Of the four of us, only Andreas Heckmair and I are still alive. So let my last words be about him. I can see him frowning angrily, for his modesty is genuine and he hates to have medals handed out to him. In any case, it is not unusual for a man to enjoy winning medals when he is young, but to prefer handing them out when older. When one is older, impartial and free from exuberance, it is much easier to decide who has really earned them.

Once when Julius Kugy was asked what kind of a man a mountaineer should be, he replied: "Truthful, distinguished, and modest." That describes Anderl perfectly. But I would like to enlarge the description by adding two attributes which he possessed to an outstanding degree; to Kugy's adjectives I should add: "Courageous and reliable."

FURTHER

SUCCESSFUL

ASCENTS

I gave little more thought to the North Face of the Eiger, though it had undeniably been a milestone in my life.

It was in April 1944 that I escaped from the British internment camp at Dehra-Dun; I reached Lhasa in January 1946 after a journey to freedom lasting nearly two years. During 1947 my hardships sought revenge in a savage attack of sciatica; the pain was often bad enough to quench my joy of living.

The doctor at the British Legation in Lhasa examined me at regular intervals. During the course of one of my visits the conversation turned to mountaineering. Like most Englishmen, the doctor was extremely nature-conscious and an enthusiastic mountain wanderer; but, also in keeping with the English tradition, he was strongly against the "extreme" school of climbing as practised on the Continent, particularly by the Germans. Presently the North Face of the Eiger was mentioned, coupled with the criticism that to try to climb it was a sign of a diseased mind.

At this I could no longer contain myself and remarked: "I was one of the first party to climb it successfully."

The Englishmen present all looked at me in a meaning kind of way. Nobody said to my face that I was a liar, but obviously no one believed a word I had said. After all, why should this Mr. Harrer, who by rights ought still to be a P.O.W. in India, not have suffered some damage to his mind as well as the lumbar pains he had acquired during the ordeal of his escape? The exertions and excitements had been quite enough to bring that about. Moreover, such attacks of megalomania and self-aggrandizement are common among sick men. First ascent of the North Face, indeed! The only answer to such a ring fence, deer park lie was a sympathetic smile; and that superior, tolerant smile was still on their faces when I took my leave.

A few months later a messenger from the British Legation came to my house in Lhasa. He brought me a cutting from the airmail edition of *The Times*, which had been sent to the Legation by special bag. I read the newspaper cutting; it was a report of the second ascent of the North Face. On it was written the doctor's name. The report included the names of the first party to climb the Face, and the doctor had underlined mine. I felt that this unspoken apology for the pitying disbelief was a nice gesture of fairness and sportsmanship.

That report on the second ascent captured my interest. Who were these men, whose names were strange to me, Lionel Terray and Louis Lachenal, two Chamonix guides? I had been away from Europe for eight years and had entirely lost contact with Alpine activities and the latest developments of mountaineering. I don't know why, but I was somehow specially glad that the pair were French; perhaps I drew some satisfaction from the fact that the "extreme" cult of climbing, which had so often been stigmatised as a conditioned degeneration of the German-Austrian and Italian rock climbers, was apparently getting a grip on France now. According to the reports, Terray and Lachenal had climbed the Face in magnificent style. My thoughts went out to these French comrades.

I did not then know that out of the ravages of war a new line of thought had begun to develop even in mountaineering—the conception of European climbing. There will, of course, always be national and personal rivalries; indeed within certain limits they are healthy. But one must always allow the other chap to follow in one's footsteps, till he becomes just as good as or even better than oneself. Indeed, one should delight in every new achievement; for stagnation leads to smugness and ultimately to sterility.

If I were to give a calm and dispassionate judgment about the North Face of the Eiger today, I should venture to say that the first ascent contributed a great deal to this new conception of European and indeed international world mountaineering. No purely "acrobatic" climb could have had this effect; for the Eiger's Face is an irrefutable touchstone of a climber's stature as a mountaineer and as a man. It does not demand the ultimate in the acrobatic skills of the modern rock climber; there are no overhanging "roofs" that can only be climbed by "nailing" oneself outwards in a horizontal position, such as for instance on the Capucin East Face, no concatenation of "Grade VI" super-severe pitches, one after another, as on the West Face of the Dru or on many of the notorious walls in the Dolomites. The Eiger's North Face calls for everything that men have learned in overcoming mountain dangers and difficulties through the centuries. On that climb the mountaineer will find every experience mountains can offer man in the menacing terror as well as in the beauty of nature at her most savage, and the mountaineer who climbs it must combine in himself every attribute that marks a true man of the mountains. The most modern climbing technique must have become second nature to him; yet he must feel in himself the same serene strength exhibited by the very first peasant who dared to put up his homestead among great and savage mountains. He must be as reliable to his teammates as he is self-reliant. He must be a "good companion."

There had been an attempt on the North Face in 1946, a year before Terray and Lachenal did their climb, by two guides from the Bernese Oberland itself. The leading spirit was Hans Schlunegger, an outstanding performer on both ice and rock, who had made his first acquaintance with the Face in 1936 during the tragic and unsuccessful attempt to rescue Toni Kurz; that same Hans Schlunegger, whose anxious voice had come down to us in 1938 during the fourth day of our climb. He knew the Face better than any other Swiss guide, though he had not yet climbed it. Now in 1946 he wanted to do so; and with his fellow guide Edwin Krähenbühl, Schlunegger climbed in a single day from the base of the wall to a point above the "Ramp." (Both these splendid mountaineers and guides perished tragically before my return to Europe from Tibet. Schlunegger was engulfed by an avalanche; Krähenbühl fell to his death when a slab on the Engelhörner broke away.) According to the observations of the brothers Fritz and Kaspar von Almen from the Little Scheidegg, the pair bivouacked on the ledge leading to the "Traverse of the Gods," that is to say above the "Ramp" and after climbing the crack and the ice bulge. On the next day, which was marred by bad weather, the two guides tried in vain to follow the "Ramp" all the way to where its upper end peters out into the Northeast Face. There they found fearful overhangs barring their way and turned back, convinced that an escape from the Face, which so many had thought to be possible, was absolutely out of the question. Nevertheless, their descent in a single day, in bad weather, after pushing their attempt so high on the Face, was a wonderful performance, which only two outstanding men could have achieved.

Terray and Lachenal found traces of their withdrawal at a number of places and spoke with great respect of their immediate predecessors, though they had failed in their attempt.

Even before the war French climbers had recorded some amazing climbs; but their fine performances and pioneering work were definitely overshadowed to a great extent by the first ascents then being made by German-speaking and Italian parties, which attracted far greater publicity.

The Schmid brothers climbed the North Face of the Matterhorn; Peters and Maier made the first ascent of the North Wall of the Grandes Jorasses; Comici and his friends scaled the North Face of the Grosse Zinne; Rudatis and his disciples opened up the "World of Grade VI" on the Civetta Wall; and Cassin and his comrades expunged the word "Impossible" from the vocabulary of modern climbers with their incomparable new routes—North Face of the Western Zinne, Northeast Face of the Piz Badile, and the Walker Buttress on the North Face of the Grandes Jorasses.

But, after the war, a great era of vertical climbing and a well-deserved triumph dawned for French mountaineers. A generation of fine climbers and splendid men grew up. The *École de Haute Montagne* came into being at Chamonix and its products began to rank among the greatest names in mountaineering circles. Names like Terray, Lachenal, Rébuffat, Magnone, Frendo, Franco, Ichac, Schatz—it is a list one could spin out *ad libitum*—can never be erased from the history of modern Alpinism. It was typical of the new spirit of French climbing that it gave birth to the idea, the planning, and finally the magnificently successful ascent of the first "eight-thousand-meter peak"[1] to be climbed—Annapurna. And two of the splendid team led by Maurice Herzog in 1950 had climbed the Eiger's North Face in 1947—Lachenal, who went to the summit of Annapurna with Herzog; and Terray, whom Herzog called the good angel of the expedition because of his strength, his calm, and his tremendous team spirit.

When Terray and Lachenal came to the base of the Wall on July 14, 1947, they could see that much of the ice described by participants in earlier attempts had melted and completely disappeared. Now it was a rock face with patches of ice in it, innumerable waterfalls pouring over it, and many stones, previously anchored in the ice, falling unchecked down it into the abyss.

They started up on the afternoon of the 14th. They bivouacked at the well-known spot on the lower part of the Face known as the

---

[1] There are only fourteen "Eight Thousanders" (peaks of over 26,250 feet) in the world. All are in the mighty chain of the Himalaya–Karakorum.—Translator's note.

"Bivouac cave" in the hope of pushing straight through to the summit on the next day; but the difficulties and the continual menace of falling stones prevented their moving as quickly as they had expected. Everywhere they found equipment of previous attempts by climbing and rescue parties; ten-year-old ropes, rusty rock and ice pitons, and snap links. Yet among them were serviceable ropes, pitons, and links, as good as new and obviously left by the Schlunegger-Krähenbühl attempt.

Terray and Lachenal had relatively good conditions on the Face, if conditions can ever be said to be good there.

The rocks were definitely less icy than when we did our climb, but this meant worse hardships at the hands of waterfalls and falling stones. In any case these were two first-class men, fully versed in the modern ice and rock techniques. And they possessed all the bodily, mental, and personal attributes that are the essentials for a successful climb of the North Face of the Eiger, unless one is going to trust one's luck on a blind throw of chance. They were guides in the best sense of the word.

They managed to traverse the big Second Ice Field without having to cut a step. They went entirely on their twelve-point crampons and after every rope's length protected themselves by banging in a piton. Their traverse of the ice field was almost an exhibition piece, as if they were demonstrating before the pupils of the French School of Mountaineering the value and possibilities of crampons. Only, in this case, the "demonstration" lasted some hours and spread itself over hundreds of feet; and, instead of a nice soft hollow a few feet below the "practice pitch," in which the interested students could sit and into which one could slide without danger to oneself, here the performance was on the edge of that colossal precipice, with a gulf more than 3,000 feet deep below their feet.

In spite of their timesaving but exhausting technique the two men could not continue their rapid assault at the pace they had hoped to maintain. Heavy volleys of stones and cascades, pouring furiously down the cliffs, delayed their progress so much that they were compelled to bivouac at roughly the same elevation as had Schlunegger and Krähenbühl.

It says much for their good sense that they did not hurry on blindly, but waited for a more favorable time of day, preferring to include an unintended bivouac rather than risk annihilation by falling stones. By doing so they acted in the true tradition of good guides.

Next morning, July 16, they traversed to the "Spider." I am not sure whether they followed our route exactly or whether they traversed higher up; but they negotiated that very difficult traverse in dazzling style. Just as they reached the "Spider," traditional "Eiger weather" overtook them; but this time the storm was a particularly severe one. Terray and Lachenal, well acquainted with every kind of bad weather which visits their native Mont Blanc and the savage spires of the Chamonix Aiguilles, reported later that they had never experienced such a manifestation of tension-laden air as on the "Spider" that day. It is of course axiomatic that a climber caught in a thunderstorm should divest himself of all iron equipment—axes, hammers, hooks, pitons, and snap links, so as not to become a human lightning conductor. But on the North Face one cannot afford to part with one's "ironmongery"; nor is it possible to follow the rules and sit patiently under an overhang or, better still, in a cave and, safe from the flashes of lightning, wait till the storm has passed. For where on the Eiger's Face is there anywhere to sit, where is the protecting overhang—to say nothing of a cave?

Terray and Lachenal had to push on, with all their ironware on them, even if St. Elmo's fire was crackling from the points of their pitons, their axes, and their hammers, and a halo of light outlined their hair.

One must have experienced a storm high up in the mountains on an exposed ridge or a steep face to understand what an effort is called for to keep one's nerve and go on climbing, while everything about you is humming like in an electricity works and you are at the centre of the static discharge of a thundercloud. Terray and Lachenal had the nerve to do it. They climbed on up the "Spider," on up the exit cracks, though they were part covered in glassy ice, part overrun with cascading water. The amazingly short time in which they climbed the final wall is sufficient evidence how well qualified these two men were to attempt this terrific Face. They reached the summit at 2:15 P.M. But they paid the Face the respect it deserves, refusing to diminish their achievement by shooting a line. They candidly admitted that they never wanted to climb the Face again. Indeed it is an admission made by every party that has succeeded in climbing it— if they were honest about it.

As we know from the earlier history of the Face, a constant source of violent polemics was the question whether it could be expected of guides to undertake rescue operations on it after harebrained attempts by "acrobatic amateurs"—a thesis now reduced *ad absurdum* by the facts. In any case, what nonsense it is to try to drive a wedge between guides and guideless climbers; there is no point in fostering a discord where none can exist. The better the guide and the guideless performer are, the better must they understand one another. They can only learn from each other. The enthusiastic guideless climber is a good advertisement for mountaineering. He awakens the interest of many in the mountains, and these newcomers take guides in order themselves to get to know the mountains. Yet, in assessing weather and the conditions on a given peak, the local guide must always have the advantage over a guideless visitor. Against that, a difficult new climb opened up by an amateur gives new impulses to the professional guides, particularly the young ones. Even the progress of a guide to maturity depends on the general development of Alpine climbing. Only bunglers and woefully inferior types dare to laugh at the guide who does not climb on super-severe routes. And only guides stuck in the old rut and opposed to all new developments, in other words those who have not really grasped the basic idea of their calling, see in the pioneering guideless climber a hostile intruder. Of course, rashness and arrogant overconfidence must be resisted just as much as persistent obstinacy, which can lead to hostile aloofness. Guides belong to that rare and enviable group of men who, in ideal fashion, combine a hobby and a calling.

Climbers and guides belong together, for they are fashioned from the same block. The North Face of the Eiger is the proof of it. Among the attempts that ended in disaster before the first ascent, we find the name of a professional guide, Toni Kurz. As far as it is humanly possible to judge, either the ascent or a safe withdrawal would have been achieved in 1936 if more had been known about the Face; but the risks taken during that tragic reconnaissance brought the possibility of success to those who came after wards. The 1937 party included Matthias Rebitsch, who, even if he hardly followed guiding as his profession, held the Austrian guide's diploma.

In our party in 1938 Andreas Heckmair was a professional guide. Heckmair, who was for many years one of the finest guideless climbers before he took out his guide's licence, combined in himself all the best attributes of a responsible guide and of the ideal type of guideless climber. The first attempt to repeat the climb of the North Face was the work of two outstanding Oberland guides, Hans Schlunegger and Edwin Krähenbühl. And now the second successful attempt had been made by two guides.

And what about the third? Once again it was a party of guides and indeed more than that, because it was the first "guided tour" on the North Face. After the second ascent we were somewhat surprised to read in the Zurich paper *Sport:*

> The two guides have achieved the same success as the Germans nine years ago. It was a great surprise to see them doing it with only two bivouacs, but there is no doubt at all about it. And while we were asking when Helvetia's own sons were likely to climb this gigantic block of stone . . .

Who was asking? Why, the Swiss themselves. Not only the guides, but a section of public opinion—that same public opinion that had at one time stigmatised the attempts as crazy and regarded the North Face as the gravestone of hordes of guides, come to grief during rescue attempts. And now it was actually encouraging the Swiss brotherhood of guides to show what they could do. The national pride in mountaineering was so far awakened that the success of the Frenchmen was almost looked upon as shame-making in the light of their compatriots' failure even to make an attempt. At the same time it read like a criticism, if a sympathetic one, of the tempo of the two Chamonix guides, in that they bivouacked only twice . . . was this not an exhortation to their own countrymen to climb the Face at even greater speed? Surely the plucky attempt by Schlunegger and Krähenbühl in 1946 justified the hope that Swiss climbers would scale the Face in a shorter time. But when would they appear on the scene?

What a turn of the wheel! The "Acrobatics of the Eastern Alps" were all of a sudden not only to be tolerated; they ought to be completely assimilated and the resulting mastery of the new technique be proved by shorter climbing times. The motive of competitive racing was slowly, and at first secretly, getting a footing in the minds of Alpine reporters. As yet there was no open expression of it, but the hint was plain enough.

The news of Terray's and Lachenal's successful repetition of the climb certainly burst like a bomb among the ambitious body of Oberland guides; but men born and bred in the Hills like Schlunegger do not allow themselves to be spurred on by personal or national dreams of glory. He for one would never forget Toni Kurz's dreadful death, nor the terrible aspect of the Face in a blizzard, veiled by sliding masses of snow, nor the thunderous moan of falling stones and avalanches. He intended to climb the Face, and he had made his intention known; but he would do it only when he considered the moment absolutely right.

Photograph continues on following pages

Photograph continues from previous page

An aerial view of the Face, showing the typically
tile-like stratification of the rock

Harrer on a running belay at
the Hinterstoisser Traverse

Kasparek traversing to
the First Ice Field

The Second Ice Field is pitted by incessantly falling stones. Sepp Jöchler's wonderful photograph shows his rope mate, Hermann Buhl, with the French climbers following. 5,000 feet vertically below lies the Eiger's own shadow, with the sunlit streams, woods, and meadows of the Alpiglen beyond it.

1952. The French climbers on the upper part of the "Spider"

1957. Rescue operations on the summit of the Eiger.
In the background the Wetterhörner

Hans won the support of his brother Karl for his plan. The "tourist" to be "guided" was a first-class climber from the Jura, Gottfried Jermann, who joined the venture enthusiastically. The trio carried out ambitious practice tours in the Bernese Oberland, so as to get to know each other, and to accustom themselves to heavy exertions, to bitter cold and to foul weather. A man like Hans Schlunegger hardly required a special training, of course; but the collaboration between him and his young brother as second guide and their tourist, Jermann, would have to be as smooth as the action of a well-oiled machine. The ingredients in the fuel for this machine were to be courage, ability, great experience, and a strong bond of friendship.

It says much for Schlunegger's conscientious, down-to-earth, and healthily slow development that it took him exactly ten years fully to absorb the shattering experience of his first acquaintance with the Face before he was ready for his first attempt on it. By then it could have no more surprises in store, and so August 4, 1947, became a crucial day in his life; for on it, at 2:30 A.M., he and his party started on the climb. Up they went over the substructure, over the "Shattered Pillar," up the "Difficult Crack," across the Hinterstoisser Traverse, as early in the day as 6 A.M. Then on over rock and ice, and rock again. They, too, met falling stones and cascades; but on and on they went up the Face, apparently moving slowly and cautiously, actually climbing more quickly than any previous party.

By 3:30 P.M. they had put the Ramp's Crack and Ice Bulge behind them, and had reached the traverse on the belt of broken rock, where the airplane had paid us a surprise visit and photographed us during our climb. This time, instead of aircraft, it was the inevitable Eiger thunderstorm which visited them with menacing fury. They were at a point which offered the only possibility of finding a bivouac site protected against falling stones. They were all three wet through from the drenching downpour and from climbing through veritable waterfalls; and Schlunegger decided to bivouac then and there. He was not influenced by the chance of winning fame through managing to be the first to climb the Face without having to bivouac, and he accepted the discomforts of a night in the open. The safety of those in his charge was for him the first consideration.

It proved a cold and seemingly interminable bivouac, which lasted fourteen hours. It snowed during the night, but in the morning there was a temporary improvement in the weather. Still stiff with the discomforts of their overnight postures, with the cold and the wet, the three men were climbing again by 5:30 A.M. They were at the "Spider" by 7 o'clock, and though they too had to grapple with snowslides, they reached the Exit Cracks without mishap.

At this point, however, the ice called a halt to their rapid progress. Even a Schlunegger had to force a way inch by inch to the summit for himself and his party. They were bombarded by stones and avalanches of watery snow; and the nearer they got to the summit ice slope the wilder grew the storm. Their wet clothes stiffened into ice armor. But, with the gale shrieking around them, they reached the summit at 4:25 P.M., and were thus spared the hardships of a second bivouac.

In spite of the total lack of visibility, the descent provided no problems for this "Landlord of the Eiger." At 7:30 Hans, Gottfried, and Karl reached the Eigergletscher Hotel in good condition. It was a major triumph, and the newspapers reported with obvious pride that Schlunegger's party had spent *only* thirty-eight hours on the Face, the shortest time ever. They handed out no medals but, besides recognising the mountaineering feat, they stressed the outstanding sporting aspects of the manner in which it had been achieved, and many of the reports sounded a note of patriotic pride, which seemed to throw at the feet of those yet to come the challenging gauntlet of: "Now who will beat *that* record?"

Such an attitude was far from the mentality of a Schlunegger— that splendid guide who met his death not on a steep face, on difficult rock, or on mirror-smooth ice, the realms in which he was so great a master, but who was buried by a freak avalanche on the

Schmadrijoch. His loss was keenly felt. He had given a shining example to a whole generation of guides through his courage, his willingness to risk his life for others, and for his modest outstanding character.

The Face had now been climbed three times. When would the fourth success be scored? Nineteen forty-eight was a quiet year at Alpiglen and on the Kleine Scheidegg. The Germans and Austrians still had too little money to visit Switzerland. The French were not entering any Eiger Sweepstakes, for, while the development of their climbing skill was mounting steeply, there was nothing hysterical about their attitude. Italian mountaineering was still feeling the effects of the war, and its Eiger losses were still remembered. There remained the Swiss themselves.

In spite of Schlunegger's achievement, which was typical of the spirit of the new era, Swiss Alpinism in the main showed no development in the direction of "extreme" climbing. The Swiss Foundation for Alpine Research became the spiritual hub of International mountaineering. Its publications were among the finest alpine literature had ever known. Men like Marcel Kurz and the late Othmar Gurtner, who had made resounding names as much-travelled climbers and knowledgeable chroniclers, with general and specialised knowledge over a vast field, as well as extremely gifted writers, set the tone. They accorded "extreme" alpine climbs no more important a place than they earned within the framework of all the climbing going on among all the world's mountains. After the war, the gateway to the world stood open to the Swiss, and they went through it. The achievements of Swiss expeditions among mountain ranges far from Europe were impressive, their successes in the field of science great indeed. And the reports about them, whose basis was entirely devoid of phantasy or sensationalism, inspired the young generation of Swiss climbers.

This did not mean that the North Face of the Eiger had been forgotten.

The thought of it hardly allowed a twenty-year-old technician, Jean Fuchs, to sleep; he had evinced a burning desire to get acquainted with it. In a twenty-three-year-old watchmaker, Raymond Monney, he found a companion of similar mind. On June 28, 1949, they made their first attempt and succeeded in climbing the lower part of the Face before the weather turned bad on them. This may have been a stroke of good fortune, for they turned back and were spared injury from falling stones and avalanches. The following spring—indeed, among the high peaks it is still winter at that date— the pair were up at Alpiglen and the Scheidegg again as early as April 7. They were fired by a plan of such daring that only the very young could have hatched it. Their idea was to climb the Face in winter conditions, when it is entirely enclosed in a breastplate of snow and ice; perhaps it might be easier then, because the stones would be asleep, the avalanches stilled to silence?

However, their judgment proved sound enough to make them abandon the idea before it ended in certain suicide. They went away, fully decided to return and climb the Face in the summer.

That summer of 1950, the Face was alive again, not only with stones, cascading water and sliding masses of snow, but with people. To start with, there were two other young Swiss climbers at work, the twenty-one-year-old gilder, Marcel Hamel, and Robert Seiler, a locksmith of the same age. They started up on July 9, climbed the Base, the "Difficult Crack," and on above it to the "Hinterstoisser Traverse," where they fixed 180 feet of rope, but were then forced to come down again by a break in the weather.

On July 14, they were back on the job. This time they reached the cliff between the First and Second Ice Fields. Once again the weather broke, and the two men were forced to bivouac in a raging blizzard. It was so bad that they were to remember it the rest of their lives. Next morning, the Face stood in a deep covering of snow down to the meadows on the Alp at its feet. Hamel and Seiler managed by the skin of their teeth to climb down to the Gallery window of the railway, but had to leave behind them 300 feet of rope that they had prudently taken up with them and used for roping down. But, then, nobody thinks twice of the value of a rope when his life is at stake.

On July 22, there was a brief interlude. The actors were two Viennese who had turned up in all secrecy, Karl Reiss and Karl Blach, both of whom will be heard of again in the Eiger story. As yet, no one had heard of them nor knew how good they were. In the "Difficult Crack" below the Rote Fluh a block came away as Blach was leading up it. Reiss managed to hold him, but Blach had broken an arm. They did not call for help. Blach somehow choked down his pain. A temporary splint on his arm enabled him at least to go through the motions of climbing, while Reiss bore the main burden and nursed his rope mate safely down to the Railway Gallery. From there Blach walked down the tunnel to Eigergletscher Station, a crime the railway authorities might well overlook. Naturally one is not allowed to walk about in the railway tunnel; but it was preferable that Blach should walk down a few hundred feet underground than to trigger off the whole immense organisation of a rescue operation.

Next day, July 23, two quiet, sunburnt young men put up their tent in a flowery meadow above Alpiglen. The latent strength in them was plain to see. They showed not the slightest trace of anxiety, they were amiable and carefree, they cooked, lay in the grass, stared up the Face in complete relaxation. One might have guessed they were "Candidates for the Eiger."

One of them was Erich Waschak, a twenty-two-year-old medical student. He was born in the romantic Wachau, with its sunny vineyards. But that loveliest part of the Danube Basin in Lower Austria boasts not only vineyards, castles, and ruins, but also some useful cliffs, on which Erich climbed the most difficult routes when only a boy. Now he was studying medicine in Vienna, though he was in no particular hurry to get his studies finished, for the most important word in the dictionary for him just then was "mountain." He ranked among the best climbers in the modern Vienna school, based on the old tradition. One of his best friends was Fritz Kasparek, and when that master climber, by now approaching forty, climbed anything with Erich, he often let the youngster take over the lead, for he recognised in the fledgling student the latent qualities of a very high-class mountaineer.

The ice axe, part of the equipment lying in front of the tent, was in fact a present from Kasparek; it was the very axe with which Fritz had cleared the ice from the rocks of the "Hinterstoisser Traverse" on July 21, 1938.

Erich's companion was a "strong, silent man," hardly any older than the medical student. His name was Leo Forstenlechner—a very appropriate name, for he was a Forestry hand in the Ennstal, near the Gesäuse.[1] That range with its immense walls, the Hochtor, the öd-stein, the Dachl, the Rosskuppe, has been since time immemorial the High School of rock climbing for Viennese, Styrian, and Upper Austrian climbers. Not only had Leo the necessary strength for his arduous career, but he was one of the most daring and safest rock climbers ever to lay hands on the rocks of the Gesäuse; and that is saying a good deal. Later on, Forstenlechner was to follow Gaston Rébuffat as the second climber ever to climb the three most famous North Faces in the Alps, those of the Eiger, the Matterhorn, and the Walker Buttress of the Grandes Jorasses. As yet, on July 23, 1950, he had not climbed the first and highest of those three huge ramparts of rock and ice. Unhurried and at their leisure, Leo and Erich were sorting equipment outside their tent.

At that moment visitors arrived—four tough lads as young as, or perhaps younger than, Waschak and Forstenlechner. They were the two Swiss parties, which had decided to join up for an attempt on the Face: Fuchs, Monney, Hamel, and Seiler. They regarded the two Austrians in a friendly but suspicious manner. Obviously they had the air of "Eiger Candidates" about them. Leo grinned and said

[1]See n. 1, p. 103.

nothing. Erich laughed and stated with the most honest expression in the world on his face: "The North Face? The very idea! Much too difficult for us."

The Swiss didn't believe this bland assurance; and the very next day they had confirmation of their disbelief, for Waschak and Forstenlechner, heavily laden, started up the lower part of the Face, intending to carry equipment up to the bivouac cave or at least to the top of the "Shattered Pillar." They didn't get there, for a volley of stones compelled them to dump their loads lower down and to scuttle off the Face. However, when they got back to their tent they noticed frantic activity in the Swiss camp, as the four men packed up for their attempt. They had been swept away by a wave of competitive feeling; they wanted to be the first on the Face. They had already prepared the "Hinterstoisser Traverse" and made various attempts. Now the glory of the fourth ascent was the lure.

Erich and Leo were calmer. After all, they cared little whether they came fourth or fifth; and if the Swiss turned out to be the faster movers, it would spare any overcrowding on the Face. Nonetheless, the Austrians also intended to start up the Face during the night.

At about midnight, Erich looked out of the tent. The sky was dark with clouds, the Face grim and fogbound; no sort of weather for starting up the North Face of the Eiger. Almost glad to have made this discovery, the medical student, heavy with sleep, crawled back into the tent. Three hours later Leo woke up and, in his turn, took a look outside. The sky was clear, and bright with stars. A short council of war followed. If they put on a phenomenal spurt, they could still start up the Face before 5 o'clock. That would bring them at the most dangerous time into the zone menaced by falling stones between the Second and Third Ice Fields, an unacceptable risk. Fritz Kasparek had drummed the lesson in. Waschak could hear his mentor saying: "Never let yourself be hurried on that Face. Blind competition on the Eiger is sheer stupidity."

Better be a live fifth than a dead fourth, they decided, and went back to sleep well into the forenoon. When they had really slept their fill and eaten an enormous breakfast, they strolled over to the Kleine Scheidegg, where the weather report announced a "high" over the whole of Central Europe. Erich and Leo were overjoyed; nor was their pleasure marred when a visitor at a telescope informed them that the Swiss had already reached the Second Ice Field.

Late in the afternoon they crawled into their sleeping bags, but they could not sleep for happiness and excitement. At about midnight they got up, and it was about 2 A.M. when they started up the Face. At the point where they had cached their equipment, they roped up. That meant no slowing-up of this well-trained pair, for they alternated in the lead, "leapfrogging" one another—the second climbing up to join the first man at his stance and then climbing straight on for a rope length above him. They met no problems at the "Difficult Crack," and the "Hinterstoisser Traverse" was ice-free and quite dry. By now Waschak confirmed at close quarters what he had suspected from a distance; a great change had taken place since the Face was first climbed. It no longer conformed to Kasparek's description. It had become a rock wall with ice patches on it; but its dangers had not been diminished by the change.

Erich was just thinking that no stones had yet fallen, when the first salvo arrived. They were at that difficult passage after the "Hinterstoisser Traverse," on the First Ice Field or rather where the ice field once was. Now it is often necessary to climb over a smooth, fearfully steep roof of stone, with neither handholds nor footholds and no crannies to take a piton.

Now Leo and Erich were introduced to the concerto of the Eiger Stonefall. The score is richly orchestrated. There are small stones with a high whistling note like flutes and fiddles. The medium-sized lumps hum fairly fiercely and yet their note can be quite a high one— like the cellos. There are no double basses, but other notes, a kind of howling, rather like an airplane before it lifts into the air after its full-powered dash from rest. The whole symphony sometimes unites in a kind of cacophonous organ-voluntary. The percussion is naturally strongly in evidence, from the side drums, with their hammered staccato, to the dull thud of the bass drum. And the cymbals are there too, not sounding metallic, but clashing away shamelessly at top volume; in fact the whole concerto is certainly not at chamber strength, but crashes and bangs so that not a word could be understood if anyone had any desire to utter one. It stinks of sulfur and shattered stone. And then, when some willful stone has beaten the drum one last time after the conductor has registered his final beat, an uncanny silence sets in.

Then one is astonished that one is still alive, up here and not down there where the stones go rippling and rattling away at the bottom of the wall. . . .

The two men went on, gaining height quickly, as if the rock step separating the two ice fields were not of any great difficulty, perhaps because the conditions at this point were unusually favourable. It was only 8 A.M. when they reached the lower rim of the Second Ice Field and found hardly any ice there; so they traversed to the left on rock, where there had been none in earlier days. Then they looked up appraising the difficulties of the precipitous ice slope overhead—500 feet of dirty grey, stone-speckled ice between them and its upper edge.

Surely those were human voices—quite close at hand, too? Quite right; up above them were four men, the Swiss party, just making for the rocks below the Third Ice Field. Leo and Erich had expected them to be far higher by now—at the "Ramp" or at least beyond the "Flatiron." They wondered what had delayed the Swiss rope— falling stones perhaps? They shouted "Good morning" up the Face, and were greeted by a friendly answering call. The two Austrians exchanged looks; Leo laughed and then set off at speed up the ice slope, which, owing to their ability to turn it on rock, was only half as high as when those engaged in the first ascent had to tackle it.

The front claws of their twelve-pointers gripped splendidly, the calf muscles of the super-fit medical student and the woodman who had grown up in the forests were tireless. Very occasionally they cut a step to stand in, very occasionally they used a piton. Their pace was not the result of a suddenly awakened rivalry, but dictated by sheer commonsense. If stones were to fall here, in the direct line of the slope, it would be no joke; so on and up, faster still, if possible.

Presently they reached the upper rim; it was only 11 o'clock. But they were not safe yet, for the rocks of the "Flatiron" caused them plenty of trouble; there were serious drawbacks to the drying out of the Face, now that so much of the ice had melted away.

As he was climbing an overhang, Waschak was hit on the elbow by a stone and injured; but this was no place in which to bother about trifles. So they pushed on and on, across the Third Ice Field, on to the "Ramp."

There was a torrent pouring down the severe crack in the "Ramp." The first of the Swiss party had just got through it and was starting to rope the rucksacks up when the Austrians caught up with the tail-enders. It was a very friendly meeting; no triumph of rivalry, no envy, no bickering about "fourth" or "fifth" climbs. There were no harsh words, no abrupt demands to hand over the lead; instead, friendliness and mutual understanding. Fuchs had been hit on the head by a stone and injured, not seriously, but sufficiently to make him hand over the lead to Monney. They were very good climbers, these four Swiss, but they admitted the astonishing superiority of the two Austrians; they had never believed anybody could climb at such a pace. With the best of goodwill the Swiss let the Austrian pair go ahead on their way to the top. And Waschak and Forstenlechner, showing not the slightest sign of tiredness, flung themselves into that shower bath of a crack and moved swiftly on upward.

Wet through, they tackled the Ice Bulge. In spite of the recession of the ice even Waschak and Forstenlechner found it in very difficult condition and only overcame the obstacle slowly and with extreme caution. Even after that overhanging ice pitch they found the traverse to the "Spider" much harder than they had dreamed it would be, harder too than any conception Waschak had derived from Kasparek's descriptions. This was no "Traverse of the Gods," but an excessively dangerous, severe piece of climbing, involving creeping and feeling one's way in a continuous battle to maintain balance.

It involved ledges that petered out, loose rocks, and slabs, which went winging their way down into the gulf as soon as touched, little flecks of ice which wouldn't take a piton, but came away from the rock beneath them at the very first blow from the axe. And just at this point the inevitable Eiger thunderstorm broke over their heads. Rain soon turned to snow; their soaked clothing stiffened till every movement became toilsome.

They drove in many a piton along that traverse, often fixing a rope balustrade to safeguard the second man as he moved on. They left every piton in, so as to ease the passage of the Swiss party moving up behind them; but by the time they reached the edge of the "Spider," with the wind and the rain raging about them, they had run out of supplies.

(It is clear from the description Waschak and Forstenlechner have given of their climb that they climbed too far up the "Ramp" ice field above the "Bulge" and consequently found far greater difficulty on their higher traversing line than we did on our route in 1938. Moreover, the recession of the ice must have been very much against them; but swift progress across the Face in the conditions then obtaining would in any case have been improbable.)

At the "Spider" they stopped and waited, not only because they had run out of pitons, which they knew the following party would have retrieved for them, but also to reassure themselves that no accident had happened on that hazardous traverse. But they found the waiting there, in the storm, with their wet clothing iced up, something of an ordeal, and time seemed to move very slowly.

At last the Swiss party arrived. They were all in good shape and presented the two Austrians with a whole bundle of pitons. Brief thanks and then away again. Waschak and his companion wanted to get as high as possible during the day; true, so did the others, but the pace of a four-man party is necessarily much slower. There was no need for the two leaders to stay with them, for a foursome can always look after one of its members who is in trouble.

So on they went. This time the "Spider" hurled down no annihilating avalanches, yet the Exit Cracks were not only icy but defended themselves with innumerable cascades, stone falls, and snowslides. The two men were so drenched that the very thought of a bivouac was appalling, even though they had dry pullovers in their packs. For, every time one of them had to wait while the other fought his way up the Exit Cracks he was racked and shaken by the cold. So they wanted to avoid a bivouac if humanly possible; and they decided to go on climbing so long as a glimmer of daylight was left. The hours passed quickly, but Erich and Leo had entered into the spirit of this race with darkness. Each of them was happy every time he took over the lead, for while one was climbing, one was warm; they were not exhausted, nor was their upward drive blunted. It was only when they had to stand still and wait that the crippling cold got the better of them.

It was still daylight when they reached the summit ice slope. It was 8:15 by their watches. They pressed on up the slope without cutting steps, and at about 8:45, their teeth rattling and their bodies doubled up with cold, they were happily shaking hands on the summit.

The last light of day was gone now; nor was the weather so good that they dared to attempt a night descent of the West Face, which they did not even know. They certainly had not climbed the famous North Face in a single day of eighteen hours just in order to come to grief while descending by the ordinary route. So they found a sheltered place close under the summit and there they hacked a big step out of the ice and fashioned a comfortable seat out of it. When they had pulled the tent sack over their heads, the cooker had started to hum, and the glorious smell of coffee had begun to wake new life in them, they forgot all about the cold. And at the very first light of day, they started down the mountain.

That same morning of July 27, the four Swiss climbers, perched on their minute bivouac spot above the "Spider," were gladly greeting the new day. They had not spent too bad a night and all four were feeling fit enough. There was the promise, too, of a fine day.

But the day didn't turn out fine. At 8 A.M., exactly when the two Austrians got down to the Eigergletscher Hotel, the weather broke completely and finally. The blizzard whirled about the ridges, whipping the flakes against the rock faces and into the Exit Cracks, turning the waterfalls into sheet ice. All four men were worn out, drenched, and frozen to the bone by their days and nights on the Face. Another disaster seemed to be imminent, and down in the valley, at the Scheidegg and at Alpiglen, alarm was growing. Would a rescue party have to go up, with the Face in that ugly mood?

But in those hours of their ordeal, one of the four grew to the stature of a great mountaineer—Raymond Monney. He led the party safely through the Exit Cracks, carefully bringing each of his three companions up on the rope at every pitch. He was only twenty-four, but the three years' advantage he had over the others seemed to provide him with the reserves of stamina and that additional element of toughness, which the very young have not yet attained. Monney battled for twelve long hours against the icy defences of those Exit Cracks. It was frequently impossible to climb without artificial aid, and Monney banged in piton after piton, fastening slings to them at places where the glazed rock offered no hold at all for a foot. Parties yet to come will be astonished to find so many pitons still in the Exit Cracks; but there is no cause for amusement or any sense of condescension. Monney put them there while carpentering a ladder to life for his friends Jean, Marcel, and Robert.

It was about 8 o'clock that night when the Swiss climbers reached the summit. The storm was still raging, the flakes were racing before it, mists veiled the mountain; it was impossible to see anything. A fourth bivouac was inevitable, but the plucky young men survived even that ordeal. At dawn they started down, and reached the Kleine Scheidegg at 8 A.M.

Many a criticism was levelled at these two ventures, which had resulted in the fourth and fifth ascents. Waschak and Forstenlechner were accused of being harebrained, a judgment seemingly based entirely on the idea that no one was entitled to "run" up the famous North Face in a single day. The claim against the four young Swiss was one of unreadiness for such an undertaking, and the well-known columnist Max Öchslin in his article in *Die Alpen*, 1950, No. 10, even spoke of a "stunt by some silly boys."

In my view, both judgments are wrong and harsh. The two Austrians just happened to be two unusually strong men in dazzlingly fine form. They made no mistakes either in their equipment or their assessment of conditions on the Face; the result was that they, the absolute cream of rock climbers, found it possible to "run" up it. As to the Swiss party, admittedly they were all young, so young that their sense of reality was mixed with almost boyishly romantic ideas. For instance, they looked for some mystical explanation of the speed and standard of the Austrians' performance, which seemed to them almost beyond belief. They believed that Waschak had been personally trained by Heckmair and that he even had that protagonist's ice axe along on the climb. It all sounds like some epic saga in which the strength of the hero is transferred to the Youth whenever he is allowed to wear his sword. Yet Waschak had never even met Andreas Heckmair and had consequently never been trained by him; on the contrary, he was Fritz Kasparek's climbing partner. And Kasparek had given Waschak the axe not as a "solemn legacy of some heroic past," but in all probability in his usual generous fashion saying dryly: "There, take it along—it'll be useful." For Waschak had no money with which to buy himself an axe.

Even if the foursome were all very young and exhibited many youthful traits, they acquitted themselves on the Face, in a fearful storm, like grown men. And it was the common sense of men that on the first day prevented them from pushing on rashly through the zone of bombardment by falling stones, and counseled them to bivouac early, even though it meant such heavy delay. As to Raymond Monney's achievement in the iced-up Exit Cracks, which thrust the responsibility for the whole party on his shoulders alone, it was one which deserves to be written into the history of the Eiger's North Face in capital letters.

As an offshoot from the theme of the development of a European mountaineering tradition, the question—albeit a somewhat idle speculation—may well be asked: "What nation has the best climbers?"

In Germany and Austria there was growing up during these years a new elite of young men, from which Hermann Buhl was later to emerge as a unique phenomenon. The Italians had many outstanding rock and ice climbers, and were to achieve the greatest success in their own climbing history with the first ascent of K2 in 1954. After Annapurna, the French were to put not one but two parties on top of Makalu, the fifth-highest peak in the world, and also to climb Fitzroy, that storm-lashed Patagonian peak. The new spirit of Continental alpinism even invaded the sacred British tradition; not only did they climb the highest and third-highest mountains in the world, Everest and Kangchenjunga, but they also scaled the notorious Mustagh Tower in the Karakorum, one of the most fantastically sheer of all the world's peaks. And what about the Swiss? At one time they were indicted for excessive self-control and accused of obstruction to every form of spiritual advance; but, after the war, their expeditions to the Himalaya were among the most daring in the climbing history of that great range of mountains. And, at home, in the Alps, they no longer frowned on the severest of climbs, they tackled them themselves. . . .

"Which country is the best at mountaineering?"

Any attempt at ranking makes nonsense.

It is at this point that I should like to remember a man who first conceived the notion of "A European Rope"—Guido Tonella, the Italian climber and journalist, who lives in Switzerland. In 1946, at a time when nobody was thinking of reconciliation, when the world was still quivering with hate and bitterness against the war and those who were responsible for its origin, he uttered the following message, loud and clear:

"Mountaineering transcends all everyday matters. It transcends all national frontiers. Mountaineers are a band of brothers. They are all one party on one rope."

1952: THE
GREAT YEAR
ON THE EIGER

There was a quiet overture to the summer of 1952. On July 22 two Frenchmen, Pierre Julien and Maurice Coutin, started up the Face, bivouacked fairly high on it, and reached the summit next day. The quick time and the splendid style in which this climb was accomplished are evidence of the complete competence of the two men. Down below, the watchers at the telescope saw nothing sensational. People were beginning to get used to successful attempts on the Face, and its hoodoo seemed to be broken at last.

July 26 awoke the visitors at the Kleine Scheidegg to new life. The reason was not the North Face itself but the names of the men who had arrived at its foot.

Hermann Buhl had come, and with him his climbing partner Sepp Jöchler. Buhl's wife Eugenie and Jöchler's brother Hans had come as their companions and supporters in their attempt on the Eiger. And on this very same day five Frenchmen, including the most famous of French climbers, arrived from the Lauterbrunnen Valley. The name of their leader was at the time even better known than Buhl's— Gaston Rébuffat, who had been on the Annapurna climb, and had twice scaled the tremendous Walker Buttress of the Grandes

Jorasses—one of the finest examples of the young French Alpine school and of the corps of Chamonix guides. With him came Guido Magnone, the first man to climb the West Face of the Dru, considered the hardest climb in the Alps at that time. And their teammates, Jean Bruneau, Paul Habran, and Pierre Leroux, were hardly inferior to their world-famous comrades. All five were well versed in each other's ways and the staunchest of friends.

But there were others present, who were not among the famous. On that same 26th of July two young brothers from the Allgäu, Otto and Sepp Maag, crawled out of a hayshed near Alpiglen, with the intention of climbing up to the bivouac hole on the lower structure of the Face and leaving their equipment up there. Nobody knew about them, and nobody was watching them.

Nor did anybody notice the fact that about 3 A.M. two members of the Viennese school of climbers, from Lower and Upper Austria respectively, had started to climb the Face; they were Sepp Larch, a baker's apprentice from Weyer, and Karl Winter, a locksmith from Scheibbs. Who had ever heard of them? Indeed, nobody even knew that they were already on the Face; so nobody had a telescope trained on them.

Larch and Winter met normal conditions on the Face, neither very good nor very bad. The ice had contracted heavily and was very hard, so that a frequent use of the axe was necessary. They crossed the Third Ice Field on a staircase of cut steps. Then they bivouacked high up on the Face and reached the summit the following day, the 27th. As they were coming down they met a young man and a very pretty young woman who knew her way about well enough in the Hills—Hans Jöchler and Eugenie Buhl. Larch and Winter were astonished when they were asked if they had seen Hermann and Sepp, the young man's brother, on the Face.

No, they hadn't seen Hermann Buhl. Was he up here too?

Yes, they were told, he and Jöchler, and seven others as well.

That'll be a pretty slow party, they thought; nine men on that huge Face at the same time! It was a pity, though, that they had missed the chance of meeting Hermann Buhl and getting to know Austria's most successful climber. And so they said goodbye and went on down, in the certainty that nothing could resist even a mass assault of that kind, if only a Hermann Buhl was along. But Sepp Larch, who, a year later, was to climb the North Face of the Matterhorn with Forstenlechner and Willenpart and, in 1955, to set foot, with his teammates Ingenieur Moravec and Willenpart, on the 26,200-foot summit of Gasherbrum II in the Karakorum, had left a greetings message—in which his partner Karl Winter also had a say: the ladder of steps on the Third Ice Field. Those steps may well have been partly responsible for the fact that none of the nine climbers on July 27, 1952, was killed by the murderous fire of the Eiger's stone fall.

Nothing can go wrong, if Hermann Buhl is there . . . so easy to say it; but on the North Face of the Eiger anything can go wrong for anybody. Even the best in the world can be hit by a stone, and nobody knew that better than Buhl and his partner, Jöchler. It was a mark of that outstanding mountaineer, Hermann Buhl, that he never lightheartedly overrated himself or underestimated his mountain. And even if many thought that he, with a team of specially chosen friends, would climb the Face in a single day, Buhl knew that he was just as subject to the law of the great mountains and the capricious rules of the Eiger-game as any other climber.

He certainly did not intend to overlook any single safety factor.

On the afternoon of July 26, he and Jöchler started up the lower part of the Face, following the usual Eiger tactics, in order to carry their equipment as high as possible. They didn't take everything they would want for the actual climb; for instance, their warm underwear, some of their provisions, and several other things were left behind. In fact, they meant to climb down again in the evening and spend the night in their comfortable tent in the meadow.

Buhl and Jöchler climbed independently, each taking his own line. As they went up, they saw two young men coming down, a little off their own line of ascent. It was the two Allgäu brothers, Otto and Sepp Maag, who had also taken their equipment up to the bivouac cave, intending to start up the Face next day. The two parties exchanged greetings, but did not climb closer to one another; in any case, they would all be meeting on the Face next day. Buhl was not particularly pleased; he would have preferred his to be the only party on the climb. Not that he cared whether his was the eighth or ninth ascent, but the more people there were on the Face, the greater the danger of being hit by a stone.

Buhl and Jöchler climbed on over the "Shattered Pillar" to the Cave. Neither of them liked the look of the place. Stones were continually falling onto the ledge and being smashed to fragments on it; and it is proof of Buhl's almost somnambulistic ability to scout out the ground on rock, that he found a virtually ideal perch for a bivouac about 150 feet farther up, diagonally to the left—a ledge protected from falling stones by overhanging cliffs, a ledge on which it was possible to sit, almost to lie down, a ledge where one could relax in comfort listening to the purring of the cooker, looking up at the sheer precipice of the Rote Fluh, a magnificent sight, a wall within a wall. At first the two men only intended to use the place as a depot before climbing down again. They sat watching tiny dots breaking away from the upper edge of the Rote Fluh, a thousand feet higher up, and whizzing through the air like birds; but these were not birds, they were stones.

For the moment a descent was out of the question. Blocks of stone were coming down, blanketing the lower face completely, beating out the devil's tattoo as they struck. Buhl and Jöchler watched the missiles spirting up into white dust as they struck the ledge by the bivouac cave and the rocks of the supporting structure. They knew they couldn't climb down till the cannonade ceased.

So long as it remained warm, the stones continued to come down; in the end the pair were forced to bivouac at their excellent depot site. They could hear faint calls coming up through the dusk—anxious, questioning calls from the wife of one and the brother of the other. . . .

They spent a very comfortable night, but they could not sleep. What should they do tomorrow? Should they climb down and postpone their ascent to the next day? On the North Face of the Eiger a lost day cannot be retrieved.

At about two in the morning they saw two tiny points of light moving up to the foot of the Face—the two boys from Allgäu, starting on their climb. Buhl and Jöchler decided to continue their climb, too, and not to waste a day. As soon as it was light, they climbed down a little and traversed to the foot of the "Difficult Crack," where they met the Maag brothers. However, they did not rope up with them.

Buhl accomplished the "Hinterstoisser Traverse" so skillfully, with all the light-footed grace of a dancer, that even Jöchler, who had often watched his friend as he climbed, could not conceal his admiration. This was not climbing in the ordinary sense of the word, nor any acquired artistry, but an inborn virtuosity, which cannot be learned even by the hardest training.

The Austrians left the traversing rope in position for the Maag brothers, who took it down after they themselves had made the crossing. Nobody seemed to be thinking of safeguarding their retreat; but then who would think of a retreat when the leader was Buhl, whom the two young brothers regarded with an almost reverently shy approach?

After the next three difficult rope lengths, the four men got onto the slabs over which the First Ice Field once spread downwards. Horrible ground, this; rock planed smooth with humps three to six feet high in it, utterly bare of holds, devoid of all lodgment for a piton. Alternating the lead, Buhl and Jöchler climbed up the treacherous, friable, holdless terrain, on which it was only possible to move up by using friction technique; for climbing on hand- and footholds was no longer practicable. Very slowly they gained height and the brothers followed them.

Buhl and Jöchler did not yet know that the two boys had woefully insufficient equipment and practically none for a cold bivouac. For the time being all they could say was that Otto and the "other Sepp" came along very well behind them and seemed to be splendid rock climbers.

The Austrians did not make for the "Ice Hose" up toward the right, but kept more over to the left towards the rock step that separates the First from the Second Ice Field. The step looked pretty bad, with ice glistening down it, and the rock was so smooth that Jöchler, in the lead at this point, had to forget all the academic rules of climbing, using his knees to get some kind of friction hold. It was climbing at the uttermost edge of the safety limit, but he dared not fall; for if he did he would hurl eight men from the Face.

Eight? Yes, eight. For in the grey twilight before dawn, as he stood at the foot of the "Difficult Crack," Jöchler had seen five figures climbing up the "First Pillar." Now those five had come up and had made contact. Jöchler heard Buhl exchanging a friendly word of greeting with the leader of the party below. Although both men knew all about each other, neither knew the other as yet; for Gaston Rébuffat, at that moment the most famous of French climbers, and Hermann Buhl, the most famous in the German-speaking countries, were actually meeting for the first time on the mightiest Face in the Alps. And, in between the Austrian party and the French, were the two Germans; nine climbers in all, who were later to join up and form a single rope—a genuinely European rope. How would it acquit itself?

Climbers are independent, thick-skinned people; each of them is a clean-cut, sharp-edged personality, complete with his personal and national pride of achievement—for each of them is only human. And, since everyone's experience on a climb is a different one, it will be seen later on that the various reports differ in minor details. For memories and descriptions are also easily influenced by individual human peculiarities. All nine of them were tremendously impressed by that mighty Face, on which the cannonade of stones was unusually fierce that July day. But neither the peril nor the deep impression made by the mountain was strong enough to counterweigh all thoughts of rivalry.

Rébuffat and Buhl, Buhl and Rébuffat—neither man had water in his veins. The spirit of competition was strong in both of them, even if differently expressed in their respective accounts later on. The difference in temperament between the Tirolese, unable to conceal anything that moved him, and the Frenchman with his relaxed self-assurance, enabling him to clothe even injured dignity with charm, aggression with friendly surprise, was too great to allow of harmonious collaboration. Given such premises, could the European rope that had been forced together on the North Face by the whim of Fate stand the test?

The question did not arise as yet. Rébuffat never even considered using a rope left on the cliff between the First and Second Ice Field by the party climbing ahead; but the Maag brothers had been glad enough to accept the assistance of the leaders at that awkward spot.

Jöchler gives an impressive account of the continuation of the climb:

Hermann climbed past me and mastered the steep ice. My stance provided an overwhelming view into the abyss; below me there were seven figures on precipitous rock and a thousand feet below them the bottom of the valley scored with gulleys and streams. Looking up, the eye could see nothing but gloomy vertical screens of rock streaming away from the ice to the very sky. We were gradually getting used to the falling stones, which were getting worse . . . to get an idea of its intensity one only had to look at the churned-up ice; they were whistling and whirring down incessantly. When I stopped to listen properly, I soon got confirmation that others beside myself were being hit, for one or another kept on crying out. . . .

We went straight up the Second Ice Field to the rocks and then traversed to the lert. It looked short enough, but we were very much mistaken. It turned out to be ten dangerous rope lengths.

If one compares the stature of man with that of the Face, man simply disappears. I would never have believed that this knowledge could oppress the human spirit like a nightmare; one felt lost and lonely. The eye could no longer find anything beautiful to behold. There was not an inch of dead ground on the whole Face; nothing but stones and stones whizzing down from overhead.

What should one do if somebody was hurt—climb down 3,500 feet or up 2,400? The seriousness of our situation slowly impressed itself on our spirits. Nature held us in the hollow of her hand. It wasn't the difficulties that were holding us back; it was simply that the uncertainty was nagging at our nerves.

At last we were up the Second Ice Field, only to find that what awaited us was even more uncomfortable than the ice— the crumbled rock leading to the Third. The leader had no time to watch for dangers from above; one simply said to one's Second—"You keep your eyes skinned. If anything big comes down, shout at once!" The little ones no longer frightened us, but the big ones could wipe one off the wall.

So we arrived at the "Death Bivouac," where the Third Ice Field begins. Protected by Hermann, whose stance was overhung by a sheltering roof, I climbed out onto that fearsomely steep ice slope. About 1,000 feet above it lies the "Spider," whose funnel catapults all loose stones from the summit cliffs straight down onto the Third Ice Field through thin air. I had to go back twice as a salvo of stones came rattling down with a terrifying din, but in the end even that pitch had to be climbed. With courage revived, I groped my way at top speed across the flank. I was about halfway across when it all started off again; I could hear the rumbling about five seconds before the pitiless storm burst all around me. It seemed an age till everything was quiet again and I took a few more quick steps before the same old game started all over again. The last few yards between rock and ice were nothing short of an escape from extinction. . . .[1]

Such were the conditions Buhl, Jöchler, and the Maag brothers met with on the Third Ice Field. The Frenchmen followed up rather later and took a fairly long rest at the place sheltered from stones before traversing onto the ice.

When describing the traverse of the Third Ice Field I think one ought to remember the little message left by Larch and Winter for their successors—the ladder of steps they had carved in the ice. None of the authors who later wrote accounts, Jöchler, Buhl, or Rébuffat, mention it. To recall this fact is not intended as censure for a trivial lapse of memory. But who can tell how Jöchler's race through the deadly barrage of stones might have ended if the steps had not been there to speed his passage of the traverse?

The first rope reached the "Ramp," where they hoped to be free from the danger of falling stones; but even here the fire was maintained, though its ferocity was reduced by the number of times it had struck on the way down. Buhl and Jöchler climbed quickly, and often simultaneously, up the first few rope lengths of the "Ramp" till they reached the chimney which narrows into a crack. Here it was not the difficulty of the rock formation that defeated Buhl; the crack was full of ice, the walls were glassy with it. It didn't seem possible to force a passage up it. So Buhl tried a daring turning movement on the right-hand retaining wall. So difficult was the ground that even this unique climber failed on its holdless, brittle, smooth slabs. Only occasion-

[1] Sepp Jöchler's personal account communicated to the author.

ally was it possible to get a piton a little way into a fissure; the turning traverse was a Grade VI maneuver. Buhl got to within 7 feet of the stance at the top of the iced-up crack, but he could get no farther. Jöchler joined him and, although he had no proper foothold, they tried to build a human ladder. Buhl climbed on his shoulders and then—risking everything—onto his head. All in vain, at the end of three hours' work.

During those three hours the sun reached the cliff, and melted the ice in the crack till a waterfall was pouring down it. The others, following up, reached the crack just as Buhl and Jöchler were roping down again to the foot of it, after their failure. Jöchler's report tells how the rope failed to end on the "Ramp" but hung clear over the gulf instead; and how the Frenchmen drew it in to firm rock. Rébuffat does not mention this, but then it could have been Bruneau or any of the other Frenchmen who gave this service, and not Rébuffat himself. This is what he says in his book:[1]

> We joined the Germans at the foot of the narrow section. Just at this moment a few rays of sunshine slipping over the crest came to warm the face and melt the ice. But this was no better, for the gulley was now flooded by a small waterfall from the melting of a little patch of snow a hundred and twenty feet higher. Here our friends Bruneau, Leroux, and Magnone arrived, and we regained our high spirits, despite all. A rope of two can take itself seriously, but a party of five Frenchmen is incapable of striking too dramatic an attitude, however sinister the wall, however continuous the suspense of disquieting the promise of traditional bad weather. Bruneau's gaiety infected us all.

Jöchler had by now joined Buhl, who started an acrobatic

---

[1] Gaston Rébuffat, *Étoiles et Tempêtes*, trans. Wilfrid Noyce and Sir John Hunt as *Starlight and Storm* (London: J. M. Dent and Sons Ltd., 1956).

traverse still farther to the right. I was certain that it led nowhere, and that the only route led up the waterfall. The Germans hesitated, but seeing me advance to climb the waterfall route they made up their minds; Sepp Maag launched away at the obstacle and got up after a struggle. . . .

Rébuffat gracefully excuses himself for having tied onto the rope of the two Allgäu boys while climbing through the waterfall:

When it came to his turn, Otto, the younger brother, turned to me without a word (he spoke no French and I, no German) and passed down the end of his rope. At first I did not understand, then he signed to me to tie on. I was surprised, then disarmed by the gesture. For a moment I hesitated, then I took the rope and tied it around me. Otto went on, evidently happy that I had not refused his overture of friendship.

It was now my turn to attack. The passage was not too difficult, but I came out drenched. . . .

Jöchler, who followed Buhl, now in the wake of the French rope of five, up through the watery crack, describes the pitch in his graphic way:

The bed of the chimney was still full of ice, offering hardly a grip anywhere. One felt rather like a blind hen looking for a grain of corn. It was hardly possible to open one's eyes and, if one tried to draw breath, sand and stones immediately filled one's mouth. Naturally, one was instantly soaked to the skin. The worst place is a very narrow bit, through which everyone has to force a way by crazy exertions against the enormous pressure of the water dammed up against him. A hundred and thirty feet, up a waterfall . . . can it be called climbing?

But one soon forgets the almost superhuman output of

energy, for the continuation of the groove with water running all over it plagued the lives out of us; and there were stones to cope with as well as the wet. It took us nearly three hours to get above the water. There we were, hanging shakily from our pitons like drowned rats, admitting that the North Face certainly has everything. We remained a long time on our stance till all our friends were out of the gulley, for the rock was so brittle hereabouts that stones breaking away under our feet could easily have been a danger to them. The moment the last Frenchman was over the ice bulge that shuts off the top of the gulley, Buhl and I rushed off like madmen—we had got so painfully cold. . . .

Rébuffat, who is a poet as well as a climber, avoids a naturalistic approach in his description of the pitch; instead he keeps the tension high by a deliberate understatement:

Paul soon joined me, followed by Buhl and Jöchler, who had abandoned their attempt on the right. They did not use the rope offered by the young Germans, who seemed disappointed on this small point of pride. While I was giving a dry pullover to Sepp Maag—who was clad, to my amazement, only in a light shirt and ski anorak—Buhl and Jöchler swept by without a word and hurled themselves at the next problem, once more in the lead.

A hundred and twenty feet more and we had surmounted the "Ramp." We came out on a steep snow patch in the center of the amphitheater. It was late, and each party set about looking for a bivouac site. The Austrians and the Germans, who had gone on too high, came down again; meanwhile we built ourselves a rudimentary platform. Magnone wielded his axe lustily to flatten the ground a little, while Leroux, ingenious as ever, built a rickety stone wall. I drove in pitons to secure the party. Habran talked hard and Bruneau, when he could, got in a wisecrack that set us all laughing. Meanwhile the Germans and the Austrians, sixty feet above us, maintained a cheerless silence, each in his separate corner.

Night came down on the mountains. Below, the rustic notes of the Alpine horn had ceased. Above, the lamplighter of the heavens had done his round. Leroux prepared a saucepan of hot drink, while the sausage, bacon, jam, and dry cakes circulated. Habran quoted from his favourite author: "They enjoyed a spicy insecurity." That was how it was. Friendship kept us warm. Then the cigarettes, smoked as we sat half-reclining on our rocky couch, tasted amazingly good. . . .

Is Rébuffat's comment that the German and Austrian ropes "maintained a cheerless silence, each in his separate corner," while the French party enjoyed life and comradeship in their bivouac lower down, born of smugness and intended to underline their own superiority? It must be remembered that the parties were still strangers to one another, only dependent on each other at times for expediency's sake; the spirit of rivalry was still alive, only moderated by the natural respect, born of common sense and climbing experience, in which they held one another. The "European Rope," as a spiritual brotherhood, had not yet emerged. Each was still complaining that the other was keeping him waiting. But the remark that the Germans and Austrians were not happy in their bivouacs arose from no sense of superiority or any hidden nastiness; it arose entirely from the facts of the case.

Compared with Buhl's rope or that of the Maags, the Frenchmen were climbing the Face with a definite advantage—the advantage of ample and first-class equipment. And that is to their credit rather than otherwise. One could rightly reproach Buhl and Jöchler for continuing up the Face without a change of long pants and a spare pullover after their first bivouac, instead of going down again to fetch their things, even if it meant a lost day. If they had done that, they would have had to forgo their climb of the Face, for the weather turned bad; and, of course, they knew best what hardships they were fit to endure. As to down-lined vests and sleeping bags, such as the French possessed, and which they had been able to collect with their best equipment and also to acquire as a result of their experiences on the Annapurna expedition and on the tempest-ridden mountains of Patagonia—Buhl and Jöchler knew of such things only by hearsay, for both of them were poor. Arnold Lunn, the chronicler and honest critic of Alpine goings-on, writes about Hermann Buhl as follows in his book:[1]

> After matriculating on his native mountains, he graduated on the terrible north faces of the Jorasses and the Eiger. Money continued to be a problem and it was with only five Swiss francs in his pocket that he left Innsbruck. . . .

After going in detail into Buhl's incredible achievements and adventures in the mountains, which included the solo climb of the East Face of the Watzmann, at night, in winter, he pays this tribute to the man:

> One can condemn such desperate ventures as contrary to all sane mountaineering traditions, but one cannot withhold one's admiration for Buhl's courage, endurance and fantastic skill.

What was that bivouac of Buhl's and Jöchler's above the "Ramp" really like? This is how Jöchler describes it:

[1] Arnold Lunn, *A Century of Mountaineering* (London: Allen and Unwin Ltd., 1957).

We looked for a bivouac site but found nothing suitable; but we promised ourselves that we would see the night through all right. Quite unexpectedly, a stone hit me on the head and made a sizeable hole. I only noticed how bad the wound must be when blood trickled down onto my trousers. I was very nearly sick, but not quite, for it stemmed from our having had nothing to eat since four in the morning, nor had we had time all day long to think about our stomachs. That was the result of being continually hunted. . . .

"Hunted" is perhaps the best word to describe the feeling under which many climbers of the North Face have laboured. Hunted by stone falls, hunted by the chasing hours, hunted by the fear of a break in the weather, which can turn the Face into a ghastly trap. The stones on that 27th of July were particularly furious. Pressure of time was worse than experienced by any party before, because there were nine men on the Face now; and that again heightened anxiety about the bad weather threatening to break over them.

Jöchler's account continues:

We sat down on a very exposed spot, pulled the tent sack over us, and had only one pleasure to enjoy—to brew and drink tea as hot as we could get it. We were unable to do anything for the first half hour, we were shivering so much with the cold. Gradually we managed to set up the cooker and melt some ice in the pan. My lighters were wet and useless; everything I was wearing and in my pack was utterly sodden. Hermann, however, had storm vestas. He struck one after another, till the last little stick of wood was scratched uselessly away; then he threw the lot—the empty matchbox and the ice which was to have become tea water over the edge with a fine "classical quotation."

There we sat huddled miserably together, very angry but

even more thirsty—so thirsty that not a morsel of food would go down our throats. A cold wind whistled outside our shelter. Continual cramps in my feet caused me violent pain. Our only consolation was that tomorrow there would be an end to this climb. . . .

The weather had taken a definite turn for the worse overnight. The sky was black with clouds, mist lowered oppressively down from the summit walls. At 4:30 A.M. we were climbing again, and once again on unpleasant terrain. First there was a traverse of a treacherous ice field that looked grim enough in the dim light of dawn. The incredibly brittle crossing to the great Traverse followed. We were sorry for the two Germans Sepp and Otto, who had not even had a bivouac tent along to soften the rigours of the night. Like ourselves, they were moving on again, without having eaten anything, under the sheer necessity to get moving again and so restore some warmth to our bodies. We joined ropes again, as we had yesterday after the Chimney, so that we were now a party of four on the rope. After traversing the ice gully the French party also asked to be allowed to hook themselves on. So we were now nine men on a single rope. We two were not long in grasping the implications. . . .

The fact that the Maag brothers had not even brought a tent sack with them is unique in the history of the North Face. It seems to merit the severest condemnation on the grounds of incredible negligence. Buhl and Jöchler can in no way be blamed, for when they met the brothers from Allgäu they could obviously not query their equipment. But it is difficult to condemn Sepp and Otto outright, for the way in which they overcame weariness, cold, and discomfort was magnificent. They not only showed great skill as rock climbers but evinced all the fundamental characteristics essential for mountaineering: willpower, toughness, and team spirit. It is true that the others were worried about them. And the French party, too, held out a hand of friendship to this lamentably equipped pair of brothers.

All nine on a single rope. One last resurgence of ambition and pride was manifest in the European Rope, now feeling its way upwards in heavy, driven snow. Rébuffat explains why he asked to tie onto the four ahead of him in these words:

> The limestone under its covering of snow was freezing to the touch. I made a long stride and found the pillar bulging convex above me. I calculated my rate of progress so as to fit in with Otto, a hundred and fifty feet higher up. He was climbing furiously in the attempt to go fast. Here was a piton, relic of the first ascent, and I hooked my finger into it for a hold. Suddenly I heard a crack above: a block as big as a curbstone had given way under Otto's feet. Suspended from my finger, which remained hooked in the piton, I swung right to avoid the block. But it burst and split above my head, into pieces that struck me. My head swam, everything spun around me. . . . But the finger hooked through the piton still held. It was very painful, and felt as if it had been sawn through.
>
> The world around me gradually came back into focus. I felt a sticky trickle down my face and a great weight on my shoulders. I looked at my finger, still in the piton, and felt happy and grateful that it had not given. Then the Germans above sent down a rope; I tied myself on instinctively and climbed up.

Buhl and Jöchler seem to have been quite unaware of Rébuffat's accident which proved so narrow an escape, for Buhl doesn't mention it either in his book, *Achttausend—drüber und drunter.* He says there:

> By common consent we now joined up as a single rope. Before us lay the so-called "Traverse of the Gods." It may be divine

in fair weather, for directly beneath one's feet the rock breaks away sheer to the "Third Ice Field." Four thousand feet below lie the meadows of Alpiglen. But under present conditions its only association with the Gods seemed to be the idea of making a rather abrupt acquaintance with them. We had to free every foothold and handhold from snow with the greatest of care. There was very little that could be used for safeguarding measures. The storm howled around the Face and the snowfall grew much heavier; the sky poured flakes down on us as if the clouds had broken apart. The snow started pouring down the walls with a rushing sound. Each one of us had to fend for himself in this Witches' Cauldron. Only the rope told each of us that he was not alone; that there were comrades sharing the ordeal, ready to help. . . .[1]

Rébuffat also describes that passage:

In the morning I had felt almost happy that the inevitable storm had burst at last. Now, with my head aching and my elbow numb, I advanced without enthusiasm. My heart was no longer in the job; and all around was a cold, white and silent hell. The human animal in me was unhappy; the snow entered by my wrists and neck, my fingers were clumsy, my toes freezing, my damp clothes formed a creaking shell. I sensed the same reflections and the same anxieties in my companions, and in the Germans and Austrians. They, like ourselves, were no more than human.

But little by little man adapts himself, as he must. Seeing a world transformed, he gradually moulds it to become his own. Confronted by the joint forces of mountains and elements, he feels born in himself a power, a balance, and a . . .

---

[1] Hermann Buhl, *Achttausend—drüber und drunter* (München: Nymphenburger Verlagshandlung, 1954), translated as *Nanga Parbat Pilgrimage* by Hugh Merrick (London: Hodder and Stoughton, 1956).

. . . a sense of brotherhood, of the rope. Hermann Buhl's: "comrades sharing the ordeal." The roped party, born of the blizzard on the Eiger's final cliff, of the fight against the storm, of the patient waiting while the next man is safely seen up in a desperate struggle to the next stance . . .

Rébuffat gives a graphic picture of the rope as it toiled up the "Spider":

> Slowly the tiny human forms moved upward, while from time to time an avalanche came spouting down from the couloirs above. Then the whole line of us at long intervals crouched against the glassy surface; each fought silently with all his strength to avoid being dragged off.
>
> It took hours to make six rope lengths of height. Three hundred feet above me was Buhl, three hundred below Bruneau. It was a fearful battle, a struggle both personal and collective. Each one of us, and so the whole rope, advanced almost imperceptibly.

Almost imperceptibly. Painfully slow was this crawl forward and up the "Spider's" slope. Only six rope lengths—but, in these conditions and with so many men, it meant seven long hours' work.

Buhl had studied the timing and the directions of the avalanches exactly. He knew that to take the direct line could prove suicidal, so he traversed the slope towards the right, till he found a narrow rib in the ice, high enough not to be continually swept by the avalanches. Up this he climbed till at last he reached the "Spider's" upper rim. The organ notes of the storm swallowed every word. It was necessary to yell if one wanted to communicate with the next man. How far, how very far, below was the last man now?

Buhl writes:

> Meanwhile the snow had become very sloppy, and so had our clothes. The ice slope shot steeply up to the rocks, now covered

with a treacherous layer of new snow. The next piece of climbing—probably not very difficult in normal circumstances—was probably the riskiest I had yet met. It wasn't really climbing any longer, but a continual fight upwards against a tendency to slide off the mountain; any means of progress was allowable provided it paid dividends; there was no question of correct method or style. Elbows and knees afforded the best technique. Whenever I managed to get a piton fixed I felt better, knowing I had wrung another snippet from the wall; every couple of feet forward amounted to a victory, as I crept forward at a snail's pace. Time raced on by minutes, hours; we couldn't reach the top anymore today. That meant a third bivouac on a wall like this, in such conditions! There was no escaping it. It was no longer a question of achieving a successful climb; it had become a fight for very life itself. . . .

We were on the spur, which parted the avalanches like a snowplow. The traverse across the main gully was comparatively easy. I could hear a piton being hammered below. Could the tail-enders have found the pace too slow and broken away into an independent party again, so as to come up past us? The rock below me fell away undercut to the "Spider."

Then, another white wave creaming down the gully.

"Look out—avalanche!"

It was a matter of seconds before the sharp jolt, all over again, and another inferno of snow smother, like some devil's merry-go-round. . . .

It lasted some minutes. By some miracle I was still alive when it ended. A deathly silence reigned down below. The Frenchmen had been struck by the main weight of the cataract. Had they been swept away into the gulf?

This is Sepp Jöchler's description of the crossing of the "Spider," the subsequent rope lengths, and the arrival of the great avalanche:

We soon found out what was going on up here. Every avalanche which comes down from the summit wall, collects here and sweeps across the "Spider" as if from a douche. The interesting thing was that a larger avalanche came down at regular intervals of about five minutes; the moral effect of getting ready to withstand it was nerve-shattering. . . .

All nine of us were now standing on polished ice. If an avalanche hurled one of us from his foothold it could prove fatal to all the others. And for that reason Hermann cut step after step in the ice—for six hours on end without a single rest. It was a superhuman performance when one remembers that only to stand upright on ice is an exertion.

Exhausted and shivering with cold, we reached the top of the "Spider." Our bodies were engulfed in an overwhelming weariness; they shook and shivered in every position, even when on the move. Added to that we were suffering terribly from thirst. Whenever an avalanche swept down on us, we automatically lay against the surface of the ice, at the same time anxiously watching the outcome and opening our mouths to let the wet snow spirt into it and allay the worst of the burning in our throats.

Then began a very difficult piece of climbing, made more so by the increasing coating of ice. . . .

We were about three rope lengths above the "Spider" when, with a terrifying roar, an avalanche—this time of tremendous volume—swept down on us. At first I thought that Hermann, a hundred feet above me, must come down with it. Then I felt a tug at my chest enough to knock my feet away from under me, but I was held, hanging from my piton. At the same time the rope went running through my hands; Sepp Maag had been pulled off too, but still my piton held.

Short, sharp exclamations sounded up the slope. Was

someone hurt? And how could we help an injured man, when each of us had to fight for his own life?

One of the Frenchmen was shouting, "Buhl! Buhl!" Hermann couldn't be expected to hear him in that raging tempest; nor could he have come down a hundred feet of hard-won ground again, after such a struggle to climb them. He couldn't even hear my shouts, for then I saw that he was hanging from a piton, shaking himself mightily.

The Frenchmen were asking for help. I let a rope down, but it was too short; so I sent down another, spliced this time, and it reached them. Sepp Maag made his way up to me and then we two Sepps both hauled on the rope with all our might for nearly two hours. Then Rébuffat joined us and patted me gratefully on the back. But Sepp and I were finished and could hardly stand any more.

The Frenchmen and the Allgäu brothers stayed to bivouac at this comparatively good spot. I had still to get up to Hermann. I could hardly climb; my strength had gone. I got him to hold a rope for me and climbed up on it. Twice I slid all the way down again because cramp in my hands bent my fingers back; the third time I tried I was more than halfway up when an avalanche came pouring down and took me with it back to my starting place. All the time, the storm was increasing in violence. I made a fourth attempt and it proved successful, but it was almost dark by the time I got up to Hermann. Now we had to face our third bivouac and that at a very bad place, hardly suitable for the purpose. But all hell had broken loose on the North Face.

By desperate efforts we managed to fix two pitons, to hook ourselves to them and to pull the bivouac cover over our heads.

Another bivouac on the Face. The third for Buhl and Jöchler, the second for the Frenchmen and the brothers from Allgäu. True, the open-air camp of the seven down below was wet and cold, but it provided at least an element of comfort. Gaston Rébuffat says of it:

> The Germans, almost at the end of their tether, preferred to remain with us in the relative comfort of our soaked down jackets. They had no bivouac equipment, no clothing apart from their thin shirts and their cotton anoraks, a short waistcoat and the sweater which I had given to Sepp on the previous day. And since last evening they had eaten nothing. We ourselves were soaked; for the snow had long ago melted at the warmth of our skin and trickled down our backs and along our arms. We had set out with the idea of bivouacking once only; and our provisions, luckily planned on an ample scale, were beginning to run short.
>
> All seven of us sat there, with our legs dangling or in stirrups of frozen rope, on those two miserable ledges, two staircase steps worn and rounded and sloping outward, yet somehow suspended on this gigantic wall. The higher one was comparatively spacious, about eight inches wide and three feet long. We managed to squeeze five onto it: Jean Bruneau was on the extreme right, the two Germans between him and me, while Pierre Leroux succeeded in sitting on my left. On the tiny step below Paul Habran and Guido Magnone snuggled against each other, with their backs to our legs. We were all attached to pitons, like goats to a stake, in case we slipped or anyone went to sleep. And we were covered with a small piece of "vinzle" cloth which Guido had had the brilliant idea of bringing. This was held in place by pitons and stretched over our heads, making a sort of roof.
>
> Meanwhile the avalanches continued to slither down the couloir. Here they were light and infrequent. They slid hissing over our cloth roof, though a part succeeded in piling up between our backs and the rock wall. From time to time the

west wind brought up a sprinkling of powder snow which got in everywhere, down our necks (despite our hoods) into pockets and sleeves and gloves, between our clothes and into our boots. Our bivouac looked like a village laid waste by storm.

And yet, despite our anxiety and the close quarters, a spark of gaiety warmed us. We had strength in numbers and still felt fit. Paul and Guido made an inventory of our provisions. Pierrot, balancing like a trapeze artist, managed to put a saucepan of snow on the stove, which I was balancing awkwardly on my knees. The matchbox was wet, but after a number of failures a tiny flame hesitated, flickered, made an island in the prevailing dampness, and like a little queen, shed its gleams of joy over the world. Otto and Sepp expressed their happiness at being with us, while Jean announced, in his even, cheerful voice that "this sets a new tradition." We shared out some sweets, some pieces of sugar, crumbled biscuits and a little tepid water from the melted snow. . . .

Buhl and Jöchler suffered torture in their bivouac. Bodily and spiritually, both were worn out, and they were shaking as if attacked by cramp. There they crouched or hung on their tiny place, wet through, cold to the marrow, unable to eat or even to exchange words. Presently they tried to consume some liquid biomalt; the viscous stuff simply stuck in their mouths, the effort required for swallowing being too great.

They had made a tremendous effort during the day. Buhl's performance had been such that even Jöchler could hardly believe it. Buhl had never for a moment thought of separating from the others, and leaving the badly equipped Maag brothers to make their own way, so that he and his partner could get along more quickly. And it was perhaps a good thing for the Frenchmen, too, that Buhl was in the lead. Admittedly, they were all first-class men, and a rope with a Rébuffat and a Magnone on it will always force a passage, if there is one that can be forced. But when the great avalanche came roaring down and darkness lay close at hand, it was the common purpose of the rope—the great international rope with Buhl out in front—that proved the saving grace.

But now Buhl and Jöchler were both completely exhausted, and during this bitterly cold night they had to pay for having used up their last reserves of strength. Pains attacked them, around the heart and in the stomach. Jöchler's sciatica, a legacy of the war, flared up. Buhl's breath came in intermittent gasps, as if pneumonia were setting in. Against these miseries was ranged the last flicker of willpower, the will to live, and the dream of life.

In spite of their discomfort, they fell asleep from time to time. Their heads banged together, they hung inert on the rope, then pulled themselves together again, crouching in their seats again, all through the endless hours of darkness.

At last a new day crept up through the dark. The storm had stopped and it was no longer snowing; but that meant a drop in the temperature to far below freezing point. Would it be humanly possible, in such cold, after such a night and in such pitiful condition, to find a way out of this fantastic Face, now overlaid with a stiff, glittering raiment of ice and snow?

Buhl and Jöchler were livid now, their faces almost greenish in hue, their cheeks fallen in, their noses unnaturally keen and prominent. But they still had the necessary willpower—willpower that was an end to a beginning.

And there on that clear, icy morning, in the gloom of the shadowy ice-plastered Face, the riddle that was Hermann Buhl was revealed, as he started the final climb to the summit.

Jöchler saw the two Allgäu boys up to him at the bivouac site; then Buhl began to climb. It was an overhanging, icy, snow-filled gully, super-severe in quality and 70 feet high. It took Buhl four hours to climb those 70 feet. He fell off, climbed again, fell off again, hung there held by his piton, forced himself to another attempt, gained height, hung again swinging on the rope like a helpless bundle. Jöchler heard him clearly as he uttered the words: "I'm finished!" But Buhl was not finished; he tried again, and he reached a stance at the top of the 70-foot pitch.

"You lead now, Sepp . . ." he said.

Jöchler commented, later on:

I have no words with which to assess Buhl's performance on that pitch. Anyone who saw him working his way up those seventy feet, ever and again coming off the ice-glazed rock and being brought up sharp on the rope, would have shaken his head and refused to believe his eyes. And Buhl battled on, stretched to the utmost, for four hours, in spite of his lowered bodily and spiritual condition. I shall remain eternally grateful to Hermann; it was he who built a bridge for us all and gave us hope of survival. . . .

In his book, Rébuffat tries to put Buhl's effort into words:

Then Buhl started. He found himself immediately on very difficult ground, for underneath the snow the rock was covered with a shining layer of hard, thick ice carpeting the whole surface. The feet skated off, the hands slid from the holds, every crack was blocked up, every hold levelled out. It was very difficult to drive pitons in; the hammer tapped, dug in, tired, tapped askew, and flaked off a chunk of thick ice. The whole body would slide, suspended from its piton. Then it would recover and hoist itself up; for a moment the laboured breathing would stop altogether. Then the hammer would dig out a hold, push off a layer of snow covering a slab, clean out another hold, and the foot would succeed in driving a crampon point into the verglas while numb fingers freed a crack of its ice and drove in another piton. Buhl gained a foot, then a yard;

his feet slipped again and he was off altogether, but the pitons held. The cold was terrible, the sky very clear. Our feet were frozen and our muscles stiff, the whole human machine was petrified; our clothes were like a suit of armour, our rope a steel thread. Buhl advanced slowly, and with wonderful doggedness succeeded in climbing the rise. Jöchler joined him and continued in the lead.

"Jöchler joined him and continued in the lead." It sounds so simple, laconically stated like that. In fact it was a highly dramatic move, which Rébuffat, waiting far behind and below, had no means of seeing and appreciating at its full value.

Buhl, the man who never gave in, who never capitulated before any difficulty, who even regarded his own weakness as an obstacle to be overcome, had used himself up so completely on that icy overhanging gully, that his last reserves of strength were exhausted. After tapping in the last piton and attaching himself to it, Buhl collapsed. He tipped forwards and hung in the rope, arms and feet limp and hanging down. He tried to straighten himself but had not the strength. "I'm finished," he said.

Jöchler was as terrified to hear Buhl, of all people, speak those words as he was at the position in which he could see him hanging there above. They were the same words Toni Kurz had spoken with his last breath. Buhl was in the same posture as Toni had been when he died. Was this the end of Hermann Buhl, too? And, just as in Toni's case, was his brave heart going to fail him just after he had achieved the seemingly impossible?

It was probably such thoughts as these, spurred by his anxiety, nay, his raging fear for his friend, which enabled Jöchler, availing himself of the rope and the piton Buhl had managed to fix, to climb up to Buhl without assistance from him and then to bring him back to an upright posture. Buhl's face was green; if only one had a drop of hot coffee, to put him right again . . . miraculously, he recovered without it. Jöchler stayed with him and helped him to bring Sepp Maag up on the rope; then trusting to Buhl's wonderful skill in rope manipulation and belaying technique, he climbed on up the vertical and at times overhanging Exit Cracks. And even if they seemed easier than the unusually severe pitches up which Buhl had led, those cracks are always extremely exhausting and uncommonly dangerous.

So Jöchler took over the lead. As so often happens where good friends and partners are concerned the realisation that Buhl needed him seemed to have lent him new strength. He led with immense care and yet astonishingly fast; and the higher he got, the faster grew the pace. The sun was breaking through light veils of mist without very much strength; but it was the symbol of life, nonetheless, lending courage and confidence.

And so the great rope of nine went steadily on, moving toward the summit, each one of them protecting and helping the one behind him as he climbed. Speed was the essence now, nothing else mattered. Every man was giving of his utmost. And then Jöchler emerged from the final crack, with nothing but the summit icecap bulking above him. One by one the others followed. . . .

At this point the French party untied from the others. By now the sun was shining warmly; so Rébuffat decided to rest and move onto the summit later with his friends. The summit was near now, the way down assured, the sun was shining and they were alive. So the single rope that bound them all together—Hermann and Sepp, another Sepp and Otto, Gaston and Paul and Guido and Pierre and Jean— was untied. Instead of a European rope climbing the ice slope to the summit, there were two, a German-Austrian rope and a French rope; and between the two there was also a gap in time. One rope was led by the most famous German-speaking climber, the Tirolese guide Hermann Buhl, the other by the most famous French-speaking climber, the Chamonix guide, Gaston Rébuffat.

What a pity. . . .

Yet it does not alter the fact that the eighth ascent of the North Face of the Eiger was made, under the worst conditions ever yet experienced, by a European Rope working together in concord and harmony. That it did not end in disaster was due to the fact that all the men on that rope were men out of the ordinary ruck, men endowed with the will to do the best for the whole party. Ambition and rivalry, those two weaknesses which men take with them up into the mountains, vanished in the great hour of their ordeal. They are two traits which it will never be possible to eradicate entirely, and maybe there are traces of them in one or other of the reports quoted above. But reports are written up afterwards, not during tempests or under avalanche fire, not in cold bivouacs or in direst time of peril.

Let us ignore the pettinesses and concentrate on the common cause—the triumph of a genuinely European rope.

THE WALL
OF LIFE
AND DEATH

Human beings allowed the North Face to rest undisturbed for exactly a week after the dramatic ascent by a rope of nine. On August 5, three more excellent Austrian climbers appeared at Alpiglen—two Viennese, Erich Vanis and Hans Ratay, and Karl Lugmayer, who hailed from Upper Austria and was studying in Vienna. Vanis was twenty-three, Ratay only twenty, and Lugmayer twenty-four years old; but Ratay's extreme youth proved no hindrance to the tempo of their climb, for in spite of bad weather and two bivouacs he was just as strong and just as tough at the finish.

The Viennese school of mountaineering is soundly based, with a tradition stretching back into the last century. It has, moreover, always frowned upon specialisation on extreme rock faces. A comprehensive knowledge of the mountains, experience and mastery on mixed ground, on a steep ice slope just as much as on a severe or super-severe rock face, all these go to make the complete mountaineer. The great protagonists, Dr. Pfannl and Thomas Maischberger, who did their most important climbs at the turn of the century, are still fresh in men's memories. And Emil Zsigmondy, who wrote the first mountaineering textbook—*The Perils of the*

Alps—as far back as the eighties, was a Viennese, as was also Alfred Horeschowsky, who, back in 1922, made the first attempt on the Matterhorn's North Face with another Viennese climber, Franz Pikielko.

The generation between the wars, in which we find names like Rudolf Schwarzgruber, Hubert Peterka, Fritz Kasparek, and Sepp Brunnhuber—one could prolong the list for pages—also held firmly to the principle of versatility in mountaineering.

Consequently young Erich Vanis not only had a record behind him of extreme rock climbs but a fine reputation as an exponent on the ice of the great classical climbs in the Western Alps, such as Mont Blanc by the Peuteret Ridge, the North Face of the Lyskamm and the East Face of Monte Rosa. Ratay, though even younger, had an almost similar history of training in the Western Alps. The pair had done many a tour together in the Eastern Alps and had even made a winter ascent of the Grossglockner's North Ridge. Lugmayer had climbed the redoubtable North Face of the Dent d'Hérens solo, then bivouacked on the ridge leading to the Matterhorn and returned to his starting point by climbing down the northern side of the East Ridge of the Dent d'Hérens. He and Ratay had already done the Lauper Route on the Eiger. All three were as familiar with ice and snow and avalanche chutes as they were with the severest rock.

On the morning of August 6, they started up the North Face and, on their first day, reached the waterfall crack on the "Ramp," or roughly the height of our second bivouac. They could have climbed farther, but the drenching at the waterfall cooled their ardour; and they had already been a little damped before that, for it had been raining ever since they traversed the Third Ice Field. The night was cool, but not unbearably so, but during the night the rain turned to snow, and when the trio looked out next morning from the cover of their tent sack, it was on a winter landscape; everything was covered with a foot of fresh snow. They hardly gave a thought to a retreat—not only because of the danger of avalanches on the Ice Fields lower down, but because they didn't see why a little snow should turn them back. Their winter climbing had made them familiar with snow-covered rock; and, then again, winter is always colder in winter than it is in summer! So they went on up.

Ratay led up the waterfall pitch, Vanis on the difficult piece up the Ice Bulge. Just as he had found a firm piton right under that obstacle and was ready to climb out onto the ice above on the protection of a rope threaded through the piton ring, an avalanche swept the upper part of the "Ramp" with a tremendous roar.

This was something new in the history of these climbs. Avalanches were previously taken for granted on the "Spider" and in the Exit Cracks; this one was certainly premature. For all that, it was upon them, and Vanis took quick avoiding action by a return to the safe piton below the Bulge. The upper part of the Face had evidently prepared an unfriendly reception. . . .

The trio climbed on, but they went up too far. Vanis judged the normal crossing from the Ice Field to the brittle rock ledge much harder than the passage offered by another ledge nearly 500 feet higher up. It proved a difficult climb and, when they got there, the shelf wasn't a shelf at all, but a thin plastering of snow on holdless rock. The weather was bad and it was still snowing; it was not cold, but that meant all the greater danger from avalanches.

So back they had to go. It meant long, exhausting, dangerous hours before they were back on the real "brittle ledge." There they decided to bivouac; but before they did so, the indefatigable Ratay, the baby of the party, displaying the spirit and toughness of a grown man, climbed the watery, ice-rimmed crack, to the top of the pillar which marks the start of the "Traverse of the Gods," then roped down again, leaving the rope hanging, so as to make the next morning's start easier.

It was a very wet and cold bivouac, differing very little from other uncomfortable nights spent in the open and survived by many climbers on this Face. Next morning, August 8, the trio climbed on, up the crack, across the Traverse—which seemed to Vanis to have nothing godlike, but only a kind of devilish treachery, about it—to reach the "Spider."

The "Spider"—true to its name—once again staged a nasty mishap, its repertoire seemingly inexhaustible. This time it was a stone as big as a fist that hit Lugmayer on the head. His companions saw him crouching down on his stance motionless for about ten minutes. When he did not answer their calls they became extremely anxious; but Vanis recalled that he himself had been hit on the head by a stone down below on the ice fields. Crouching had quickly restored his balance and dulled the pain; Lugmayer must be in the same case.

In fact, he suddenly got to his feet again and climbed up to join them. More than that, he was once again so fit that he was able to take over the lead and tackle difficult rock and ice in equally brilliant style.

The weather continued to improve, and when towards evening the trio reached the summit, the sun was going down in glory. It was like a greeting and a triumphal reception on the part of the mountain for three climbers who had made their way up the Face and climbed faultlessly, in spite of bad weather and having taken the wrong line on the way up.

The descent of the West Face, with which they were unfamiliar, dictated a third bivouac. It was neither dramatic nor perilous, just uncomfortable, cold, and wet. To quote Rébuffat's strikingly simple phrase: "The human animal was unhappy." But next morning at 8 o'clock when they were already enjoying breakfast down at the Eigergletscher Hotel there was nothing, either animal or spiritual, about the trio which could be described as unhappy.

Down on the meadows near Alpiglen there was a red tent, occupied by a solitary inhabitant, a young chemist from Vienna, Karl Blach—the same Karl Blach who had already been on the Face in 1950 with Karl Reiss and had broken an arm when a slab came away in the "Difficult Crack."

He had come back again, but Reiss was not here, nor was there anyone else with whom he could attempt the climb. But on August 13th of this very active year a green tent was pitched quite close to the red one. It was inhabited by Jürgen Wellenkamp from Reichenhall and Bernd Huber from Munich, two very fine mountaineers. Wellenkamp, especially, was to develop into one of the best, most intelligent, most companionable, and most successful climbers who ever embarked on difficult new routes in the Alps or elsewhere in the world. (By a grim irony of fate, only a few years later, Wellenkamp slipped on a safe path in the Bregaglia and was killed.)

The inhabitants of the green tent made friends with the occupier of the red one. They told him they intended to climb the Face next day. Blach did not force himself on them, nor in any way suggest that the great climb might be undertaken as a threesome. Instead he unselfishly proposed to go with them as far as the "Difficult Crack." "I can show you the way," he said. "I've done it before."

During the night the tents awoke to furious activity. Wellenkamp cooked a meal and brewed masses of strong coffee. Unfortunately the good breakfast and so much coffee did not seem to agree with Bernd Huber. He climbed up the base of the wall through the night and the early dawn without uttering a word. Then, suddenly, he said: "I don't feel nearly fit enough for such a big climb."

It looked as if Wellenkamp would have to forgo his climb; it would certainly be a risk to go on with an apathetic partner, who was not feeling well. It certainly does not do to talk anyone into climbing the North Face of the Eiger. But was the discovery that Blach could wear the same size boots as Huber and that he could also wear his crampons blind chance or the machination of fate?

So Wellenkamp and Blach roped up together, while Huber, in no way put out, but glad not to have robbed his friend of a great experience, turned back and went down again.

The two men, one from Bavaria, one from Vienna, proved to be an almost perfect Eiger partnership. Each of them rejoiced at the supreme skill he recognised in the other, without a trace of envy, rivalry, or competition. Neither had to show the other what a grand chap he was, because both were such grand chaps. They too were bombarded by stones, but the harmony between them was so great that they never experienced that "hunted" feeling.

It was only 1 P.M. when they reached the bivouac site on the "Ramp." There was no ice in the crack this time, but the waterfall was coming down in such volume that it was almost impossible to see the rocks. It was still early enough for them to complete the climb in one day, which had not been done again since Waschak did it; but this was the kind of idea that might spring from that "hunted" feeling, and they did not feel hunted.

They had plenty of time, so they rested and made tea for more than an hour and a half. This is how Wellenkamp himself described it later:[1]

> We gazed and gazed and gazed. We had enjoyed a rest at many a magnificent spot in the mountains; but that rest on the North Face of the Eiger was unique.

Wellenkamp was the first to say it. Everything had been said about the North Face, how big, how savage, how grim, how high, how magnificent it was; but no one before him had said that to rest on it was lovely, that one could enjoy the beauty of the scene from it at one's leisure. Was it the result of the unusual understanding between these two men of similar mentality and outlook, or were the conditions on the Face so much easier? We cannot tell, but we must all be grateful to Wellenkamp for this simple yet all-embracing statement.

Now for the waterfall crack. They spent a long time trying to turn it on the right, as Buhl had tried to and as Terray, according to his

---

[1] Jürgen Wellenkamp, "Ein Bergerlebnis: die Eiger-Nordwand," *Südost-Kurier,* September 10, 1952.

account, succeeded in doing. These two failed, and in the end found themselves back, breathless, at the foot of the crack. Wellenkamp reports how they finally mastered it: "Karl just swam puffing up the waterfall. I took a great deal longer, laden as I was with the heavy rucksack and two ice axes."

Short as the description is, one can recognise at once how good Blach was. Wellenkamp led the next rope length—we know by now how difficult it is—and just as he was beginning to get ready to bring the packs up on the rope, there was Blach himself with both rucksacks and the two axes. Wellenkamp was so thrilled by this further performance on his companion's part that—undemonstrative though he normally was—he felt compelled to shake him by the hand. Blach just grinned back amiably and somewhat breathlessly.

The two men found the right crossing to the "brittle ledge," climbed on up the crack to the great Traverse, which seemed to both of them to justify its godlike name; but they had to wait before taking to the "Spider," mainly on account of falling stones, not, this time, avalanches. They waited till after sunset, then hurried up over the "Spider" and on through the darkness onto the rocks above it, where they found a wretched little place for a bivouac.

They changed their underclothes, in spite of which the night, at 11,800 feet, was bitingly cold; but it would have taken more than that to quench their high spirits. It was the most impressive night either of them had ever spent. "The human animal" within them was unhappy; but their mind rose superior to their hardships and their spirit kept a joyful hold on life.

Next morning they found the Exit Cracks difficult under a heavy coating of ice—nothing new in that. They reached the summit just before noon and Wellenkamp described the moment in these words:

During my thirty-three hours on the Face I seemed to have been in a dreamland; not a dreamland of rich enjoyment, but a much more beautiful land where burning desires were translated into deeds. . . .

I learned how genuine his reaction had been when, in 1953, we climbed together to the 20,940-foot summit of Ausangate, an icy throne of the Inca Gods of Cuzco in the Andes. Wellenkamp was a sensitive, musical type, and I shall never forget how he learned to play in Indian fashion on an Indian flute, which he had first heard the native porters playing only a short time before. In him were combined in complete harmony a perfectly fashioned body, a bright, courageous mind, and a receptive spirit.

Maybe as he stood on the Eiger's summit that August 15, 1952, he thought of his partner Karl Reiss, whose care, two years before, had brought him safely, in spite of his severe injury, to the Gallery window. He could have no idea that his onetime companion was at that very moment only about 2,000 feet below him, just above the "Death Bivouac."

Only the day before, the Viennese Reiss and another climber from Wels, Siegfried Jungmeier, had arrived at Alpiglen and had proceeded straight to the climb next morning. It says much for Reiss's courage and skill that he was not satisfied to traverse the Third Ice Field from the "Death Bivouac" to the "Ramp" in the usual way, but climbed straight up the cliff leading to the "Spider" instead. There he found some old pitons, which Sedlmayer and Mehringer must have left behind, for who else, if not those first two to leave the mark of human endeavour on the Face, had tried to climb straight up at that point?

Reiss reckons that he got to within 250 feet of the "Spider." He found the rocks difficult, but no more so than anywhere else on the Face, and he would have pushed on with his attempt if he had had more than six rock and six ice pitons with him. With so little equipment it seemed too risky a venture, so he and his partner turned back and climbed down again to the "Death Bivouac." The attempt had taken four and a half hours; but Reiss had established beyond any doubt that the direct climb is possible—in the right conditions, especially when stone falls and avalanches are inactive.

Reiss and Jungmeier were the first to turn the waterfall pitch since Terray and Lachenal, but even that detour took three hours and a half. Their day's work was quite extraordinary. A cold bivouac linked it to the next day. At the "Traverse of the Gods," the Eiger led them the usual dance with snowflakes and, finally, an unusually heavy thunderstorm caught them on the summit.

In spite of that, Reiss said: "We had good conditions."

Two years later this splendid climber and good companion died of pneumonia at a high camp on Saipal, a lonely white peak of over 23,000 feet in northwest Nepal. There could be no better example of human courage and humble gratitude for the gift of life than those words: "We had good conditions."

This successful climb by Reiss and Jungmeier brought an end to the 1952 "Season" on the North Face. It had been a good year and an important year. Nobody had perished on the Face, nor had a single rescue expedition been called for. As to successful ascents, it was an unexampled year in the history of the North Face: there had been five of them, involving eighteen men in all. Of the ten Austrians, eight either came from Vienna or belonged to Viennese climbing circles. These successes added to those of earlier years brought the total up to twelve. So it was not surprising when, among Viennese "Extremists" and even elsewhere among Alpine know-it-alls, the question was being asked:

"Aha, so you did the North Face of the Eiger. And—what else?"

It is also understandable that those who had actually climbed the Face protested energetically against any such downgrading of the climb.

In a notable study of the North Face, Erich Vanis has raised the interesting question whether the Face has become "easier" during the course of the years. He himself gives a negative answer, setting off the greater volume of the waterfalls and the more serious danger from stones against the drying out of the rock and the shrinkage of the ice. Indeed, only one who has climbed the Face several times could really say definitely whether it has become easier, more difficult, or remained the same; and there is not, probably never will be, such a person. For up till now, everyone, no matter how comparatively good his passage up the wall may have been, has said: "Never again!"

Besides which, the Face has a different aspect, evinces different conditions, every time. In fact it often changes in the course of a single day. The "good conditions" for Wellenkamp and Blach were quite different from those affecting Reiss and Jungmeier, although both parties were on the Face on one and the same day.

The fact that eighteen men climbed the Face safely in the summer of 1952 is no criterion of its degree of severity. All it does indicate is that they were all superb climbers and mountaineers. The very aura of death which had veiled the whole history of the climb brought to it the elite: only the very best dared the attempt and succeeded in it. And let us not forget that even in this summer of successful climbs the finest Alpine climbers in a world climbing-elite had often to fight very hard, not only to reach the summit but to preserve their own lives.

Erich Vanis dealt with those know-it-alls and Alpine loudmouths who minimise the North Face of the Eiger and try to downgrade its standard of difficulty—armchair mountaineers, who would probably never dare to climb. Vanis warned them clearly that talk of that kind could easily restore the aura of fatality to the Eiger's North Face.

A warning and a prophecy. . . .

And how right Vanis was. For, even if the accidents of later years did not, for the most part, arise from lack of skill in the climbers who attempted it, they certainly proved that the North Face had remained and would always remain what it has always been: the ultimate test of a mountaineer.

In the summer of 1953 the veil of death once again descended on the Eiger, not to be lifted again for five long years. On July 26, two climbers started up the North Face without any fuss or bother. Both were good, experienced rock climbers with a fair amount of experience on ice. These two Germans, Paul Körber and Roland Vass, were watched by the few visitors to and staffs of the hotels as, on their first day, they reached the "Flatiron" and bivouacked there. During the night the weather broke, bringing snow and a sharp drop in temperature, obscuring visibility the whole of the next day. How were the two men faring? Even down at Alpiglen and on the Kleine Scheidegg it was bitterly cold; it must be frightful up there on the Face. On July 28, the pair could be seen again, climbing down now, crossing the Second Ice Field. Suddenly, the uppermost of the two slipped out of his holds—struck by a stone perhaps, or his balance maybe impaired by cold and exhaustion?—to go sliding swiftly past his companion, whose numbed hands could no longer hold the iced-up rope. He, too, was hurled outward by the shock and both went catapulting in a great curve down into the bottomless gulf.

At about the same time, two particularly fine climbers met at the Oberreintal Hut in the Wetterstein Range. They were Uly Wyss, a thirty-year-old Zürich climber, and Karl Heinz Gonda, a twenty-three-year-old amateur from Dresden. Wyss was an exceptional ice exponent and equally good on rock; Gonda one of the best rock climbers ever to graduate on the Elbe's sandstone hills. When we remember that Fehrmann, Strubich, Dietrich, and Wiessner all tried out their first climbing boots on that same sandstone, the phrase speaks more than any superlatives could.

Gonda and Wyss climbed together, got to know one another's ways perfectly, and became one of the most perfect of climbing partnerships, fit to tackle the severest and most perilous climbs. But it was not the difficulties of the Eiger that proved fatal to them; for the mountain had let them escape from its greatest difficulties before it undermined the bridge that led back to life.

They started their climb on August 20. No one knows what conditions they found on the Face, for they left no record, of course, and observation by telescope was much hampered by cloud and mist. When the telescopes were trained again on the third morning, two little dots were visible. Wyss and Gonda were not only alive, they were climbing the icy Exit Cracks as swiftly as if they had just risen from a warm bed instead of having lived through a second bitterly cold bivouac after two days of fearful exertion.

The report given by those at the telescopes—Hugo Hansjörg Wyss, Uly Wyss's brother, and Werner Stäuble, a famous mountain rescue man from Zürich—was shattering in its brevity and simplicity:

> Towards midday we could see them about 150 feet below the summit, then clouds hid them from view. When the curtain of the mists parted again, all we could see through the glass was that their steps disappeared into a snowslide. . . .

So an insignificant snowslide on the summit ice slope claimed the lives of those two fine climbers—*after* they had climbed the Face, and only a few feet below the summit.

The Gallery minder of the Jungfrau Railway saw two shadows hurtle past the windows of Eigerwand Station, enveloped in a cloud of snow, at noon. It was only a momentary glimpse, but long enough for him to recognise the shape of bodies. . . .

Horrified, he reported what he had seen. Later on, Werner Stäuble found parts of Heinz Gonda's body, battered to pieces in its 3,000-foot fall, below the Gallery window.

Wyss and Gonda were proof against everything on the mountains except the caprice of an avalanche sliding down a smooth ice slope and an unexpected blast of wind. Could their fall have been prevented by better belaying or by ice pitons? Perhaps, but, again, they may have run out of ice pitons. Perhaps their nerves were dulled against danger at a moment when by all human calculations there was no more to fear. Perhaps they let themselves be mastered by the feeling that their agony was over and the summit already won—before it was. Perhaps they suffered too soon that tremendous sense of relaxation which is only justified when the last step to the summit has been made. No one will ever know.

There were long deliberations whether their effort could be allowed to stand as the thirteenth climb of the Face; but the historians of the Eiger are hard-hearted. The verdict was that the record only counts for him who climbs the very last foot of the Face and lives to tell the tale.

Nineteen fifty-three saw another successful climb. Two excellent Bavarian climbers, a butcher's assistant, Erhard Riedl from Reichenhall, and a customs officer, Albert Hirschbichler from Berchtesgaden, made the ascent in splendid style. Unconsciously, the memory goes back to Hinterstoisser and Kurz, from Reichenhall and Berchtesgaden respectively; and, like their precursors of seventeen years before, these two had learned their climbing in the hard school of the Watzmann and the Mühlsturzhörner, graduating from severe to super-severe, from rock to ice. By the time they set foot on the Eiger's Face they were both masters of their craft. Life went with them all the way, and their successful climb was a memorial greeting to their predecessors, who had opened the gate to the climb but had not been able to find their way back through it alive. . . .

Körber and Vass, Gonda and Wyss: their names will always be remembered. But their deaths shrouded the North Face in grief and horror once again. Not a party dared the climb in 1954 and 1955, and it was not till 1956 that climbers gathered once more at its foot.

The first to come were two Munich climbers with fine reputations, Dieter Söhnel and Walter Moosmüller. As usual they put up their tent above Alpiglen; they started the climb on August 3. At the end of the "Hinterstoisser Traverse" they were overtaken by a heavy storm, so they climbed down again, arriving at their tent safe, but wet through.

As soon as the weather improved, up they went again, on the 5th, with the intention of preparing the Traverse more thoroughly; once again they were driven back by bad weather.

It was on this same day that two more aspirants arrived in Grindelwald and took up their quarters to start with in a hayrick; they were Klaus Buschmann and Lothar Brandler, who had come from his native Saxony to live in Munich and was a noted performer on sandstone. Brandler was only just nineteen, as daring and nimble as a cat on a rock, but lacking in ice experience and so not yet quite ready for the great ordeal the North Face imposes on all its attackers. Yet he and his partner had a guardian angel along with them, a grim and grisly guardian angel—who, for two others, proved to be the angel of death. . . .

At first Brandler and Buschmann went about things like old and experienced mountaineers; they had read too much about the North Face to treat it lightheartedly, and in the existing conditions, they never even thought of going anywhere near it. The weather did not clear till the morning of the 7th, when the two men went down into the village, listened to the weather forecast, and studied the weather chart. To their joy, the promise was of fine weather for the next four or five days. They hurried back to the station, travelled by train up to Alpiglen and, during the afternoon, climbed as far as the bivouac cave above the Second Pillar, where they arrived at 4:30 P.M. The temptation to climb further was great, but they were determined to counterbalance their lack of experience by extraordinary care. They looked up at the dripping cliffs and decided to camp for the night.

The next morning dawned cloudlessly fair, but the two climbers didn't feel in the right mood for continuing the climb at daybreak. They might even have preferred bad weather as a welcome excuse. Somehow they couldn't make up their minds. Their equipment was complete, but too heavy. It would be much better to go down again, go through their gear again, and come up again next day with lighter baggage. . . .

By this time—6 A.M.—it was broad daylight, and at that moment they saw another party—Söhnel and Moosmüller—climbing past them towards the "Difficult Crack." That gave the boys new confidence; they followed the others and came up with them in a gully below the Crack. The parties exchanged a friendly greeting. It was good to know that there were other, older, more experienced men nearby. Everything would go all right now.

From the shelf below the gully the first party climbed up to a pitoned stance about 30 feet higher up. Then Moosmüller moved out to the right to a position some 10 feet above his partner Söhnel. Brandler moved up into the gully and drove in a temporary piton, to which he belayed himself, with Buschmann 6 feet below him.

Suddenly, Brandler heard Moosmüller exclaim: "Hold it!"

Immediately, he felt a blow on his shoulder. Aha, he thought, Moosmüller has come off and fetched up next to me; but when he looked, there was no Moosmüller, nor was Söhnel on his stance anymore. Down below there, two bodies were hurtling down the Face, striking the rocks with a hideous dull thudding sound, hurtling out again, striking the rocks again, finally disappearing from sight. . . .

Brandler instinctively lowered himself to join his friend; then both stood rooted to the spot, staring into the abyss, into which the two others had vanished. The two boys could hear the rushing of their own blood in their ears, their own heartbeats thumping in their throats. It was some time before they recovered from the shock and slowly began the descent.

Down below, they found the others, both dead. They could hardly grasp that two men, with whom a short time ago they had been talking and laughing, could be dead now. But there was no doubt about it; they were past all human help. This was the first time they had witnessed death in the mountains. Shaken to the core, they climbed on down, reported the accident, and paid their fellow climbers the last duty due, by taking part in the recovery operation. But they turned their backs on the North Face for that year. Nor did anyone else attempt it during 1956.

It was left for 1957 to stage the grand catastrophe, the tragic disaster, which once again directed the full blaze of publicity onto the Eiger's North Face, so that the newspaper headlines were full of it, the press and radio reporters came streaming to its foot, even more than in 1936—the appalling tragedy that befell Nothdurft, Mayer, and Longhi. . . .

THE TRAGEDY

OF 1957

The tragedy of 1957 from its prelude to its dramatic end was a thing of riddles and secrets. It began on a Saturday, August 3, before night had faded into day; it ended on Monday, the 12th, the day after a man had been rescued from the North Face.

So one man out of the four who had started on the climb was in a position to give an account of what had happened and to clear up any mysteries. It is not for us to doubt his word; but it is clear that the incredible stresses of nine days spent on the Face, of eight bivouacs often in an upright posture or hanging on the rope, of weakness and pain caused by falls and injury from stones, had somewhat blunted the clarity and accuracy of his memory and his powers of judgment. For his reports are full of contradictions.

One must try to get rid of all sources of error which stem from the human imagination; that includes those which so frequently occur in the reports of the people who man the telescopes. One must seek absolute clarity, not in order to satisfy the inquisitive or the sensation seekers, but to lessen the nagging doubts surrounding a mystery, to stifle all guesswork and to replace mere surmise by knowledge of the truth leading to a solution of the riddle, however grim that knowledge may be.

But clarity and knowledge are unfortunately not possible in this instance, it seems. And however hard I try to be an impartial historian, approaching my assignment cautiously and scientifically, I know I shall fail in that aim. I cannot solve the riddle, cannot lift the veil from this human tragedy, can provide neither knowledge nor clarity.

The actors in this drama were, first, two Italian climbers, Stefano Longhi, aged forty-four, and Claudio Corti, twenty-nine, both from Lecco in the province of Como. Lecco, at the gates of the Bregaglia, a savagely beautiful group of sharp granite peaks, faces, and ridges, is a little mountaineering realm of its own. This was the home of Ricardo Cassin, the first man to climb the North Face of the Western Zinne, the Northeast Face of Piz Badile and the sky-raking Walker Buttress of the Grandes Jorasses. To be recognised as a good climber by the climbers and guides of Lecco carries the weight of a diploma.

The other two protagonists in the tragedy of 1957 were two Germans—Günther Nothdurft and Franz Mayer—who, in spite of their youth (both were only twenty-two), had made a resounding name for themselves in Alpine circles.

Günther Nothdurft—he and Mayer were both from Württemberg — was so fine a rock climber that Hermann Buhl himself acknowledged the youngster's achievements with surprise and approval. Young Günther was already familiar with Cassin's great face climbs. He had climbed the great overhanging precipice of the Western Zinne in good time, mastered the neighbouring Yellow Arête on the Kleine Zinne solo in 45 minutes and the Northeast Face of Piz Badile, also on his own. Only Buhl had done that daring climb solo before him. The time taken by Nothdurft shows what an outstanding rock climber he was. The first party ever to climb Badile's uncommonly smooth face had to bivouac twice, as did the next successful team, which included such redoubtable names as

Lionel Terray and Gaston Rébuffat. When Buhl completed his solo climb of the face in 4½ hours, the Italian climbers gathered on the summit were so enthusiastic that they wanted to carry him off, down to Lecco, in triumph. Yet, a year or two later, Nothdurft, hardly more than a boy, came and did the solo climb in only 3½ hours.

Martin Schliessler, perhaps the most successful German climber since the war, a man who is extremely sparing with praises, wrote to me about Nothdurft in a letter:

> I will tell you straightaway what bound me so closely with Günther Nothdurft. We were the best of friends and had in mind to do many a climb in days to come. In my eyes he was the most gifted young climber of recent years. It is sad, the way the North Face of the Eiger time and again takes the very best to itself. . . . About a month before the disaster, Nothdurft started up the Face, intending to climb it solo. It took him only a few hours to get above the Second Ice Field. When the weather turned bad, he climbed down through the night and a snowstorm using a miner's headlamp which he had taken up with him. He said it had been a tough fight.

Schliessler was a critical man, and that was his opinion. We learn from him that young Günther knew the Face up to about half its height and had been the first ever to dare to tackle it alone; moreover, that in doing so he had climbed up and down at a pace nobody would ever have believed possible. So this young mountaineer, who wore out his first pair of boys' climbing boots on the rocks of the famous climbing school called "Battert" in the Black Forest, proved that he could move equally swiftly and safely on ice. All the same, the proprietor of the famous Munich sports shop Schuster and the famous mountaineer Steinmetz both tell of the indelible impression left on Nothdurft by the North Face. He described it as the most difficult and dangerous thing he had ever been on and said he would never try to climb it again.

Yet only a few weeks later here he was, with Franz Mayer, starting up it once more. They knew each other to perfection, and had done a winter training climb together, which must have been the severest test on snowy, icy rock, under winter conditions, ever undertaken: the direct ascent of the West Face of the Totenkirchl in the Wilde Kaiser range by the Peters-Eidenschink route. So they were two climbers of whom anything might be expected, *except* that they should climb slowly and find the severities of the Eiger's North Face too much for them. Yet, it was just the slowness of the four men on the Face that brought about the tragedy culminating on Monday, August 12, in the death of Stefano Longhi.

The prelude began on August 3 in the early hours, when Corti and Longhi started to climb the Face. It looked as if they intended going up by the "Most Direct," for they climbed straight towards the windows of Eigerwand Station, as Sedlmayer and Mehringer had once done. But it turned out that they were doing so unintentionally, simply because they found old pitons as they went up and so thought they must be on the right route. It was late before they realised that they had gone astray, and bivouacked accordingly. Next day, Sunday, August 4, they roped down and at long last traversed out onto Hinterstoisser's original route, still on the lower part of the Face.

Here, for the first time, they saw two other climbers coming up by the same route—Nothdurft and Mayer. What happened when they met?

This is what Corti said in the report he gave in hospital at Interlaken to a United Press reporter after his rescue—according to a number of reports published in the press it was recorded on tape:

On Sunday, when we had found the correct route, we met the German climbers Günther Nothdurft and Franz Mayer, who had started up the Face the same morning. We could only communicate by signs, as they knew no Italian and we no

German, but we understood that they had lost their rucksacks which contained their crampons and the rest of their equipment, so that they were in no position to continue their climb. Since we had enough equipment, we pooled it and went on climbing together: I led the party, which now roped up as one, with Longhi bringing up the rear.

And where was it that they met? It is impossible to fix the spot from Corti's description; for he apparently lacks the gift of pinpointing a given spot on a mountain. However, it must have been below the "Difficult Crack." And we are asked to believe that Nothdurft and Mayer had already lost both their rucksacks and their crampons, of such critical importance! Nothdurft already knew part of the Face and he must certainly have been aware that during his solo descent, a month earlier, he would have been lost without crampons. Now we hear that after the loss he had still continued to climb at least some way without them. It all sounds very peculiar. We also learn that Nothdurft was satisfied with the use of the Italian's surplus equipment. Was a man who was always used to leading suddenly so harebrained and easily satisfied that he was prepared to tag onto another party just because it had equipment which he had not? Or could it just be that Corti wanted to have the Germans with him, because they knew the way? Puzzle upon puzzle. . . .

People who watched them reported that the two ropes certainly did not tie up together from the moment when they met; on the contrary, they went on climbing separately for a long time. An argument arose out of the divergent narratives and reports; the inexplicable differences resulted in heightened tempers. Weeks after the disaster, the Central Committee of the Italian Alpine Club ordered Corti to furnish a precise report on the attempted climb. I was sent a translation of that report.

I will try to reconstruct its factual content on the broadest lines. The first thing that strikes anyone who knows the Face is that—as already mentioned—Corti is never able to pinpoint the exact spot at which he happened to be at any given time. Significant points that for years, indeed for two decades, have been known by definite names, are depicted in vague terms, as if he were on completely new ground. The name Hinterstoisser keeps on cropping up everywhere, not only at the "Hinterstoisser Traverse," which is quite unrecognisable as itself. Corti keeps on climbing a Hinterstoisser Passage, a Hinterstoisser Traverse, a Hinterstoisser pitch, a Hinterstoisser overhang. It is only with the greatest difficulty that one recognises the long traverse at the upper rim of the Second Ice Field or the rock pitches on the "Flatiron" arête. Was it that Corti had no notion at all of the Face? Had he not even studied its route-finding history?

The fact that Corti and Longhi had already lost their way on the lower part of the Face, so that they were compelled to spend a whole day and night and part of another day down on the frontal structure of the base, shows how absolutely clueless they were. (It was brought to light later on that they actually lost two full days down there.)

Guido Tonella, the Italian publicity man and himself a first-class mountaineer, who has already been mentioned and who will be extensively quoted later on, interviewed Corti in hospital. It was Riccardo Cassin who arranged their talk. Now Corti told Tonella that his only foreknowledge of the Face lay in a postcard-sized photograph on which the route was painted in. Corti's burning ambition was to be responsible for the success of the first Italian party on the North Face of the Eiger; but his knowledge of the mountain and of the Face did not match his ambition. Tonella published this interview. He wrote no unfriendly word against his countrymen, but simply indulged in objective criticism, as his sense of journalistic responsibility dictated.

Now, how does Corti describe the meeting of the Italian and German parties in his report to the Italian Alpine Club? This is what he says:

We climbed two rope lengths vertically . . . at that point we saw a rope of two coming up our way, about two hours away from us. We decided to halt for a meal and to see of whom this other rope might consist. It was exactly 3 P.M. on Sunday August 4. Then we noticed that the other party had stopped, so we decided to climb on. We climbed a rope length straight up on ice and found a piece of rope fastened to a piton. At this point the guide in our possession showed that we had to get over a 200-foot vertical pitch (traverse?) leading to the Hinterstoisser Ice Field . . . [obviously Corti is referring here to the "Hinterstoisser Traverse"].

At this point the party we had seen earlier caught up with us and after exchanging the usual greetings we finished the traverse across the vertical wall, followed by the two Germans, and so reached the Ice Field. Then we climbed about two rope lengths straight up, where we decided to bivouac, at 8 P.M. After preparing a bivouac place by digging a hollow in the ice where we could spend the night, we were subjected to bad weather with a high wind and icy temperatures. The Germans were about 10 feet from us.

At about 3 A.M. on Monday August 5, we got ready to eat something warming and noticed that the Germans, though provided with every other kind of comfort, were not eating anything. We asked them why, and they gave us to understand that during the night their pack containing all their provisions had fallen off the Face. So, out of sheer humanity we shared our breakfast with them and asked them whether they had decided to continue their climb or not. They gave us to understand that they wanted to go on, come what may. So we decided to keep on in separate ropes of two. It was about 5:30 and we began the ascent of the ice. We climbed vertically for about five rope lengths of about Grade V severity and after about four hours reached Hinterstoisser's Traverse. At this point the second German began to suffer from cramps in his stomach and to show signs of weariness. We then decided to tie up as a single rope of four. I led the rope, the leader of the German rope came second, then the second German (whose condition had in the meantime deteriorated) and Stefano last.

Here the "Hinterstoisser Traverse" begins. We traversed about 25 rope lengths (always on loose ice). . . .

Let us forget the constant and misplaced repetitions of Hinterstoisser's name. Corti had no idea of its correct application, and simply attached Hinterstoisser's name to everything of great difficulty he met as far as Sedlmayer's and Mehringer's "Death Bivouac." According to Corti's inexact indications, the first joint bivouac was at the "Swallow's Nest" or thereabouts. According to him it was the Sunday–Monday night; but even that doesn't make sense, as we shall see presently. The roping up of the two parties as a single rope did not happen, if we believe this report of Corti's, until the great traverse on the Second Ice Field, and certainly not, as stated in the interview he gave to the United Press, right from the start. Moreover, the facts, as seen perfectly clearly by Fritz von Almen and many other observers through the ×72 telescope, from a distance of only two miles, each day, are firmly established. Its magnification was such that they could distinguish snap links, slings, even the features of the men's faces, through it. According to their observations, the two ropes only joined up just before the "Spider"—and not till Friday, August 9. Till then they behaved exactly as if they were enemies. The same observers also established that the common bivouacs were as follows: Monday to Tuesday at the bottom of the Second Ice Field on the same knob of rock on which we spent our first night; Tuesday to Wednesday at the "Death Bivouac"; Wednesday to Thursday on the upper part of the "Ramp"; Thursday to Friday just short of the "Spider" and high up on it, and finally Friday to Sunday at the foot of the Exit Cracks.

The most vital question, however, is this: how and when did the Germans lose their rucksacks and equipment? The first version is that they had lost everything, including their crampons. Now we suddenly hear that they only lost the pack with their provisions in it, during the first night's bivouac. Which is right?

The certain fact is that both ropes, and later the united rope, moved forward uncommonly slowly. Observers record that the two parties not only failed to cooperate, but were often clearly working in opposition. Consequently, several papers reported that the second man on the leading rope always retrieved the pitons his leader had fixed, thus forcing the second party to knock in new ones. This would, of course, be an unfriendly act on rock, and points to a lack of harmony, nay almost to enemy action. On ice, however, such behavior is normal and intelligible since each party needs its pitons to belay itself and go on climbing. But the most incomprehensible thing of all is the way in which they climbed steep ice, where the two ropes cut separate ladders of steps for themselves.

The Bernese *Bund*, normally a very well-informed paper, wrote the following article about this climb under the title line of "Strange behavior on a mountain":

The two ropes that started on the climb a week ago have been under continual observation from Grindelwald as well as from the Kleine Scheidegg. The extremely wary and cautious progress by both Germans and Italians led to the possible conclusion that the conditions were unfavorable (heavy icing), but to an equally possible one that the people concerned were insufficiently experienced on ice.

This view is supported by the fact that incredibly long and exhausting bouts of step cutting were indulged in on the ice fields. And it struck one as equally odd that the two parties, which had already met on the second day, were not working together . . .

The corps of Grindelwald guides, too, signed a report that tried to deal with the circumstances, development, and aftermath of the tragedy. This is a section from that report:

> This is not intended as a biased criticism of the dead men, and if, in spite of that, we venture to state our views, they are intended simply as a warning for young climbers, who may still come, not to risk their promising young lives. We admit that the climbers involved were above the average in skill. They were picked men from the "extreme" school of "Specialists"; but their experience was gained on rock, not on ice. And this feature was very noticeable during the climb; for it was established from favorable observation points and by independent observers that the victims when on ice or frozen snow hacked regular bathtubs of steps, and were consequently far too slow on the ice passages.
>
> Add to this the fact that the North Face is always being underestimated. The men who first climbed it had studied its problem most thoroughly; they knew its topography by heart, and in spite of that we learn from their reports and those of later successful climbers that they had definitely underrated one pitch or another. This year's aspirants are also reported to have made a searching study of the Face. Why, then, did they repeatedly lose their way on it. . . . ?

Lionel Terray, too, whose kindly nature would always lead him to pass an objective, truthful judgment on a fellow climber, expressed his great surprise and misgivings at what he saw when we watched the four climbers from the Kleine Scheidegg. And Wolfgang Stefan, one of the best young climbers from Vienna, and his partner Götz Mayr, an equally accomplished performer from Innsbruck—about whose attempt on the Face we shall shortly be hearing—could find no reasonable explanation of the slow progress made by the two ropes. An apparent twist of fate had saved these two Austrians from meeting the others on the Face. Who knows what would have happened to them if they had had to climb behind the other four? They might, of course, have succeeded in getting past somewhere or other and, with their tremendous drive, have reached the summit; but they might just as well have come to grief through lending them assistance, out of sheer comradely feeling. It is impossible to say. Stefan and Mayr were thoroughly fitted to climb the Face, both being equally good on rock and ice. The North Face of the Ortler, the direct ascent of the "Whipped Cream Roll," the cornice of the North Face of the Königsspitze, the North Face of the Matterhorn, and the North Face of the Fiescherhorn in the Bernese Oberland provided a sufficient certificate of competency. On Sunday, the 4th, the pair carried their packs of equipment up to the Bivouac Cave and then climbed down again. On the gentle slope of Alpiglen's meadows Mayr turned his ankle and was unable to walk for two days. It was not till Wednesday, August 7, that they started up the Face again on their actual climb. While they had been waiting, the weather had been fine, and so it was in the early morning of that Wednesday. By eight o'clock they had put behind them the "Hinterstoisser Traverse" and two difficult rope lengths beyond it, when the weather broke. Experience and wise forethought dictated a painful decision—to climb down again.

Neither of them could believe that Günther Nothdurft was one of the joint party of Italians and Germans proceeding at such an unbelievably slow pace. Nor could anyone else. Could this be the Günther Nothdurft who had climbed to above the Second Ice Field and down again to the valley in a single day—the same Nothdurft who had proved his mastery of crampon technique beyond any doubt on that occasion? Why couldn't the Germans climb on ahead? Why were they all so terrifyingly slow? And if on the second day Nothdurft showed signs of stomach trouble, why did not he and Mayer turn back then? All these questions and mysteries remain unanswered and unsolved.

If Corti's statement in his interview with the United Press reporter was correct, namely that the two Germans had no crampons, it would explain a great deal. If so it still remains impossible to explain how Nothdurft's party could be talked into continuing the climb with inadequate equipment. They were both familiar with the history of the Face and knew how fearfully I had had to exert myself to complete the climb without crampons and to avoid delaying the others, although my boots were splendidly nailed. And *we* were a homogeneous company, able to communicate in the same language of heart and mind, while these two parties could not even understand one another's mother tongue.

Who can answer all these questions? Was there tremendous competition between the two ropes? Was rivalry between two age groups a factor, over and above the friction of personal and national ambition? Corti was a grown man, his partner Longhi, at forty-four, could easily have been the father of the Germans. Were the younger generation trying to prove that they were as good as or better than their elders? One riddle after another, all unanswered by anything in Corti's reports. . . .

Let us try to reconstruct the progress of the four men up the North Face purely by time, using only Corti's report as a basis. According to it, the bivouac between Monday and Tuesday—the second for the Germans, the Italians' third—was probably at the start of the "Ramp," though Corti's description is so inexact that one can tell nothing for certain. But when Corti speaks of a great indentation slashing the Face, he can only mean the "Ramp." According to his statements, one of the Germans—Nothdurft—was in such a bad way that an injection of Coramine had to be administered to boost his heart. Yet, apparently, no one thought of turning back.

Corti then explained the slow progress by Nothdurft's weak state.

By 2 P.M. they had, he says, only "managed 9 to 10 rope lengths." He then goes on: "We then came to a great overhanging cliff which it took two rope lengths to climb, the severity being VI plus. . . ."

Corti continues:

> After four more rope lengths we came to the foot of a great waterfall, barring all progress. It was 6 o'clock, and we agreed with the Germans to stop and bivouac. After consulting the photographs that the Germans had with them, it was clear that the route lay straight up the waterfall. We therefore made ourselves as comfortable as the place permitted. The condition of the sick man remained unchanged.

This description contains a suggestion which at first might seem unlikely—that the Germans had the photograph with the sketch of the climb on it. But Corti's explanation to Guido Tonella must be remembered, namely that the Italians' only aid to route finding was a postcard-size photograph with the route sketched in on it.

Where, then, was this bivouac from Tuesday to Wednesday? According to observers' reports, the four men climbed far too high on the "Ramp," probably even higher than Vanis's party five years before. It therefore seems reasonable to assume that the bivouac was in the "Ramp" about two rope lengths above the brittle ledge leading to the "Traverse of the Gods." Attempts have proved that the "Ramp" affords no means of escape from the Face; as so often on the North Face, the hope is illusory, for the "Ramp" has many overhangs and becomes impossible to climb. There is no door to freedom here.

Corti's report about Wednesday, August 7, reads:

> At about 7 A.M. we struck our bivouac and roped up intending to make a direct attempt on the waterfall pitch, something over 100 feet high and of Grade VI severity. Meanwhile the weather conditions had improved; it had turned fine and the

sun was shining strongly. We were at the top of the waterfall
by about 10 o'clock and stopped in the sun, as best we could,
to dry ourselves, for we were absolutely soaked through. [On
August 7 it is quite impossible for even a ray of sunshine to
penetrate this part of the Face at 10 o'clock!] The German's
condition was now worse, and we were beginning to doubt
whether he would be able to see the rest of the climb
through. . . .

This is where we began the traverse leading to the
"Spider," which was on our right. We started on it at about
noon, and it proved to be very severe, being coated in ice and
with an inclination of from 70 to 80°. We moved forward
about six rope lengths; by the time we had got near the
"Spider" snow had begun to fall heavily. In addition we could
hear heavy avalanches of snow and ice sweeping down the
"Spider." At about 4 P.M. we all agreed to bivouac for the
night, which proved clear and very cold indeed. The sick
German's condition was unchanged. I spent a great part of the
night, with the assistance of the German, Franz (Mayer), in rub-
bing Stefano's hands with alcohol, to check the progress of
frostbite, symptoms of which were continually increasing. . . .

There can be no doubt from this that the climb of the new waterfall pitch in the upper part of the "Ramp" and the traverse, some 250
feet above the brittle ledge, which is the correct route, turned out to
be extremely difficult. We also learn that Nothdurft was in such miserable condition that it seemed more than doubtful whether he would
be able to carry on. (Indeed, if Corti's diagnosis had been correct
Nothdurft should have died long ago.) Yet Nothdurft—whatever his
physical condition may have been—climbed rope after rope of what
Corti classifies as Grade VI pitches, in other words the severest demands which a fit man can be called onto meet. This was indeed a
strange effort on the part of a man weakened almost to death! And,

of course, one would in these circumstances have expected this fourth bivouac to spell the end for Günther.

Yet, next morning, Thursday August 8, the two Germans not only took the lead, but they climbed as a separate rope, thus proving that Nothdurft cannot have been seriously exhausted. And Corti confirms the fact—intentionally or by an oversight—in the continuation of his report:

> At 6 A.M. on August 8 we set out for the "Spider," moving horizontally. . . . I caught the two Germans up and authorised Longhi to retrieve the two pitons and come up to me. . . .

So Mayer and Nothdurft were definitely leading, for Corti says he caught them up.

It was while Longhi was moving up to join Corti that the first accident took place, though at the time it did not seem to herald the catastrophic outcome of the venture. This is how Corti describes it:

> I had taken in about 10 feet of the rope when Longhi slipped and shouted "Hold me, Claudio!" I got ready to take the shock of his fall. When I look back on it, it seems a miracle that we didn't all follow him in his fall. Somehow I managed to hold him. . . .

This was a remarkable feat of Corti's. When he was rescued from the Face three days later, the palms of his hands still showed the deep cuts and burns inflicted by the rope as it ran through them with Longhi's weight upon it. The report continues:

> Longhi called up to me to let him down about six feet, as he was dangling in thin air and had seen a comfortable ledge below him. I let him down, as requested, and secured him with two pitons and both ropes. Then I enlisted the assistance

of the Germans in letting me slide down about 50 feet of the ice slope on the rope—it was from 70 to 80 degrees steep. I could then see Longhi another 60 feet below the overhang and asked him if he had suffered any damage or injury. He only answered that he had had to let go with his hands because he had no longer any feeling in them. He then asked me to rescue him. I tried to jolly him up into helping himself a little. Then I tried several times to haul him up from the ledge of the overhang—it seemed easier there, for there was less friction on the rope—but always in vain. The two Germans could not assist me much, for one of them was exhausted, while Franz, the other one, had to belay me and his partner too. Moreover, Franz was so placed that he only jammed my hands against the ice when he hauled on Stefano's rope, so that he was really hindering me in my attempts to pull him straight up the cliff.

Obviously it was a very serious situation. But even fresh men could never have pulled Longhi straight up from under the overhang. It could perhaps have been done with the aid of an emergency "block and tackle"; but that would have called for a row of firmly anchored pitons, and at this point it would probably have been almost impossible to fix enough pitons, even for men in good physical condition. It is, however, obvious that Longhi was unfamiliar with the "Prusik-knot" technique. For, even with one's hands partly out of action, it is possible to work one's way upwards by the use of a couple of loops of line fixed to the main rope in that special fashion. According to Corti, Longhi was in good condition in spite of his fall. Perhaps he was in the best condition of the four men—such good condition that he lived, as it turned out, five more days on his tiny stance. . . . It would not have taken Longhi half an hour to "Prusik" himself by his own efforts up to the overhang at whose edge Corti was standing; but the North Face of the Eiger is no place in which to learn the tricks of rope manipulation. One has to familiarise oneself with them and have them in one's repertoire before getting there.

Let us follow Corti's report still further, in the belief that he and the others did their very best for Longhi, but that direct aid was out of the question. According to Corti, Longhi had spoken to him and agreed to everything they discussed. This is what we read:

Then, after considering the position in which we found ourselves after three hours of vain attempts at rescue, I cheered Stefano up, by telling him we thought we were not far from the summit and urging him to make himself as comfortable as he could on his shelf. I promised him to do everything in our power to get to the top, there to organise a rescue operation and to fetch him in safely. When Stefano agreed, I let my bivouac sack and some medicaments down to him. I said goodbye, cheering him up and promising him again that help would reach him as soon as humanly possible. That was the last I saw of poor Stefano.

It was exactly 9:30 A.M. I got Franz to pull me up and after reaching him I led on up, with the exhausted German next and Franz last.

Two rope lengths of horizontal work brought us onto the "Spider." On it I climbed five lengths straight up. While I was 60 feet above a belaying piton, a stone hit me on the head, causing me to lose my grip with my hands. I fell about 100 feet, where Franz at last succeeded in checking my fall. When I stopped, I was head-downward about 60 feet below the German. Franz completed my rescue, which, owing to the head injuries it had inflicted on me, was a fairly dangerous operation. Then he bandaged me with some muslin he had along. When he saw the concussed state I was in, he told me to stay here while he and his partner tried to reach the top, which was, he thought, still about 650 feet above us. He would then come back and rescue me and Stefano. He left me his bivouac tent with the pitons and cords belonging to it, so that I could anchor it properly, and I made myself as comfortable as I could. My two companions bade me goodbye and climbed on towards the summit. It was about 3 P.M. . . .

According to Corti's report they parted at about 3 P.M. on Thursday, August 8. So, at that rate, we are asked to believe that not only did the Germans not spend a night in the bivouac above the "Spider"; they didn't even arrange a bivouac, but simply left their tent and accoutrements with Corti, said goodbye, and on an afternoon of bad weather, with a thunderstorm threatening, climbed away towards the summit. Toward the Mittellegi Ridge? Or toward the West Ridge? Or up the Exit Cracks? No detail is given.

Well, here, the only possible way out lay, in fact, up the Exit Cracks.

And they are supposed to have gone off up them without food and without a tent sack. . . . Franz Mayer with his companion Günther Nothdurft, who—according to Corti's report—had for the last two days been so exhausted that he hung dubiously between life and death?

Everyone who has studied the history of the North Face knows how difficult and dangerous those cracks are and how infinitely slowly one has to fight one's way up that last bastion—inch by inch, foot by foot, yard by yard. Corti could therefore have watched his comrades for hours as they climbed out of sight, could have described how Mayer and Nothdurft grappled with at least the first hundred or two feet of that terrible ground. Don't let us forget how graphically Gaston Rébuffat described Hermann Buhl's effort at this point, though he was further from him than Corti was from the two Germans. And for Corti, remember, this close scrutiny would not have been attributable to mere interest; his very life depended on whether the Germans succeeded or not. True, Corti knew that the people in the valley below were already aware of the tragedy being enacted on the Face; airmen of the Rescue Flight were circling the mountain and had interpreted his waving as a distress signal. Assuredly he would be sent assistance. But the really important consideration for him was whether the Germans succeeded in getting to the top.

Well, how did they go? And where did they go? We have already said that the only possible way out was up the Exit Cracks. Corti says not a single word about them.

This is how his account goes on:

From that instant till the arrival of the German Hellepart on Sunday August 11, I spent every moment between hope and despair. I kept on thinking of Stefano and the two Germans. The weather remained horrible, rain following periods of wind and snow. I was very lucky that the good weather on Saturday and Sunday allowed of my rescue. My poor friend Stefano had less luck, for just as they were going to rescue him, the weather took a turn for the worse again and my brave rescuers found it impossible to bring him to safety.

I would like to emphasise that, in spite of various suggestions to the contrary, my preparations, as were Stefano Longhi's, were excellent. Regarding the carelessness someone ascribed to me I consider it essential to underline that I and poor Stefano had studied the Face in every detail on photographs and with the aid of a German climbing guide of the district translated into Italian. I already had in my head many other details of the route to be followed, from reading the reports of climbers who had climbed the Face before me. I found the Face under winter conditions and so was confronted with severities from Grade V to Grade VI.

I should add that we tackled the climb with high-altitude equipment fully equal to the requirements.

In the name and service of truth!

I have prepared this report at the request of the headquarters of the Club Alpino Italiano, of which I am proud to be a member.

(Signed) Claudio Corti.

"In the name and service of truth. . . ."

That constitutes an oath, which we have no wish to doubt. A man has sworn it. I should be happy to believe it, although observers and eyewitnesses saw much that differs from the matters in the report, and although Corti gave various versions of the drama. We want to believe this version, because it is given under oath; in the name and service of truth. . . .

Who was this "someone" who ascribed carelessness to Claudio Corti? None other than that courageous man who has throughout his life campaigned for truth, heedless of any threats to himself, as a journalist, as a mountaineer, and as a man—Guido Tonella.

Nobody would dare accuse Tonella of being a "bad" Italian. But what he will never do is to confuse truth and deceit, clarity and mystery, common purpose and selfishness, just because an Italian happens to be concerned. Moreover, he wants to preserve the scutcheon of Italian mountaineering unblemished. Italian climbers do not suffer from any complex just because no rope composed of Italians has yet succeeded in climbing the North Face of the Eiger. A nation that has produced Comici, Cassin, Lacedelli, Soldà, Bonatti, and countless other superlative mountaineers can well recognise the greatest feats of other nations ungrudgingly and with the assurance of an equal. The best Italian climbers have not yet attempted the Eiger's Face; that is all there is to it.

In the name and service of truth. . . . This book, too, is written in the service of truth. It does not set out to condemn or absolve, but simply to provide a conscientious report. That is why I asked Guido Tonella to tell me all about his difference with Corti, who went so far as to initiate a slander action against him. And Tonella replied simply, clearly, unmistakably, without reservations, and with the precision of a man who is fully aware of his responsibilities.

He wrote to me first about the interview he had with Corti in the Interlaken hospital in the presence of Riccardo Cassin. Tonella had published this interview, which contained nothing that could not be confirmed, in the Italian periodical *L'Europeo*, and it was reprinted verbatim in *L'Illustré*. After its publication Cassin had of his own accord written in a letter to Tonella: "Bravo! How right you were to publish the truth!"

Tonella, however, wrote telling me that he had not repeated the whole truth, for Corti had said much that was still worse. In spite of that, Corti, badly advised by his lawyers, brought a libel action against *L'Europeo*. Tonella had no intention of revealing too much; but Corti tried to rebut suspicion before it had ever been voiced.

What Tonella wrote me was that Corti had obviously not been too fastidious with the truth, as was already self-evident from his accounts. The costly rescue of Corti on the Dru, in the Mont Blanc Range, was still in everybody's memory; Tonella confined himself to stating that, long before his Eiger attempt, Corti had suffered an accident with a painful sequel. Admittedly he stood by his judgment that Corti had undergone insufficient preparations for his climb of the North Face; but this was a judgment already expressed by the whole world, including such important men as Lionel Terray, and it is the established right of a journalist to express an opinion and a valuation. Tonella understands that Corti is defending himself against doubts and also against the presentation of his true character; but it is Corti himself who first invited those doubts, for the details of his reports are all too contradictory. For instance, in his interview at the hospital in Interlaken he assured Tonella and Cassin that the two

Germans had left him on Friday, the 9th, at about 10 A.M., about three hours after Longhi's accident. In his own signed report in the Milan paper *Tempo* the date and the hour are quite different: there he speaks of Thursday, the 8th, at 3 o'clock in the afternoon.[1]

Tonella concedes Corti every possibility of a mistake resulting from his unusual physical and mental state at the time. He admits that one could possibly make a mistake about the days; nor does it matter very much whether it was Friday or Saturday. But not to be able to decide whether it was early morning or in the afternoon is inconceivable. It is impossible to establish any clear impression from such a mass of inconsistencies and inexactitudes.

> It is my belief [Tonella says] that Corti doesn't want to tell the whole truth! Worse still, I believe he has something to hide, some secret to keep, I am forced to the conclusion that Corti is trying to make us forget his mistakes on the Face and his errors in the execution of his duties and responsibilities; above all the fact that he persuaded the unfortunate Longhi into joining him on the climb—a man who, quite apart from his forty-four years, brought with him no qualifications for so difficult a climb and had, in fact, never climbed a mountain of more than 10,000 feet. And Corti does not seem to have thought it worthwhile at least to study the leadership of the route exactly in advance. That was the mistake that resulted in his taking six days over a route which good climbers usually cover in two. . . .

Tonella next deals with the photographs, which were published in many newspapers and periodicals as early as Sunday, the 11th. The photograph on which one is said to be able to see three figures in the bivouac above the "Spider" was, according to the investigations

---

[1] See also above, p. 225.—Translator's note.

carried out by Tonella, taken at about 3 P.M. on Saturday, the 10th, from an airplane, by a reporter of the Zürich *Photopress*. In other words, thirty hours, in one of Corti's versions, forty-eight in the other, after the Germans had left Corti!

On that photograph one could definitely distinguish more than one figure, partly obscured by the bivouac sack. Tonella explains the fact that, in the papers that only featured the picture on Monday or later, the caption only mentions one person, as due to its being known by that time that only one man had been identified.

He wrote to me:

> I was already seized of the importance of this question when I was preparing my article for *L'Europeo*. I felt it my duty, to get in touch with *Photopress*, whose Director—with the negative in his hand—assured me that there were on it three people, two at least quite plainly, and not only Corti by himself.

Tonella then reports that the photograph of Longhi hanging in the ropes was taken at the same time—about 3 P.M. on Saturday, August 10. On Monday, when poor Longhi was already dead, it was noticeable that his body had fallen some fifteen feet lower, thus proving that on the Friday he had climbed by his own efforts to look for a better stance. In Tonella's view this confirms Riccardo Cassin's horrifying suggestion that Longhi was abandoned by Corti while he was suffering from concussion and his mind was still confused. I can give no opinion about this; it is a question calling for the verdict of a neurologist. But the whole of Tonella's letter is redolent of his fairness and his conscientious approach. He is a man who cannot be tricked. And, about the enlargement of the picture of the controversial bivouac above the "Spider," he writes that he was unable to decide beyond all doubt how many people are visible on it. "The picture," he says, "was flat, rather like a radiophotograph. One could have recognised just whatever one wanted to on it."

Tonella did not want to recognise anything that put a heavy onus on Corti. In spite of his doubts he remained impartial, but his doubts were in no way diminished.

There was one more remarkable thing in Tonella's letter to me. Corti was not the last person to speak to Longhi while he was still alive. When on the afternoon of Saturday, August 10, those two splendid Italian climbers, Cassin and Mauri, and the Swiss Alpinist Max Eiselin climbed the Eiger to join the rescue operation, they saw Longhi on his exposed stance in the Face at a direct-line distance of about 300 yards from a point in the West Ridge. Cassin and Mauri shouted a greeting over to him and asked: "What's become of Corti? What do you know about him?"

Longhi shouted back: "*So Nigot!*"

In the dialect of Lombardy that means: "I don't know anything."

That mysterious answer seems to be another factor in support of Cassin's theory. Corti, lodged in a gully that screened every sound coming from outside, could not hear the shouts; all he could hear was the tumult of the wind. Max Eiselin, too, called to the two Germans, but there was no reply to his shouts, no single sign of life.

Longhi's voice was to be heard only once more. On Sunday evening when they were bringing Corti down the West Ridge and someone shouted over to him again to say they were coming to fetch him the next day. Longhi only shouted back two words, two shatteringly simple words, clear and intelligible: "*Fame! Freddo!*"

"Hunger! Cold!"

That night brought the snowstorm, and Monday brought death to end Longhi's agony.

Tonella never says anything about which he is not sure, but what he knew was evidence enough. In spite of Corti's declaration, in *La Suisse* of August 14, 1957, that, on the summit, after his rescue, he never said he wanted to have another go at the Face, Tonella's exact inquiries into every detail resulted in his being able to report precisely how Corti had behaved after his rescue. His first words after a sip of cognac and his thanks to his rescuers were: "That's grand! Now I can have another go next year!"

Corti is hagridden by the idea of leading the first successful Italian party up the Face. He cannot see his own mistakes and is so sure of himself that he actually believes he will get financial support for another attempt. In that respect his naïve ambition and vainglory border on complete cluelessness.

In Cassin's presence he asked Tonella: "Do you think my climb will be counted as the first Italian success?"

Climb? What climb? Had Corti forgotten that he had been rescued from a position of extreme distress on the Eiger by Hellepart and a steel cable?

I also possess a letter from Lionel Terray. That sensitive, amiable Frenchman, who carried the exhausted Corti on his back across the knife-edged ridge of the Eiger's summit after his rescue, was shocked by Corti's words after he had been brought to safety: "Grand! What a lucky break for me. Now I can have another go next year!"

Terray got Mauri to translate those words for him because he couldn't believe his ears and mistrusted his knowledge of Italian. About Corti's "insufficient experience on ice," Terray wrote: "It was not only in the Exit Cracks on the final wall that this would have proved a handicap. Even if he had managed to climb them; the descent over the iced-up normal route would have been more than he could have managed in the existing conditions."

Terray is staggered by the riddle set him by the character of the rescued man whose words on the summit appeared to him outrageous, and the question a mountaineer must ask himself is a profoundly shaking one: "How presumptuous can a man get?"

I am sorry that the verdicts of my trustworthy informants must necessarily throw a shadow on the great joy over the rescue of

Claudio Corti. It is the hardest assignment I have had to carry out in this book. I can only lay the reports on either side of the scales— on the one side sober criticism and judgment, on the other self-justification or an attempt at it.

It is not for me to say; but it should not be very difficult to decide on which side the balance will come down. . . .

THE

INTERNATIONAL

RESCUE TEAM

The tragedy enacted on the Eiger's North Face in 1957 appears to have been a true tragedy of errors—errors on the part of those who underrated the Face; on the part of the rescuers, who committed many organisational mistakes; on the part of the Grindelwald guides, who declared any attempt at rescue to be impossible; on the part of many reporters, who trumpeted facts that never were facts all around the world.

The only people immune from error were the gogglers who took no part in it. They came in their hundreds and then in hundreds more, crowding Grindelwald, Alpiglen, and the Kleine Scheidegg to capacity for a whole week, besieged the telescopes, paid inflated prices. There wasn't a single bed to be had in the district, and the more often the Radio and Press gave the North Face front-page publicity, the greater became the number of those who came to gape. The weather did all it could for this spectacle, enacted on the most savagely wild natural stage in the whole world; it stayed fine for days on end, and when clouds came up and hid that stage intermittently from sight, they merely provided a welcome drop scene, which only served to heighten the suspense of the play. True, the drama which was being staged occasionally had its moments of tedium. A good director would have introduced cuts. . . .

Yet the director was good—too good. His particular method was not to follow the usual theatrical conventions, but, in a manner all his own, to save up all the dramatic effects for the last act. A director with unrivalled experience in staging last acts, this director of directors—Death.

Many of the watchers knew well enough that death was in charge of the production, but they wouldn't let that upset them. They only enjoyed a stimulating thrill, while at the same time tasting a modicum of smug self-satisfaction at the thought that they themselves would never be mixed up in such nonsense.

But it was not only these gaping hundreds, avid of sensation, who were watching the incredibly slow progress of the four climbers; mountaineers, guides and men with their roots in the mountains, were following it with burning anxiety. It was Lionel Terray who was saying to his Dutch client Tom de Bloy: "They could still turn back now; they *must* turn back now, if they aren't to walk straight to their deaths."

Those words were dictated by no love of sensationalism. They were uttered by a man who would gladly have been up there, where the stones come whistling down, where the waterfalls plunge from ledge to ledge and the rocks are veneered with snow and ice. He would have liked to warn his comrades, though they were strangers to him and came from different countries, because he knew he was competent to do so.

On Friday, the director of the drama had a new idea: Longhi fell and hung there on the ropes. One could see he was alive in spite of his fall, one could see him opening his rucksack, clearly helping himself to food, putting on extra clothing. The others, however, moved on, even more slowly than before. The rubbernecks nudged one another; in a moment they would be reaching the "Spider," where every party had always had to fight for its life. "You wait, there's sure to be something interesting now!" So they waited. . . .

Aircraft took off, circled the mountain, flew close to the Face, animating the scene, but the audience soon got used to that, too. They heard that one of the planes was piloted by the famous glacier-rescue pilot Geiger and that Herr Balmer, the chief guide of Grindelwald, had been in the cockpit with him and had declared that nothing could be done, in present conditions, to bring any assistance.

Nothing to be done. . . .

But not everybody agreed. Erich Friedli the leader of the Blümlisalp Rescue Section, for one. Nor did Ludwig Gramminger, the Head of the Munich Mountain Guard, nor Lionel Terray, Riccardo Cassin, Carlo Mauri. The members, too, of a Polish climbers' camp and many other mountaineers, who knew something about the Face, refused to accept this death sentence, which had been passed on the four men.

Admittedly, the guides were right, in so far as it was absolutely no use trying to do anything with the traditional means of ropes, pitons, and sheer self-sacrifice. But everyone who knew anything about the latest steel-cable apparatus and had practised with it, was aware that there was now at least a possibility of bringing aid to exhausted men marooned on the Face.

Friedli, who was in charge of this modern apparatus in the equipment store at Thun, not only placed all his cables and winches at the disposal of a rescue operation but himself hastened to the Eiger with the other volunteers. Among them, too, was Robert Seiler, who, while climbing the Face with his three companions in 1950, had witnessed the fantastic speed record set up by Waschak and Forstenlechner,[1] never equalled till this day. The Rescue Organisation suffered from many arbitrary mistakes, and many things could have been better done; but everybody showed the greatest goodwill and enthusiasm to help as quickly as possible. Unfortunately there was all too little experience of the great strides made by modern rescue tech-

[1] See above, p. 158.

niques and there may have been many clashes of personality in their operation, but the very mix-up at the beginning was a splendid token of a comprehensive goodwill.

Perhaps things might have turned out differently in many respects had the Rescue Operation gone into action on the Thursday.

It was on Friday, August 9, that Friedli rang through to Grindelwald. Frau Balmer answered and told him: "Grindelwald is setting nothing in motion, because it is impossible to do anything up there."

Ludwig Gramminger had been given the same answer when he rang up from Munich on the Friday morning; but Gramminger, the most experienced man in Germany in the field of mountain rescue and one of the people who had helped to develop modern rescue appliances to their present level of efficiency, didn't believe that word "impossible" either. He asked the responsible Rescue Centre at Grindelwald whether he and his assistants could come and join the rescue operation, and was given leave to do so.

On the Saturday a stream of rescuers, all volunteers, made their way to the summit of the Eiger from two different sides, by easy routes. A new spectacle was being unexpectedly mounted for the audience. Would there after all be a happy ending? Would Death the director resign at the last moment and give way to the great comradeship of the guides and a steel cable only a fraction of an inch thick?

But by now no one was thinking of the audience, greedy for thrills, anymore; they were no longer a subject either for astonishment or anger. The men on the Eiger's summit had other things to preoccupy them. It was cold up there. Up on the summit ridge, the cornices jutted now to the south, at another point to the north. The gale went howling over the top. The only shelter to be found was in caves dug out of the cornices. And, because everything had to be done with undue haste and didn't allow for methodical planning, many things were in short supply, above all food, tea, and protection from the wind. But there was no time now to bother about that; all that mattered now was to find a solid anchorage for the cable winch as quickly as possible. The rocks underlying the snow were brittle, the cornices treacherous; one never knew for certain whether the caves one had already dug were suspended over the abyss. Yet caution had to be the first law for the rescuers, too. And then there was that other big question—where to site the bivouac gear? It was essential to avoid any swinging traverses; the cable must go nearly as possible straight down to the little red tent above the "Spider," where Corti and the two Germans were thought to be.

The direction was fixed by a radio link with the Kleine Scheidegg. At 4 P.M., at long last, they were ready for the first man to be lowered down the Face. It was Robert Seiler. He descended nearly 500 feet, looked down onto the "Spider," located the red tent; but there was only one man to be seen and he did not answer when Seiler shouted. Perhaps the wind was too strong. Seiler was hauled up again and climbed down from the summit.

The same evening, with darkness falling, Erich Friedli went down on the steel cable. He could not distinguish the red tent, but his shouts were answered, though he could not make out the words nor even in what language they were uttered. He could only hear the sounds; but one thing was certain—only one man was answering. Were the others, then, so exhausted that they could not raise a shout?

Darkness threatened. There was no more to be done that day. Friedli radioed the word to the top, to haul him up again. It was almost night by the time he reached the summit.

It was a cold and stormy bivouac for those on the Eiger's summit. How would the four men on the Face get through the night? They *must* be rescued tomorrow! It was decided to lower Alfred Hellepart, one of Gramminger's Munich team, early next morning, Sunday, the 11th.

The endless night gave way to dawn and daylight. They began to lower Hellepart down the Face on his historic, decisive descent. He described it as follows in his report to the Munich Mountain Guard, under the title: "The Rescue on the North Face of the Eiger":

At precisely eight o'clock on that Sunday morning I stood at the notch in the cornice which juts out over the Eiger's North Face. I fastened on the climbing belt, strapped the radio on my back and put on my helmet for protection against falling stones. Erich Friedli, the leader of the Swiss volunteers, gave me some last briefing about the radio and then it was my turn to go down. I cannot now describe the feelings that moved me at the time. But I knew that our "Wiggerl" Grammminger was safeguarding me down the Face on the cable; and trusting to his skill and care, that of my teammates of the Mountain Guard, and that of all the grand lads on the Eiger's summit, who had wished me luck, I started slowly to climb down the summit ice slope.

I tested the radio several times while I was going down and it all worked splendidly. Slowly I moved farther and farther from my comrades and finally, when I climbed down into a steep snow gully, I lost sight of them altogether. At that moment I felt absolutely isolated, but I could hear Erich Friedli's voice on my radio's speaker and then I knew that all their thoughts were with me down here on the Face. Slowly I went farther and farther down. Every now and then I was told to stop while they coupled on a new length of cable.

I could see a black rift coming nearer to my right. I knew that my route must be down it, for there just was no other. And then for the first time, I looked right down the North Face. . . .

That glimpse took my breath away, and I think I stifled an exclamation. This grim, menacing blackness, broken only by a few snow ledges, falling sheer and endlessly away into illimitable depths, had such a strong effect on me that I instinctively looked up at my cable, which went winging up above me like a thread of cotton till it lost itself in the greyness. Here was I, an insignificant little human being, swinging out in space between heaven and hell, so staggered by this sight that I had nearly forgotten what I was here to do. And I particularly remember the soothing voice of the radio control down at the Scheidegg, where Wiggerl, who restored my composure, reminded me of my assignment to bring aid to others.

As I slowly moved farther down that terrible wall— everyone who proposes to climb it should first dangle his way down it on a steel thread; it would make him think again!—I got in touch with Friedli on the summit again.

During this brief radio talk, I suddenly heard a human voice. At first it was hardly audible against the hollow howling and singing of the wind which ceaselessly swept the Face. But when I moved across to the right onto a shattered pillar, from which rubble and rocks, loosened as I traversed it in my crampons, went clattering dully down the Face, I could hear the shouts clearly, and after a minute or two I suddenly saw a climber sitting on a small finger of rock at about the same level as myself. He was about 60 feet from me and was waving to me. I immediately reported by radio that I had found a man.

Then I called to him and he told me his name was Claudio. I tried to get near him by traversing, on crampons dug into the rubble, across the pillar. His first request was for cigarettes; unfortunately I had not a single one with me. When he also asked for food I gave him—or rather threw across to him from a distance of about 7 feet—half a bar of chocolate, which he grabbed and began to eat ravenously.

I had meanwhile realised that I could not get to him this way and told the summit to haul me up some 150 feet so that I could look for another route down to him. I explained to

Claudio that he must be patient for a few minutes; but he only nodded, so busy was he with his food.

My comrades pulled me up on the winch, following my instructions. Then I let myself slide straight downwards to above the Italian, down a sheer gully. While I was doing so, a lot of loose stone again came away, and I shouted warnings down to Claudio to look out for them. He pressed himself as close as he could to the cliff. When I joined him on the little platform, no bigger than a tabletop, which was his stance, he shook me by the hand and wanted to rise to his feet; but I told him to remain seated. Then I asked him how he was. He showed me his bandaged hand, which had been burned by the friction of the rope. He had head injuries from falling stones and I gathered that, in an attempt to climb up farther by himself, he had fallen about 100 feet. Then I asked him about his partner Longhi and the two Germans, who must also be somewhere on the Face. He explained that his Italian partner was hanging on the ropes about 300 feet farther down and that the two Germans, after leaving him their bivouac sack, had tried to climb through to the top together. Since then, he had seen and heard nothing of either of them.

Then we both tried several times to shout to his companion; but there was no answer. The only sound we could hear was the horrible blustering of the wind.

As I was fairly impressed by Corti's physical condition, I radioed up to Friedli asking him to fetch the Italian, Cassin, to the mike. He could talk to Corti and ask him if he felt fit enough to climb the Face independently in front of me on the cable. Even while these exchanges were going on, I realised that Corti was in no state to attempt it; so I broke in on the conversation and told Friedli that I had thought it over and now proposed to transport him to the summit on my back.

Friedli approved my decision, saying he thought it would

be better for a man in Corti's condition. Then he asked me to be patient for a little while as the winch would not haul us up quickly enough; they would, in the meantime, change over to man power on the summit.

I had meanwhile also noticed that the straps of the Italian's crampons were all torn off. For this reason alone it would have been impossible for him to be taken up by the method I had previously suggested.

I packed Corti's rucksack, made his ice axe fast, and put his pack on for him. Then I strapped him firmly into the Gramminger Seat-Transporter, propped him up away from the rock, and myself slipped into that apparatus. I now had him firmly seated on my back. Unfortunately I had to strap my radio equipment on my chest because I could find no other place to put it. This was a considerable impediment and I had to lengthen the girths by using snap links to make it reasonably bearable; but it all went fairly smoothly and I had at least got Claudio safely on my back and firmly on the cable.

I had to wait a few more minutes sitting there while they completed their preparations on the summit. Then Friedli gave me the word that they were ready to haul me up. With a great sense of relief I gave the order to haul away, glad to get away as quickly as possible from that inhospitable spot.

I felt the steel cable tighten and heard it begin to vibrate. Although I have unbounded faith in our apparatus, I couldn't avoid a sickly feeling of apprehension as the cable, grating over the rock edges, pulled us slowly towards the top. Swinging across into the steep gully and bringing away lumps of rock as the cable whipped, we swayed foot by foot upwards. Claudio's weight was not inconsiderable, and hampered by the radio equipment too, I tried to pick the best line.

The rock was overlaid by a centimeter-thick film of ice and, whenever I broke through that crust with my crampons, the rubble went pounding down the Face by the hundred-weight. I had come a thousand feet down the wall and now I had to retrace the same distance foot by foot with two people to care for.

The ground gradually became a little easier and I also found it easier to keep the cable on the direct line upward. That put an end to the uncomfortable scraping on the rock. Very naturally the Italian moaned about the cold; and I too could feel the cold in my fingers, for while I was roping on down there on the Face one of my pairs of gloves had fallen off. Gradually we gained height and a little sunlight stole down to us from between tatters of cloud. I could hear Claudio's expressions of delight at that and tried to hearten him, telling him he would soon be better.

After the ascent of yet another ice gully I experienced a thrill of inexpressible joy at seeing my comrades on the summit ridge again. The Italian's head fell forward from exhaustion. Quite erroneously thinking he had lost consciousness, the summit party quickened the pace, and I had to use every ounce of strength to keep up with the cable. Already somewhat breathless from the ascent and the rarefied air, I was pretty hard put to it by the final slope, and I was at the end of my tether when we reached the summit.

I only had time to shout to Friedli to relieve me of my load with the least possible delay before measuring my length in the snow. Corti was quickly lifted out of the seat and I tore off the radio, which was causing me the most trouble. They set me on my feet, thumped me on the back, shook me by both hands.

At that moment I thought of Wiggerl Gramminger, who had devotedly protected me at the top of the cable, and felt that most of the praise belonged to him and his equipment, which had made such a rescue possible at all. The crowd of volunteers then set to work to get the injured man to safety. I stayed quietly tucked away in a bivouac hole, so as not to be in anybody's way and to have a quiet smoke at last.

I just had time to give a short report before Lionel Terray, that great climber, started down on the second cable descent of the Face. As ill luck would have it, his radio packed up and he had to be hauled up again without achieving anything. It would have been so wonderful if he too had succeeded in snatching a fellow climber from certain death! They were looking after the rescued Corti as best they could in the circumstances. When he had smoked a cigarette and drunk some hot tea, I went over to him; he gave me a feeble smile and said, "Grazie."

A warm feeling enveloped me then and I knew that it was not for nothing that I had been afraid on that hellish Face. . . .

The very simplicity of Hellepart's report testifies to the greatness of his feat. It was neither more nor less than the greatest success so far achieved with modern rescue equipment, an up-to-date triumph of steel cables, and the frog couplings now used to joint them. A thousand feet down the face of the Eiger . . . who would ever have thought such a thing possible? But surely to label the men who brought it about "Cable-railway specialists" or "High wire acrobats" is rank ingratitude and spite, and poor sarcasm into the bargain.

Even now, with the best apparatus available, it is man who is the decisive factor, his courage, his prudence, his team spirit, and his will to spend himself even to the point of giving his own life. Hellepart's report is evidence of such a man. He started down the Face and what he found there was fear. He conquered his fear, because there were other men who needed to be brought back to life; and he was able to conquer his fear because his trust in the scientific skill and ability of his friends gave him complete confidence.

That day, Sunday, August 11, was a great triumph for the steel-cable apparatus and the brave men who worked it. But it was a very hollow victory, because it proved possible to rescue only one man, Claudio Corti. Stefano Longhi, after enduring ten days and nine nights on the Face, failed to survive till the weather improved; hunger and cold—*fame e freddo*—killed him first. It proved extraordinarily difficult to transport Corti down the mountain by the ordinary route; yet another bivouac was necessary, but the volunteer helpers were unsparing in their efforts and their succour.

On Monday, Grindelwald received a pitiful visit, shattering to behold. A sixty-five-year-old man, whose kindly face was frozen with grief, came to the place. He could not see those whom he met, for he had been blinded in the war; and he had lost two sons in that same war. Now the third son, the youngest, had come to the Eiger and he, too, had failed to return home. . . .

The elderly, sightless man was Günther Nothdurft's father.

One hope was still alive: perhaps Franz and Günther had got up the Face and then climbed down by the Mittellegi Ridge, to reach the Hut in safety? On Wednesday, the 13th, Max Eiselin and three other climbers returned from the Mittellegi Hut.

No, they had not found anyone. And what about the tracks the flying men thought they had seen on the topmost part of the Lauper Route? Those weren't any tracks; they had seen nothing of any tracks.

And so an old man was left in his loneliness, a loneliness beyond tears for him now. . . .

More than anything else it was the agonised, insistent questions put by the parents that moved the German authorities to pursue in closer detail both the early history and the final tragic circumstances of this attempt on the North Face. The chief of police of South Württemberg, Dr. Hermann Lutz, got in touch with the appropriate Swiss authorities. He himself is an enthusiastic mountaineer, a member of the Tübingen Section of the German Alpine Club, and a personal friend of the young German climbers involved, who also belonged to that section. He made no complaints or recriminations;

he simply sought clarification. But the last secret, the secret of how Günther Nothdurft and Franz Mayer died, could not even then be solved.

The official Swiss report, based on Corti's statements, makes nothing any clearer. It leaves open several questions that Dr. Lutz deals with as follows in his own compilation:

1. The photograph in the *10-pfennig Bildzeitung* of August 15, 1957, shows that on the Saturday, i.e., August 10, there were still three climbers at the red tent sack. It is understood that this picture was taken from an aircraft at about 4 P.M. on the Saturday. It is impossible to establish from here whether the time is correct or whether the photograph has been touched up. In any case this newspaper report is in direct contradiction of the communiqué issued by the Police Force of Canton Berne and also of Corti's own accounts.

Guido Tonella has already been reported as having gone thoroughly into the question of this photograph. In spite of obtaining the best possible information about the circumstances, he failed to obtain any clear explanation, free from all doubt.

2. The time given for the German party's start up the Face during the night of Saturday–Sunday does not seem to tally; for, according to the statement of the local police at Gutenstein near Sigmaringen, the two Germans did not start for Grindelwald till about 8 A.M. on Sunday, August 4, so that it is most likely that they did not start the climb on Sunday night but on Monday morning.

What kind of a statement was this, which claimed that Nothdurft and Mayer only left Baden-Württemberg on Sunday?

Willi Heppeler, the innkeeper, born on August 30, 1914, at

Hausen im Tal, Kreis Stockach, Baden, and himself a resident there at the Gasthaus "Adler," made an affidavit on August 19, 1957, to the following effect:

> The two climbers, Günther Nothdurft and Franz Mayer, who died by accident or from some cause unspecified, had been staying with me on and off for some time. [Note: the practice rock-climbing grounds frequented by the Tübingen climbers were close to Hausen im Tal.] Till now there has been some doubt as to when the two men entered Switzerland. The rescued Italian Corti makes contradictory statements, among them that he met the two Germans as early as August 4, 1957, when they had already lost their rucksacks containing their crampons and the rest of their equipment.
>
> The two climbers, Nothdurft and Mayer, did not leave my hostelry till Sunday, August 4, 1957, in the morning, somewhere between 8 and 8:30 A.M., on a "Puch" motorcycle, red in color, intending to go to Grindelwald, Switzerland. Both men informed me before they left that they would probably start to climb the Face on Monday, August 5, 1957. It therefore seems improbable that they could already have lost their equipment on the day they entered Switzerland (August 4, 1957). Yet that is what Corti says, though his statements are all confused.
>
> I feel it is my duty to make this statement primarily to establish it beyond any doubt that the two Germans only entered Switzerland on August 4, 1957. The time required for the journey from Hausen im Tal to Grindelwald would be at the very least six hours, so that they cannot have arrived there before from 2 to 3 P.M.
>
> Maybe the declarations I have now made will be of the greatest importance in clearing up this affair.
>
> Signed: Willi Heppeler.

In my view a letter I received from Max Eiselin is of greater importance. Written at Krienz-Lucerne, it contains the following statements:

Günther Nothdurft and Franz Mayer were at my home a day before they started up the North Face, and that was on Sunday, August 4, 1957, at about 1 P.M.; moreover I should like to underline most carefully that there is no possibility of an error in the date. I myself was away from home on that Sunday, but my parents entertained Franz and Günther—he had often visited me at my home. Even now my mother can remember every detail of the visit. One of the reasons why any mistake in the date is absolutely out of the question is that I would have been at home on the afternoon of Saturday, August 3. Another proof is that Franz and Günther were made aware of the contents of a telegram which only arrived late on that Saturday afternoon. Yet another is that they wanted some repairs done to their motorcycle, but were unable to do so just because it was Sunday. And at about 1:30 P.M. on that Sunday they resumed their journey.

As I happened to be in the Bernese Oberland at the time and had planned to take about a week's leave there, my mother brought the telegram to their notice and asked them to acquaint me with its contents. Unfortunately the message in that telegram, sent me by a Viennese friend from Grindelwald, read: "Climbed Fiescherwand stop Conditions excellent stop Proceeding Alpiglen tomorrow." According to my mother, Franz Mayer had immediately become extremely nervous and he and Günther had exchanged a meaning look. They had actually mentioned Mont Blanc as their ultimate objective.

Another remarkable thing is that Günther Nothdurft, who had visited me a few weeks before and had left his traversing rope from the "Hinterstoisser Traverse" with me, did not take it along on this second occasion. (It is still here.) Moreover, after his solo attempt, which took him to the crossing from the First to the Second Ice Field, he told me that he was no longer particularly interested in the Face—it was all too "floury." He also told me that the conditions on the Face had been very good, the rocks being pretty dry and the névé on the First Ice Field easy to move on in spite of that. All the same, in his bivouac at night a falling stone had knocked his tea flask right out of his hand, a circumstance which—taken with the general "flouriness" of the Face—had made a strongly negative impression on him. . . .

Günther Nothdurft was definitely of the opinion that the best way to tackle the Eiger's North Face is solo. He explained to me that he had gone into it thoroughly with Hermann Buhl, who agreed with him about it. That is why it is absolutely inexplicable to me—as it must be to countless others who knew him—that he should have joined up with the Italians; for it was his view that speed was the essence of the matter and a bivouac below the level of the "Ramp" not to be contemplated for a moment.

Furthermore, I watched the four men at the Third Ice Field on the Wednesday. In disagreement with all the other "observers," I thought they were moving quickly, and wondered how they could have taken so long in reaching it. And because they were moving relatively quickly across the Third Ice Field while I was watching them that morning, I reckoned that they would get to the top that same evening or at least the following day. I consequently fixed a congratulatory card to Günther Nothdurft's motorcycle as it stood outside Grindelwald-Grund Station. My friend Hajdukiewicz and the other members of the Polish climbers' camp got ready to go up and meet them on the summit. It never occurred to me at the time that the situation looked in the least "dicey." But when I came down to Rosenlaui after a climb on the Engelhörner and put in a telephone call to ask about the success of the venture I was informed that the climbers were still on the Face and a rescue operation had been set in motion. . . .

So much for Max Eiselin's letter. He too was unable to solve the riddle; he too failed to remove the nagging uncertainty. The unexplained remains inexplicable. But one thing stands out like a beacon: Nothdurft and Mayer were still in Lucerne at 1:30 P.M. on the Sunday, which agrees with the deposition of Heppeler, the innkeeper. It therefore seems proved beyond any doubt that Corti is continually in error, not only in his topographical descriptions but in his times, equally as to days of the week and hours of the day. One must accept it as proved that Nothdurft and Mayer caught up with the Italians not at 3 P.M. on Sunday but at 6:30 A.M. on Monday. That forces one to the conclusion that Corti's claim was intended to cover up the fact that it took him two whole days and bivouac nights to get onto the correct route. Fritz von Almen saw both parties together at the "Hinterstoisser Traverse" at 6:30 A.M. on the Monday. That proves that Nothdurft and Mayer were in the normal form exhibited by good parties and had caught up the two Italians, who had started up the Face forty-eight hours ahead of them, in less than four hours after they themselves began to climb. This is not meant to throw too damaging a light on Corti's ability as a climber, but to show up his route-finding capabilities and his lack of thorough preparation.

Dr. Lutz continues:

If the two Germans had lost their rucksack down the Face on the first day, it is absolutely incomprehensible why they did not climb down again. Everyone who knew the two climbers is of the opinion that after seeing their rucksack fall they would definitely have climbed down and never risked an at-

tempt on an exceptionally difficult face without food and vic-
tuals. I myself cannot believe that Nothdurft, whom I knew
personally, would ever have risked climbing on without
provender, after giving serious thought to the matter.

We already know—as Dr. Lutz could not, when he wrote the
above passage—that Corti revised his first statement and in his report to the Club Alpino declared that the Germans had only lost their
provision pack (there is no longer any question of a rucksack carrying their equipment) at the bivouac near the "Swallow's Nest." At
the same time the newly established facts seem to prove that this
bivouac was occupied during the night of Monday to Tuesday, not
Sunday to Monday, as claimed by Corti. But let us not dwell on his
time-fixing statements any longer.

There remains only the great, unanswerable query, how these two
ropes climbed onwards about five times as slowly as average parties,
according to Lionel Terray's assessment. How does this fit in with
the established fact that the two Germans climbed so quickly before
they ran up against the Italians? Was it simply the iced-up state of the
rock? Of course, Corti's statement that Nothdurft was suffering
from stomach or bowel trouble could be perfectly true. The declaration by Günther's mother, that he was always 100 percent fit, is neither here nor there. A drop of cold glacier water with some granite
dust mixed in it can induce in the healthiest body diarrhea or colic,
resulting in serious weakness. Yet we notice that the weakness was
certainly not so serious that it occurred to the German party to turn
back.

But why didn't Mayer—also described by Corti as "good"—and
Nothdurft climb past the much slower Italians and take over the lead?
The answer is very simple: on the North Face of the Eiger, it is impossible to overtake if the party in front doesn't want one to. The
only way would be to engage in a race on the Second Ice Field, which
would force one into a carelessly imprudent pace, such as a scrupu-

lously sound climber like Nothdurft, however daring, would never have accepted. The only reason why Waschak's party had been able to overtake that of Fuchs in 1950 was because the latter of its own free will let the quicker, better rope climb past. Remembering Corti's red-hot ambition, it seems highly probable that he would have been cut to the quick if the youngsters had climbed past him. That Mayer and Nothdurft accepted the inevitable is shown by the fact that they later on joined the Italians in a single roped party. But I would like to point out that there is nothing so stamina-sapping—physically and psychologically—to very young climbers as having a pace imposed on them which does not suit their temperaments.

Dr. Lutz continues:

> The cession of the tent sack to Corti was a comradely mountaineering gesture on the part of the two Germans. All the same, to climb on without food or shelter in the face of an imminent thunderstorm would seem, when quietly considered, an almost suicidal thing to do; it looks as if the two Germans when they decided to go on were bent on reaching the summit quite soon or else getting off the Face somehow and so managing to fetch help for their teammates reasonably quickly. Yet it seems almost impossible to believe that they could have cherished any such hope, after the past days of struggle against the Face. . . .
>
> Not only the parents, the Tübingen Section, and all mountaineers interested in the fate of the unfortunate climbers, but I myself would be grateful for any further light on the mystery of their death. Somehow, I think, the ultimate truth will never see the light of day. Those who died will keep to themselves the secret of their last hours. . . .

At the beginning of September 1957, a search party, including once again the trusty Max Eiselin, combed the whole base of the North Face.

This plucky team climbed up to Eigerwand Station in spite of the danger from falling stones, and thus thoroughly explored the whole "field of fire" of the "Spider." They found no definite signs to prove that Nothdurft and Mayer had fallen from the Face. A search party working farther over to the west did, however, find a purse belonging to Roland Vass, who had fallen on July 28, 1953, and in it his club membership certificate, still astonishingly well preserved.

Nonetheless, the mystery could yet be solved. Up to the time of writing, the bodies of the two dead men have not been found. When they are, it may well prove possible to tell from their position on the Face where they fell or died. That they will be found is a certainty, for the Face is such that anything which is not firmly fixed to it must sooner or later fall down it. It may be that they will find Günther Nothdurft's notes, for the lad always kept an exact diary, even on the severest face-climbs. That could result in the clarification of many a dark doubt. It cannot give them back their lives.

I do not propose to take leave of this mighty, terrible, and yet so gloriously beautiful mountain face at the end of my book with the thought of these tragic deaths. For mountaineering is life, sheer concentrated life. . . .

With the miraculous rescue of Corti a bridge was built between the Wall of Death and life itself; and every mountaineer is glad that he was rescued and that a life was saved. He too must have suffered terribly. One would have to have spent nine days on the Face to know how one would react when the only driving force is the naked urge for self-preservation. True, mountaineers worthy of the name, who of their own free will and with a common purpose commit themselves to ventures beyond the ordinary, must only recognise a common urge for self-preservation in time of extreme peril, as in the case of the European Rope of Buhl and Rébuffat in 1952. I sincerely hope that Corti was also possessed of that true mountaineering spirit.

As already stated, I do not wish to take part in the polemics, which flared up after the rescue and were widely fanned by the Press,

between the guides and the voluntary helpers. I would only like the
guides to consider that no new development in Alpine technique and
practise will stop at the guides' behest—however much it seems to
them to conflict with tradition. Practice with the steel-cable apparatus is no ropeway engineer's course. It is essential. According to information given to me, when a course in the new technique was
organised in Grindelwald under that splendid guide Hermann Steuri,
only five pupils applied, and for a second course later on there was
not a single application. Against that, we know from experience in
the Eastern Alps and in Chamonix that guides learn to man the new
equipment in masterly fashion. And when the new art is harnessed to
the unrivalled powers of achievement and endurance that are the
hallmark of the guides, then the optimum in the field of rescue work
will have been achieved.

And to the volunteers I would like to say: "Don't rate yourselves
as better than the guides. Follow their advice and don't ignore them.
They have grown up in the mountains, they live near the mountains,
earn their livelihood from the mountains, and know them as no one
else knows them. Never forget that, even at transient moments when
you may be technically superior. I have already said that guides and
amateur climbers are chips off the same block. And if ever there was
a mountain face made for guides and amateurs alike, it is the North
Face of the Eiger. Surely that is a lesson that everyone can learn from
its history and from the terrible tragedy of 1957. . . .

But now let us stop talking about death; let us think of and believe
in life and the beauty of mountaineering. Let us not now worry about
the lack of organisation at the last rescue on the Eiger; let us only see
what was uplifting, grand, communal, the will to help.

At the end of his report on the rescue operation in 1957, Alfred
Hellepart says:

There we learned true mountain comradeship, transcending
all national frontiers and the true will to help. Nor must we

forget our good friend Tom de Bloy who, with his knowledge of five languages, was called in to overcome our purely language difficulties and so bring us mutual understanding. Yet our handshakes and what we saw in each other's faces as we said goodbye were proof enough that, language or no language, we understood one another.

And may that always be so, everywhere in this great and lovely world!

EPILOGUE

Since this book was first written, the North Face has once again become a focus of public interest. On July 31, 1958, a party consisting of Hias Noichl, Herbert Raditschnig, and Lothar Brandler started up the Face soon after midnight. All three had gone through an exceptionally thorough preparation and were superbly equipped. By about 5 P.M. they had already reached a height of some 10,800 feet on the "Flatiron"; but at that point they were subjected to a heavy burst of stone fire from the "Spider." Their plastic crash helmets protected them from the worst effects, but one of the stones smashed the left hand of the thirty-eight-year-old guide Hias Noichl. Then began a retreat that will be recorded as a highlight in the history of great performances on the Face. After Noichl had been given a first-aid bandage the three men spent the night at the "Death Bivouac" of Sedlmayer and Mehlringer. At five in the morning they started off again and, after a descent lasting ten hours, safely reached the Gallery Window of the Jungfrau Railway. A party in undamaged condition would not have been able to cover the distance any more quickly. Noichl kept going in spite of his injury and considerable loss of blood. It was only in the car on the way to hospital, once he was relieved of any responsibility for his rope mates, that he collapsed.

Once again the Eiger had repelled an attempt which, so far as anyone could judge in advance, promised success; but all those who, in Grindelwald and at the Kleine Scheidegg, lived through those days with the unsuccessful climbers, knew that the "siege" of 1958 was not yet over. Not even Noichl's bad luck would scare the others away.

Hardly had the meteorologists promised a little fine weather, when on Tuesday, August 5, at 3 A.M., two students from Vienna, Kurt Diemberger and Wolfgang Stefan, started up the Face under a cloudless sky. They, too, had prepared themselves most thoroughly for their attempt. The same evening, after a safe and rapid ascent, they bivouacked for the first time at about 11,000 feet. Wednesday morning brought one of the Eiger's frequent breaks in the weather, with up to 11 degrees (centigrade) of cold and many inches of fresh snow. During the morning, Diemberger and Stefan were seen climbing out of the "Ramp" up to the "Spider" before clouds closed down on the Face. Raditschnig, Brandler, and the Bernese photographer Albert Winkler climbed to the summit by the normal western route, to receive the two climbers there or if necessary to go to their assistance. About 7 P.M. Diemberger and Stefan answered their shouts, and exactly an hour later the two men reached the top. The fifteenth climb in the history of the Face had been successfully accomplished. After a chilly bivouac below the summit they were safely back on August 7 at the Kleine Scheidegg in astonishingly good condition. Once there, Diemberger reported: "We were never in trouble, nor did we ever for a moment consider a retreat. All the same, I never want to climb the North Face again. It is one of those climbs which one does in a lifetime, and finds it enough of a good thing."

So 1958, the twentieth year after the first ascent, brought yet another success. It showed too that there are many ways in which the dangers of the Face can be minimised. The most important and absolutely indispensable requisite is outstanding skill as a climber; but that alone is not enough. Another definite essential, apart from terrific powers of endurance and first-class equipment, is an exact knowledge of the route. That is why I have added a precise description of the route as an appendix to this book and have enlisted the aid of Diemberger and Stefan in bringing it right up to date. Without such a route guide perhaps even their ascent would have come to grief, once the weather had turned bad. Equally important, and a *sine qua non* for future attempts, are the new plastic crash helmets. Noichl's party as well as Diemberger and Stefan reported that during murderous volleys of stone fire they were glad to crouch down under the full protection of their helmets. Stefan's had a great dent in it from a falling stone and but for its protection he would probably not be alive now.

But in spite of all security measures, the North Wall of the Eiger remains one of the most perilous in the Alps, as every man who has ever joined battle with it knows. Other climbs, the North Face of the Grandes Jorasses for one, may be technically more difficult; nowhere else is there such appalling danger from the purely fortuitous hazards of avalanches, stone falls, and sudden deterioration of the weather as on the Eiger. I know well that ambitious climbers will not let themselves be scared away by those dangers in days to come. And so I would like once again to utter an express warning to them.

The North Face of the Eiger demands the uttermost of skill, stamina, and courage, nor can it be climbed without the most exhaustive preparations; to attempt it without the finest equipment is abysmal folly. Even when all these requisites are fulfilled, the most brilliant climbers need plentiful reserves if they are to succeed. For these cogent reasons, let everyone whom the North Face ensnares in its lure first weigh his intention well.

There are many other targets for the climber's ambition, his dreams of achievement, and his love of adventure. I myself have discovered, in the course of several expeditions during the last few years, innumerable blanks on the map, promising everything that a genuine mountaineer can ask of his climbing.

We are still a long way from having experienced the ultimate adventure on this globe of ours.

ADDITIONAL CHAPTERS
BY HEINRICH HARRER,
IN COLLABORATION
WITH KURT MAIX,
JULY 1964

FATE

MADE THE

AMENDMENTS

As will shortly be seen, fate was to change the order in the list of successful climbs, and I hasten to make the necessary adjustments. To start with, there were Karl Heinz Gonda and Uli Wyss, who fell to their deaths from the Summit Ice Field on August 22, 1953—the marks seemed to show that they were carried down by a snowslide.

Before this book was first published, I tried everything I knew to get their climb recognised as the twelfth ascent. I carried on a correspondence with the ranking authorities in the climbing world and the field of sport generally, discussed the case from every angle with them; in the end, I felt bound by Othmar Gurtner's[1] ruling that, in order to achieve recognition as a successful ascent, the climbers must reach the summit of the Eiger alive. On my return from New Guinea,[2] I was delighted to hear that this brilliant attempt, which ended so tragically, was after all to be recognised as the twelfth ascent.

[1] The late director of the Swiss Foundation for Alpine Research.—H.M.

[2] See the author's book *I Come from the Stone Age* (London: Hart-Davis, 1964).

As a result, the ascent by those quiet, courageous Bavarians, Albert Hirschbichler and Erhard Riedl, becomes the thirteenth—a fact that will not bother Riedl, who never courts notoriety, nor would it have worried his partner. For he, too, was a modest man, for whom happiness did not depend on public opinion.

His shy and pleasant personality, his ability to fit into a team, his skill as a mountaineer, and his utter reliability won him an invitation to join a British expedition to the Karakorum. It was the fulfillment of every climber's dream for the youngster from Reichenhall, but he did not return from his journey. We know from Mathias Rebitsch, Anderl Heckmair, Martl Schliessler, Rudl Bardojez, and others how perilous are the unexplored peaks of over 23,000 feet in the Batura massif of Hunza. It is a region of fast-flowing glaciers, of ever-changing seracs, of crashing ice pinnacles. Hirschbichler and his British companions were engulfed by an ice avalanche.

One might think that, after these amendments to the list, Kurt Diemberger and Wolfgang Stefan could claim the fourteenth ascent. But no—that must now go—surprisingly—to Günther Nothdurft and Franz Mayer. . . .

I heard by letter while I was in New Guinea that Claudio Corti's last companions had been found—not on the North Face or the South, not on the ordinary way down, but at the rim of the gulley that falls to the western snowfield. They were found on September 22, 1961, and from their positions it was deduced that they had not suffered a fall nor been swept away by an avalanche, but had simply died where they lay. Was it cold and exposure that led to exhaustion and death? How can one establish, four years after the event, whether a man's circulation or his heart failed first?

With the news of the discovery of the bodies came other letters, saying: "Now Claudio Corti is cleared." There were many who thought it my duty to make immediate amends by a postscript, rehabilitating Corti. But I felt my duty lay in being a true friend to all the world's climbers, particularly the younger generation. It is not my fault that his pronouncements, descriptions, and reports were so full of dark riddles and still remain so.

If I could not then convert the confused report of the Italian into a document of crystal clarity, it was because of my special regard for Italian climbers. Nor can I do so today, though the discovery of the bodies of Nothdurft and Mayer on the West Face certainly seems to have substantiated Corti's report thus far: the pair left him at the bivouac by the "Spider," complete with tent, equipment, and the remains of their provisions, in an attempt to complete the climb and fetch help. But the description of the route and the events of the days from August 3 to 8, 1957, however we may try to sort them out from Corti's report, remain confused and frequently unintelligible.

Many suggest that Corti's confusion was merely the result of the intense nervous strain and nights of delirium on the Face. That view simply enforces the opinion that Corti was not fit to be on it, since his mental and spiritual powers failed to match so great a demand on them. What climber worth his salt ever went crazy as a result of exertion, deadly peril, or fear? Did Walter Bonatti go crazy on the Southwest Buttress of the Dru? Or Lino Lacedelli and Achille Compagnoni, at 28,000 feet on K2, when they found that their oxygen containers were empty and they would probably suffocate? No. Choking and blue in the face, they climbed onto the summit of the world's second-highest peak, took pictures with shaking hands, and then stumbled down, over difficult ice pitches, dangerous snow and rock, to the point to which the faithful Walter Bonatti had somehow dragged up some full bottles.

Nor did Willo Welzenbach and Willy Merkl allow themselves the luxury of going crazy before they died on Nanga Parbat in 1934. None of the men on Everest ever went crazy. At the 26,000-foot level, Lionel Terray managed to keep sane through tempest and trial, the perfect team man who thought last of himself. Cesare Maestri did not go out of his mind when, after a six days' struggle on the Cerro Torre in a fierce Patagonian blizzard, he lost his rope mate and our never-to-be-forgotten friend, Toni Egger. Nor did Anderl Heckmair and Hermann Kollensperger during their five days with four bivouacs in snowstorms on the Walker Buttress of the Jorasses. Not one of the nine climbers who in 1952 fought their way up the Eiger Wall (and incidentally combined to form the first truly international rope in Europe), in weather conditions Corti never even dreamed of, lost his reason; not even Hermann Buhl, who would probably have died in the final bivouac, if he had not had with him a comrade of Sepp Jöchler's caliber. Let us rather think of Gaston Rébuffat's grim, Gallic sense of humor when he wrote of those bitter hours: "The human animal in me was unhappy."

There was no room for madness in those places. Nor does Corti need any further rehabilitation from me. The spot on which stood the little tent, given him by the Germans, from which Alfred Hellepart rescued him, is today known in climber's jargon as the "Corti bivouac." That name is an award of honor, which will sooner or later give him equal rank with Hinterstoisser, Terray, and all the other pioneers after whom salient points on the Face have been named. No one will withhold a kindly thought for a man who, just because of his failings as a man, suffered greater fear and terror than others who came to climb the Face. The fact remains that this bivouac spot above the "Spider" has been named after Corti, not after the two men who in all probability pitched and secured the little tent to ensure his safety.

Walter Seeger, one of the best climbing partners and intimate friend of Günther Nothdurft, in a letter to Kurt Maix, wrote as follows:

By mere chance Nothdurft and Mayer were found on September 22 or 23 in a couloir on the Eiger's West Face. Werner Stäger, Head Guide in Lauterbrunnen, and his party had brought down rescue material and thrown part of it down the snow slope to the west of the ordinary route; it was then that they came upon the two bodies. On September 25 I travelled to Lauterbrunnen with Herr Nothdurft[1] and at the police station there they showed me various articles, such as a camera, identity papers, etc., which I was able to identify beyond all doubt as Günther's. I was then taken into the mortuary, a shattering experience.

After that I got in touch with Stäger, to obtain further facts. According to him it cannot be certain whether they were overwhelmed by an avalanche and swept into the couloir or died during a bivouac. From Stäger's description, one of them seemed to be in a belaying position; but, after four years, external forces might well have altered the position of the bodies.

I also saw Günther's much-discussed diary both at Lauterbrunnen and later, when the experts had examined it, in Berne. There were no definite entries in it. But from my own experience I can say that Günther never made notes while he was actually on a climb; he did this afterwards, either in his tent, or not till he got home. In the special case of the Eiger, I cannot believe that he would have made a single note.

Seeger goes on:

Günther's climb of the Face to his death is full of question marks for me. Why, for instance, did the pair change their plans and decide to do the climb at the start, instead of the end, of their leave? Why did Günther not give a short report which might have been his salvation? Why did they join the Italians? It is a whole chain of queries, in none of which did Günther

---

[1] Günther's sorely tried, blind father, who died on Easter Saturday, 1964, aged eighty-three. — Author's note.

behave according to his predictable reactions over all the years I knew him.

And then, the mysterious finding of the rucksack by Raditschnig, Noichl, and Brandler in 1958, at the "Shattered Pillar," raises more questions. According to them, there were crampons in it, though I never saw them; against that, there were two carabiners marked "WS," which were clearly mine. If we accept that the pair lost the rucksack right at the start of the climb, how can one explain their going on with only one pair of crampons? From all my long experience of Günther, I just cannot believe they would have done such a thing. On the other hand it would explain their slow progress on ice, which everyone remarked on at the time.

What cannot be explained is their joining the Italians as a foursome on the rope. They were only on the lower third of the Face, and there was no earthly reason for it, no compulsion whatever. Moreover, language difficulties must have militated against establishing a good understanding so quickly. Could the difference in age have influenced their decision; or did they feel they could not overtake the Italians for considerations of sportsmanship or safety? Equally incomprehensible are the reasons for leaving Longhi behind. Günther was fully familiar with every form of assistance known in rescue methods. Can a serious illness or a decision of Corti's have been responsible for deserting Longhi? Yet, surely Corti, as his partner on the rope, should never have climbed on without him? But what use is there in asking all these questions? A dark shadow will always lie heavy on what happened during that particular climb of the Eiger's North Face.

Today, my own theory seems to have been confirmed. It was good companionship, sheer humanity, which moved Nothdurft and Mayer to stay with Corti and Longhi. Obviously the young and highly trained climbers would have moved more quickly than that odd rope of four. But there is a climber's law, unwritten, yet binding on climbers of whatever nationality, and it is generations old: the strong are responsible for the weaker vessels, no matter whether their rope be a foreign one.

Nothdurft's indisposition cannot have been as serious as Corti, the leader of the Italian pair, thought or described later. A trained climber can of course get over a slight upset during a climb lasting several days; but the Eiger Wall is not so constituted that it would permit a seriously sick man to recover, regain his strength, and reach the summit after five days of tremendous exertions—and that, climbing free and without the protection of a tent.

That yellow tent is the proof—a memorial to an act of comradeship on classic lines. After his injury Corti seemed the weakest; he had definitely exhausted himself severely while trying to rescue Longhi. So he got the tent. That is why Nothdurft and Mayer made him a present of their only chance of survival. Let us all rejoice that Claudio Corti is alive; but let us give an occasional thought to the two who died—Günther Nothdurft and Franz Mayer, whose climb became the fourteenth successful ascent of the Eiger's North Face.

And so the first successful Italian ascent did not take place till 1962, when, between August 11 and 17, a team consisting of Acquistapace, Airoldi, Aste, Perego, and Solina completed the climb. I am not going to say here whether the very long time taken, seven days with six bivouacs, was a sign of internal harmony, relaxed nerves, and caution, or whether a virtue was made of necessity. I have often said and the years have confirmed my conviction that the Face does not suit the mentality of Italian climbers, and, further, that the very best of the broad front of great Italian climbers had not even attempted the climb till then. As long ago as 1938 Mario Menti and Bartolo Sandri had come to grief on it. It is a clear sign of the healthy attitude of the Italians towards mountains and mountaineering that they did not build upon the tragic death of that pair any form of duty for successors to go and avenge it. The best of them never came near the Face; and the six men whose successful ascent in 1962 was the twenty-seventh, good as they were, were not the cream of Italy's climbing elite.

But, after them, one of the very best did come; not only one of the best Italians, but one of the world's best. For in July 1963, Walter Bonatti came, and he came alone. Everyone watched him and everyone was disappointed. The know-it-alls passed judgment: ringside spectators of the Eiger drama uttering criticisms of the man who first climbed the Southwest Buttress of the Petit Dru, the East Face of the Grand Capucin, the Walker Buttress in winter! Bonatti, they decided, was going too slowly, too tentatively. Would this attempt—it would be, of course, the first solo climb—end in another fatality?

Italian headlines were already shouting: "Bonatti on the Eiger North Wall, solo." Spectators at the Kleine Scheidegg reported the presence of a whole publicity corps, talking of exclusive rights and the rest. Bonatti would have to climb the Face now, come what may; his whole reputation was at stake.

Of course. And then, after bivouacking once, Bonatti came down again, just as carefully as he had gone up, only yesterday. By midday he was at the bottom again. What could have happened? Had he been hurt by a stone, at the Second Ice Field? Or some other injury, perhaps? Would Bonatti ever be able to climb again . . . ?

Nothing so dramatic. Bonatti did not indulge in histrionics, nor let himself be photographed with a sad look of heroic self-control on his manly face. He said little, but did not seem depressed, or in the least bothered about his "reputation." Walter Bonatti had turned back for no better reason than that it seemed sensible to do so. Perfectly relaxed, he voiced the pregnant thought: "No mountain is worth as much as one's life."

FOUR SHIRTS
AND AN
OVERCOAT

I have thought it essential to clarify my exact attitude toward Italian climbers, so as to eliminate the slightest doubt on the subject. Now, to keep the history of the Face in its proper order, we must turn back to 1958.

In that year, Kurt Diemberger and Wolfgang Stefan, whom we already know so well, achieved not the thirteenth but the fifteenth successful ascent. I think this is the place to clear those two superlative Austrian climbers of the reproach, levelled at the time, that they failed to take part in the search for the missing Viennese, Engelbert Titl. Their all-too-zealous critics had overlooked the fact that they were already committed to the Face before he was posted missing. Titl had last been seen on the Mittellegi Ridge climbing solo at an incredible speed. He was not found till three years later, in 1961, in the couloir on the West Face, already of tragic fame, a few yards below the bodies of Nothdurft and Mayer.

The sixteenth ascent belongs to two very unusual lads, two bricklayers from the Grisons, resident in Zürich, Adolf Derungs and Lukas Albrecht. Both were poor but plucky; both felt the spur of regional loyalty. They knew all about the type of modern equipment in general use in the Western Alps and essential on the North Face of the Eiger; but they did not buy it, for the good reason that they could not afford it. They hadn't even a modern anorak. However, one of them wore four—or was it five?—shirts, on top of each other, which is one way of keeping warm; the other took an overcoat along, an old, tattered overcoat, but still an overcoat. This was instead of a bivouac bag; two people huddling under an overcoat can manage to find some warmth—enough to prevent their freezing during the night and to start off again upward next morning. And, farther up, when it seemed certain that another bivouac would be unnecessary, they abandoned the old coat to the laws of gravity and threw it over the side. It slid across the "Spider" and shot out into the abyss. A coat has sleeves, just as a man has arms; and who can distinguish from a distance, even through a telescope, between sleeves and arms? So there were the most exciting stories flying around, about the "third man" who had fallen off, while the onlookers watched the other two climbing happily on above the "Spider."

The facts are that Albrecht and Derungs made the sixteenth ascent between August 10 and 13, 1959. The weather was most unkind and they both showed great courage. The shirts and the old coat proved their worth; but the decisive factor was the toughness and grit of these two young men from the Grisons. It was quite ridiculous to reproach them for having worn old metal motoring helmets instead of the modern anti-stonefall plastic ones.

Alpine Scrooges attacked the two Grisons labourers enthusiastically. The old favourite, "irresponsibility," reappeared in all papers more or less interested in Alpine affairs; but Mathias Rebitsch, that old warhorse of the mountains, came out strongly in favour of them. "Two splendid lads," he said. "They proved that even today, men are more important than equipment!"

Derungs and Albrecht, incidentally, were the first ever to be filmed while on the "Spider," not as paid members of a cast, but rather by chance, though gladly enough. There were in Munich two film personalities called Edmund Geer and Wolfgang Görter, who were complete fanatics about the North Face. Geer had taken part, as a mere boy, in the 1938 German expedition to Tibet, and brought home, as its cameraman, a most interesting film of the country. At that time, of course, I did not know that Tibet was to become a landmark, indeed a turning point, in my own life; but now the theme gives me a strong fellow feeling for Edmund Geer. His career as a photographer brought him from freelancing, through the post of cameraman, to the role of producer. Görter started as a mountaineer, and a very good one at that; with Ludwig Steinauer he made the first ascent of the North Face of Mont Blanc de Seilon, and the pair later mastered the highest face of Iran's famous "Five Thousander," Demavend. He began to film for fun; the filming climber was to become a climbing cameraman.

I do not know which of them first had the idea of doing an Eiger film, but Kurt Maix tells me that he saw the Geer-Görter film *Eiger-Nordwand* as early as the 1959 festival of mountain films at Trento. Its chief stars were Toni Hiebeler and Lothar Brandler; there were shots on the lower part of the Face and close-ups on ice that were obviously not shot on the Face at all, which agrees with Toni's report that they turned back at the Hinterstoisser Traverse. Then there was an excellent sequence of a break in the weather, and pictures of Lothar and Toni coming down. But not only that, there were also shots of two climbers on the way up. The two ropes met on the approach to the Face and exchanged greetings. The newcomers were Derungs and Albrecht. And the telephotos I have mentioned, showing the two men on the "Spider"—taken, by the way, from the shoulder of the Northwest Ridge—were really sensational, largely owing to the continual intervention of driving mist.

To return to the history of the Face. In 1959 there was for a time much talk of another very remarkable ascent, particularly notable for the short time in which it was supposed to have been accomplished.[1] Uli Link, that experienced chronicler of the events on the Face and a professional journalist, brought the pictures of it to Trento, and showed them to all the experts. The unanimous opinion was against their having been taken at the points on the Eiger Face they were alleged to represent.

Be that as it may, my own investigations lead me to believe that the "Seventeenth Ascent of the Face in Record Time" took place in a room, and partly even in a courtroom. Now, the North Face of the Eiger still surges up above the meadows of Alpiglen to the 13,025-foot summit. For which reason, mountaineers the world over accord the true seventeenth to Ernst Forrer and Peter Diener, for their ascent—a truly meritorious one, on account of the heavily iced state of the Face—on September 13 and 14, 1959.

---

[1] In 1959 two Swiss climbers claimed to have climbed the Face, utterly unnoticed, inside a single day. The photographs they offered in support were later shown, during the course of a libel action, to have been taken on the lower rocks of the base structure. —H.M.

ASCENDANCY

OF THE

ARMCHAIR

In February Geer and Görter were at work again with their cameras at Kleine Scheidegg. This time the "stars" were Lothar Brandler, Jörg Lehne, and Siegfried Löw, three Saxons who had taken up residence in Munich and, at times, Salzburg. The film made at that time has acquired a special value in Alpine history, for it clearly shows Sigi Löw, the broad-shouldered champion gymnast who had found a new home in Salzburg. He was destined, two years later, to share with Toni Kinshofer[1] and Anderl Mannhardt the second ascent of 26,660-foot Nanga Parbat and the first of its gigantic Diamir Face, which we attempted way back in 1939. Löw fell to his death on the descent.

The three ex-Saxons, all "Direttissima" experts in the Dolomites—the "Superdirettissima" had not yet been thought up then—Brandler, Lehne, and Löw, now made a winter attempt on the Eiger Face. They were nearly drowned in snow on the approach pitches. It was quite useless to attempt the Face in such conditions,

---

[1]Later, in 1964, Kinshofer died tragically during an easy practice climb near Baden-Baden.—H.M.

but they did their best, reaching roughly the level of the gallery exit (though they did not take advantage of its escape facilities) and climbing down again, while the cameras whirred.

Cameras and actors alike had tried their hardest, but the Face acted a dramatic and repellent part, which robbed them of any spoils worth having. The "gentlemen of the jury" at Trento acknowledged the painstaking labours, the difficulties, the dangers involved, and awarded the film quite a good place. Geer and Görter, whose single-minded aim was *the* documentary of the Eiger North Face, were far from satisfied. Kurt Maix saw the second edition of the film "North Face in Winter" at Trento in October 1961, when Geer and Görter won the first prize with it. The true 16 mm documentary of the climb had been produced at last.

That winter climb was a wonderful performance on the part of all four men constituting the rope. Toni Hiebeler organized it, acted as spiritual leader, and operated the camera. Toni Kinshofer, aged twenty-two, led the climb, the other two members of the team being Anderl Mannhardt and Walter Almberger. The ascent took them seven days, with six nights out on the Face. There would never have been the slightest ground for criticism of this wonderful venture, or the men who took part in it; indeed, the armchair experts could have done nothing but admire and marvel at it. It was Toni Hiebeler himself who handed them the right to interfere; and Bruno Erath, the mountaineering correspondent of the Bayerischer Rundfunk, started the ball rolling, by revealing the little rift, the hole in the mountain, the gallery entrance, the Stollenloch.

The final attack had been launched from that point, not from the foot of the mountain. Nobody would have minded that; nobody would have questioned it as the first winter ascent of the most fearsome face in the world. Not a mountaineer but agreed that, even so, it counted as the first winter ascent, for him and his friends. That was not the bone of contention; what they were contesting was the claim that it had been done in one unbroken effort, from the bottom of the mountain, without making use of the tunnel.

If one reads Toni Hiebeler's account of that great climb[1] and forgets his gratuitous remarks before the armchair jury, one cannot help being thrilled and gripped; it is not only tense and dramatic, but truly sympathetic. For Hiebeler, in setting up a fine testimonial to his companions, never obtrudes his own personality but produces a psychological study of their three widely divergent characters. There is the first and best of them, Toni Kinshofer, utterly unflappable, answering every tense question, however grim, however dubious the situation, with his inevitable "quite all right." And then there is the second, Walter Almberger, safeguarding Toni up and up the Face, even in places where it was *"assistance only moral,"* he was getting from the rope. And then Anderl Mannhardt, the sceptic, not conceding the certainty of success until a split second before success itself. Truly a well-knit and harmonious team, these four magnificent climbers, who achieved a magnificent feat in climbing the Face for the first time in winter.

[1]*North Face in Winter* (Barrie & Rockliff) which I had the pleasure of translating into English. — H.M.

THE SILVER

TRENCH

The "Silver Trench" is a pleasant name for a feature in so grim a Face. It was invented, not by the men who climb it, but by the spectators at Kleine Scheidegg. It is visible only late in the afternoon, this "Silver Trench," when the sun throws a few brighter shafts even into so dark a wall. Its position is at the foot of the "Waterfall Chimney" in the "Ramp," and it only has its being when ice lying in it catches a gleam, or the water falling into it throws back a mirrored sheen. Early in the day, when the Face lies shadowed, when everything looks frozen in the stillness of death, there is no "Silver Trench." Nor do climbers want to hear any mention of its existence, however gaily it may sparkle and shine through the lens of the ×72 telescope on the Scheidegg terrace. They have not wanted to hear its name since Adi Mayr plunged from it to his death on August 28, 1961.

The year had opened with a resounding fanfare, heard by the whole excited Alpine world, which exulted in that first winter ascent in March. No Eiger year had heard such a prelude, which left everyone tense with expectation of great things to come.

At first poor weather and the bad condition of the Face forbade any successful ascents. There were attempts, withdrawals, awkward moments, but no disasters. Even August had almost passed without bringing the nineteenth climb of the Face.

In the last week of August, Adolf Mayr, an Austrian climber, arrived at Scheidegg. He was very young, but had already acquired great experience in the Eastern and Western Alps, as well as in Norway. He had done the severest of rock climbs, and also big combined ice-and-rock routes in the Western Alps. Young Adi—a native of Bad Hall in Austria, but domiciled for some years in Innsbruck—had accomplished all these climbs sensibly, stylishly, and with a natural technical mastery of his craft. His highly developed imagination ensured that prudence and preparations were for him a *sine qua non,* for he could visualise the dangerous moments in a climb before he reached them.

Adi Mayr was a lovable type. All his climbing friends said so; so did Fritz von Almen, the famous proprietor of the Scheidegg hotels, who had been taken into his confidence—a confidence which he returned with the best advice he commanded, given out of his great knowledge and experience, as with every care and support he could lend. Adi knew every inch of the Face from books, reports, verbal accounts, daily observation; Fritz von Almen filled in any gaps there might be in his knowledge.

Among other things, Fritz told him that the traverse of the Third Ice Field after midday was extremely exposed to falling stones, for every stone and ice fragment loosened by the afternoon sun from the "Spider" and the cliffs above it sweeps in an incessant curtain of fire across it. From this knowledge von Almen gave the young man sound and responsible advice: "If you get there after two o'clock, bivouac first, at the 'Death Bivouac.' The long hours of waiting are naturally tedious, but they are better than being hit and killed."

Adi had enough imagination to envisage the dangers of that traverse. He decided to start very early and climb as quickly as possible, so as to get through to the "Ramp" by the afternoon. Where would he make his first bivouac? Up on the Ice Field by the "Ramp," on the "Traverse of the Gods," in the Exit Cracks, or perhaps even on the summit itself?

He was in splendid condition, full of drive and enthusiasm. He did not say so, but the idea of the first solo ascent acted as a powerful spur. What a year 1961 would be: the first winter ascent and the first solo!

So, all alone, he moved off into the darkness with no companion save Fritz von Almen's words of encouragement, and the memory of the hotel keeper's kind young wife, who had got his breakfast ready soon after midnight. It is a bad thing to think too much about the earth when embarked on an unknown and hazardous adventure between earth and sky, and Adi soon shook off the moment of weakness which can so easily envelop a climber in those dark early hours. After all, he had often been alone on great and perilous faces.

By the first grey glimmer of morning Adi had reached the rocks; he soon warmed up over the first easy ground. As soon as there was enough light, Fritz von Almen looked for him through the big telescope and found him at the "Difficult Crack." He saw the solitary climber master the first real buttress of the mighty Face, moving smoothly, steadily, and without hesitation. Occasionally he made use of the rope which had been hanging there for two years though it was not altogether to be trusted; but Adi Mayr was well aware of that and used it with great caution, as a minor aid, never coming on it with his full weight.

On the easier rock above, the solo performer showed himself truly in his element, gliding unhurriedly and evenly over the rocks like a well-oiled machine. The "Hinterstoisser Traverse" hardly held him up at all. That redoubtable feature has, it is true, long ago had its teeth drawn; there were perhaps not so many ropes hanging on it as a year later, when they were so plentiful that good parties hardly took more than ten minutes over it. Even now, Adi did not take much more than twenty. He was not only climbing well, but making masterly use of all the artificial aids—ropes, carabiners, stirrups, and the rest.

The longer von Almen and other guides and climbers watched him, the more reassured they felt. They were all sure that this was no young seeker after fame moving to his destruction, but a man, sure of his skill and power to do what he had come to do.

The ice, when he reached it, seemed brittle and hard, and he had to resort to occasional step cutting. Adi was admittedly more at home on rock than on ice, but so were most of the climbers from the Eastern Alps who came to pit themselves against the North Face; and it was they who, in the end, were the first to climb it. He took no notice of the ice in the "Ice Hose" between the first two ice fields, turning the obstacle by climbing straight up the rocks to its left. Ever since Erich Waschak first tried this variant in 1950, we all know how friable and uncomfortably stratified the rock is at that point; but Adi moved on up as quickly as if he were on his native limestone cliffs. (The Eiger is, of course, also limestone.)

The Second Ice Field, that huge, endless shield of ice which cannot be climbed direct but the whole of whose half-kilometer length has to be traversed diagonally, damped the young man's swift upward tempo to a slow, measured, cautious—perhaps surprisingly cautious—pace, from step to step, yard by yard. It seemed as if the lonely climber had for the first time sensed the monstrous size of the Face.

The Second Ice Field is terribly impressive. When we climbed it for the first time in 1938 it had the same effect on us. One suddenly feels that one is on a journey with no end to it. How can I describe the place? Imagine the roof of a Gothic dome, 1,500 feet diagonally across, which you have to climb from bottom to top, from right to left. According to your position you see the lower edge of the roof 700 or 1,000 feet below you; but there is no gutter or friendly waterspout. Beyond the edge is thin air, two or three thousand feet of it. That means you can fall clear in a vertical plunge, hardly hitting anything on the way, to the rocks at the base of the wall. So it was not surprising that even a first-class climber like Adi

Mayr went slowly and carefully up the endless diagonal across that gigantic roof.

On the steep rocks leading to the "Flatiron," the solitary figure quickened pace again. They could see that through the telescopes, but they could also see that stones had started to come down. It was 2:30 P.M. when Mayr reached the "Death Bivouac." The mountain barrage was sweeping the Third Ice Field by then, and the crest of the "Flatiron," too—the way ahead and the way back. The weather was fine and would have allowed the climber another six hours of daylight, during which he could perhaps have reached the "Traverse of the Gods" or even the "Corti Bivouac" in the Exit Cracks. If he had been harebrained he could have said to himself: "Oh, hell! Every stone doesn't find a target," and gone on up.

But Adi Mayr didn't want to take any risks. He wanted to climb the Face by all the good rules of the mountaineer's art. So he tried to fight down his anxiety and followed the dictates of good sense, the command of the mountain that was sparing only one spot on its Face its notorious bombardment of stones—the "Death Bivouac." And there he stopped.

It was a long bivouac—a night that lasted fifteen hours, at whose start the afternoon sun was still shining brightly for six hours of broad daylight. It seemed an endless age before it really grew dark and before Adi could give the agreed torch signals, which Fritz von Almen answered from Kleine Scheidegg; an even more unending age before the first pale grey of a new day, August 28, crept out of the darkness. Nobody can say how the young man spent those long hours in his bivouac, how he coped with his loneliness, his innermost thoughts, his fears and his doubts, setting against them all his courage and purpose.

Next morning the big telescope revealed his every movement as he climbed on alone, but it was difficult to interpret his state of mind or the level of his spirits from them. Fritz von Almen was only a little worried to note that he did not seem to have recovered his rhythm of the day before. Of course the whole great Face was still in the grip of extreme cold; in its chill shadow the very movements of a human were strange enough. Were they really, as they seemed to the on-lookers, angular, stiff, hesitant, and less coordinated than yesterday?

The ground ahead of him gave Adi no chance of warming up. This was not the simple terrain of yesterday's lower terraces. Here he was met at once by the traverse slanting obliquely down to the Third Ice Field, the steepest ice field of all. Slowly he moved out to the left, cutting steps, technically correct, perfectly normally, if a lit-tle more slowly than usual. Nonetheless, von Almen, watching in-tently, could not rid himself of the feeling that all was not well with the lone climber up there. Was it perhaps some bodily ailment, re-sulting from the long, cold night? A lowering of his spirits, affecting his limbs, following on fifteen hours of lonely bivouacking at the very place where, twenty-six years earlier, the first two men to at-tempt the Face had died?

There were no stones hurtling across the Third Ice Field. Silence lay on the whole mighty wall. Nothing moved, except a human be-ing—a tiny point of life, of willpower, of sheer courage in a cold, shadowy vastness, inimical to all life.

Adi Mayr negotiated the Third Ice Field and reached the "Ramp." The first few pitches are by no means difficult and the rock is very good; yet the expert rock climber did not seem to be in top form even there. Was there ice on the rocks? Up there, in the shadow, it was dif-ficult to say; only his movements, still cramped and less masterful than yesterday, hinted at it. Against that, it was observed that he had nowhere belayed himself, which he would certainly have done if he found the going hard; so Adi couldn't be finding it dangerous, or he would definitely have given himself the necessary protection. Everybody had seen on the previous day how careful he was. No, they all said, he'll soon climb himself warm, even in that shadow.

Then he was on the traverse at the foot of the "Waterfall Chimney." It isn't an easy place. The "Silver Trench" was still invisible, for it does not glitter till in the afternoon. Water was coming down the chimney, so the rocks were probably icy below it; the shadow was too deep for anyone to be certain, but they could see the man and his movements. They saw Adi take the big stride out to the left. His left boot seemed to slip and he withdrew his leg. They saw him working at the hold—with his ice axe. Then he tried the stride a second time. Again he seemed unable to find a foothold; again he returned to his stance, only, this time, more jerkily.

A tired man moves like that, or one who is nervous, or at a loss. Yet Adi had not fixed a protecting rope, even here. What could be the matter with him?

They watched him make his third attempt. The same long stride as before. Nothing was different from the two previous times, and yet at 8:12 Adi Mayr risked that long stride out of the "Silver Trench" again—the trench that was dark and shadowed like the rest of the Face. And in shadow, too, was the body that slipped that morning from the "Silver Trench" and hardly struck the Face during its fall of nearly four thousand feet.

CLIMBERS HAVE
A LANGUAGE OF
THEIR OWN

My friend Guido Tonella first advocated the principle of the "European Rope." As long ago as 1957 international comradeship had proved itself, as already described, during the great rescue operation that saved Corti; for there were Polish climbers in the team even then—the first representatives of the Eastern Bloc to be associated with Eiger and its North Face. Tonella's principle was to be put into practice again.

For 1961 brought two East European parties to the Face, and two successful ascents by them. On August 30, only two days after Adi Mayr's tragic death, two Czechs, Radovan Kuchař and Zdeno Zibrin, were at work on the Face. They were well enough known, not only in the Elbsandstein Range, the Tatra, and the Caucasus, but also in the Western Alps, where they had won a fine reputation, particularly in the Mont Blanc massif and around Zermatt. Only a short time before, they had succeeded in climbing the North Face of the Matterhorn.

So these two intimate climbing partners went quietly up the lower sector of the Face—so quietly that one could almost describe their climbing as relaxed. Fritz von Almen told me that they missed not a single opportunity for belaying, and though they climbed a little more slowly than other first-class climbers in good weather conditions, they impressed every watcher with the resolution and mountaineering skill they exhibited. What the watchers could not see was that one of them lost his axe on the Second Ice Field. This, however, did not disturb them; two days later they were to provide ample evidence that the loss of even so important a piece of ice equipment was not allowed to interfere with their climbing.

Starting their first day at 3 A.M. they prepared their first bivouac on the upper rim of the Second Ice Field before 6 P.M., close under the foot of the rocks which sweep up to the "Flatiron." They could have used the two or three remaining hours of daylight to press on up to the "Flatiron" or the "Death Bivouac"; but it was late afternoon and the "Flatiron" not yet unmenaced by falling stones. And the basis of this party's climbing was safety first, second, and third.

Next morning, August 31, they climbed on in the same steady, measured way by the "Death Bivouac" and over the Third Ice Field to the "Ramp." Here they ran into ice on its lower rocks, which explains why Adi Mayr had gone so slowly there. They found the "Traverse," the "Stride," and the "Waterfall Chimney" heavily iced, and technical protection measures proved time-consuming. So they elected to bivouac on the "Brittle Ledge," as early as 5 P.M., with the Face still in sunshine; but Kuchař and Zibrin were merely demonstrating, to themselves and the world of the watchers, that they had plenty of time.

Next day, on September 1, they moved fairly quickly up the "Brittle Crack" across the "Traverse of the Gods" to the "Spider." And there a surprising thing happened, which gave the onlookers their first inkling that something might have gone wrong with the party's ice equipment. For Zibrin and Kuchař made a variant at this point, a kind of new route. Avoiding the "Spider" altogether, they went straight up the rocks to its left, eventually reaching the Exit

Cracks without meeting any insuperable difficulties. Obviously they did not like climbing on ice with ice pitons and ice hammer, and perched on the front teeth of their crampons. East European climbers still mistrust the Western gymnastic technique and its toe dancing; they prefer the classically safe and safety-ensuring methods. So if one's ice equipment is not good enough, one just takes to rock, even if nobody has ever done so before.

They bivouacked a third time high in the Exit Cracks. And on the fourth morning, September 2, soon after 8 A.M., the first East European rope to climb the North Face reached the Eiger's summit. The weather was perfect all the time. There were no sensations, unless it be sensational to observe complete safety measures all the way up the Face. They did not make a single mistake, barring the loss of the ice axe. But then who, of the younger generation, wants to cart a thing like that—a prehistoric legacy of his father's bygone days, an ice axe—about with him on a climb? Radovan Kuchař and Zdeno Zibrin set a good example of this on their climb, the nineteenth successful ascent.

The second East European success followed hard on its heels, indeed later the very same day, when two Polish engineers, Jan Mostowski of Gleiwitz and Stanislaw Biel of Cracow, reached the summit ten hours after the Czechs, though they had not started their climb till twenty-four hours after them.

There is no point in trying to draw any weighty conclusions from a comparison of these times. The Poles came under stone fire because of their greater speed, the Czechs avoided any risk of it. They seemed to have calculated everything on the basis of complete safety.

About the time when the Czechs were approaching their first bivouac on the afternoon of August 30 at the rim of the Second Ice Field, two Swiss climbers were settling down for the night at the "Swallow's Nest" far down the Face. Both bore famous names— Ernst Schmied and Alois Strickler. Schmied had been the leader of the second party to reach Everest's summit. Strickler belonged to the group of young "Extremists," bent on catching up the arrears which, in their view, Swiss mountaineering has incurred through its loyalty to traditional climbing. Every climb that a man should, in modern eyes, have done in order to qualify for world class, is down in his climbing diary as accomplished.

At the "Swallow's Nest" Schmied was attacked by pains in his stomach and intestines; so Strickler had to come down with his sick friend next day, August 30. On the way down they met two parties coming up—the Poles, whose climb has been described above, and two Swiss climbers, Sepp Inwyler and Kurt Grüter. They felt very sorry for Strickler and informed him that there was an Austrian down at the Scheidegg looking for a partner with whom to attempt the Face. Strickler hit it off well with this Austrian, Leo Schlömmer, whose Tirolese partner had been unable to get away from work, so they teamed up.

Schlömmer, a Styrian and close compatriot of mine, is full of healthy zeal and energy, necessary qualities in one whose main occupation is playing tag with the clouds. He is a staff sergeant-major of the Austrian Federal Army, and a flight instructor at the flying school at Aigen in the Ennstal. He teaches flying between high mountains, in narrow valleys hemmed in by mighty precipices, which he climbs when off duty. Leo is very practical and invariably takes the right means to a given end, as do all who live dangerously but love life itself.

Schlömmer and Strickler started their climb at first light on September 1, the morning on which the two Czechs were still sleeping on the "Brittle Ledge" and the Poles were making their early tea at their bivouac to the right of the "Flatiron." The Swiss pair, Inwyler and Grüter, who had spent the night about 100 feet lower down to the right, were early awakened by the morning cold, but were slow to get going. When at about 7 A.M. the Poles started on their climb to the "Flatiron" and onto the "Death Bivouac," they looked back and could hardly believe their eyes. Right down there, at the start of the Second Ice Field . . . two small dots . . . people . . . climbing at an incredible pace. Inwyler and Grüter saw them too and shook their heads in amazement. Then Inwyler laughed and said: "That can only be our friend Strickler, and the other one must be Schlömmer!"

Early in the afternoon the three parties met at the "Waterfall Chimney." It was icy and in bad condition. The Poles were halfway up, quietly and safely negotiating its difficulties. They let a rope down and safeguarded the Swiss up to them. As for the last pair, Strickler and Schlömmer, the strongest party, did anyone let them climb past, since they were clearly the quickest movers? Not a bit of it. Everyone laughed and passed the time of day, happy to be to-gether—Poles, Swiss, and Austrians alike. So the last party, too, ac-cepted the proffered aid of the dangling rope; and all six of them joined up on a single rope of men who did not speak the same mother tongue but understood the international language common to climbers, whose chief features are laughter and friendly greetings and mutual enjoyment.

To the left of the Ramp Ice Field they found a bivouac site for six—probably the very spot that has earned the rough name of "the comfortable overnight stop" on the Eiger Face, ever since the French spent the night there in 1952.

The next day was full of surprises. Strickler and Schlömmer took over the lead, but the rope remained a rope of six. Strickler lost a crampon, so Schlömmer had to do some step cutting on the "Spider." In spite of the delay, the party drew gradually nearer the Exit Cracks. The Poles and the Swiss were hit by stones, but there was always someone at hand to help, and the six men climbed as one party till they reached the top of the Cracks. There the single rope split up again into three separate pairs. At about 6 P.M. on September 2, Schlömmer and Strickler reached the summit, where two friends were waiting for them. Half an hour later, the Poles arrived. Grüter and Inwyler did not get there till 7:30, but the others had waited for them. Good companionship had greater appeal for them than a bed or a mattress in the Scheidegg camp. The eight men then climbed down into the darkness and bivouacked together. This climb was a triumph of harmony and fellow feeling; a climb to be remembered and retold again and again.

I hold this twentieth ascent—it need hardly be said that the six men agreed that it was a single common success and not three separate climbs by separate pairs—to be the highlight of the year 1961, even if there were other meritorious performances.

Between September 19 and 22, the two Bavarians Georg Huber[1] and Gerhard Mayer with the two Austrians Karl Frehsner and Helmut Wagner brought off the twenty-first ascent. It has been done much quicker and it has been done more slowly; but there was no reason for haste, as the weather remained fine throughout. Their three bivouacs were: above the Second Ice Field, below the ice bulge on the "Ramp," and on the rocks just above the "Spider."

The weather was, indeed, amazingly reliable that September, always set fair. The ice was comparatively hard, stones a great source of danger. Speed can often be a decisive factor. Schlömmer and Strickler, for instance, had moved at a wonderful pace before they caught up with the others at the "Ramp" and put considerations of friendship before those of records. But the tempo seen on September 23 and 24, when Hilti von Allmen and Ueli Hürlimann climbed the Face, was not mere pace, but a whirlwind speed such as no one had seen since Waschak and Forstenlechner's feat of eleven years before.

Hilti is not related to Kaspar, Fritz, and Albrecht, as witness the extra "l." He is a guide and a ski instructor and a very attractive young man, as Luis Trenker was to discover a year later, when he made him costar with Toni Sailer and Dietmar Schönherr in the Trenker-Eigerfilms productions. But in 1961 he was not yet an actor,

---

[1]"Schorch" Huber perished on Cho Oyu, during the Monsoon of 1964.—Author's note.

far less a "star," but simply an outstanding climber, guide, and ski instructor.

He and Ueli started up the wall late in the afternoon of September
23, and reached the "Swallow's Nest" very quickly. Granted the
"Difficult Crack" was already somewhat "prepared," and there was
a fixed rope at the "Hinterstoisser Traverse," which meant a great
saving of time. But on the 24th the pair made the pace right from the
moment of leaving their bivouac. In fourteen hours, practically non-
stop, they raced from it to the summit, arriving there at 8 P.M.

It was natural for the climbing world to talk about so fantastic a
time. The press took it up, too; the young guide became world-
famous and became known familiarly as just "Hilti." Naturally, too,
voices were raised in warning against a thirst for records. Chief
among them the voice of Arnold Glatthard, uttering dark prophecy
that the North Face would become a racetrack. Actually, there is no
danger of that; but that is no reason for making fun of Glatthard, as
so many Alpine chroniclers chose to do. If Glatthard has something
to say on the subject of the Eiger, he is entitled to do so; we older ones
will never forget that, and it is time the younger men learned it. I have
already told the story: how Arnold saw Toni Kurz die. Die, because
at that time there was far too little knowledge of mountain rescue
technique; because, too, the best Swiss guides were not equipped
with the aids that today's "Extreme" climbers have at their disposal.
It was a tragedy that Glatthard has never been able to forget; nor
should we forget the simple, sympathetic words he wrote in his letter to Gunther Langes in memory of those who had died on the
Face—way back in 1936!

"I saw them climb and I can do no other than honour them. My
poor friends, the Face was unkind to you . . . it was the saddest moment of my life."

He said that at a time when there was little good feeling towards
the German and Austrian climbers who kept on coming to attempt
the unclimbed Face. His words of human warmth stood out against

a chorus of derision, misunderstanding, and hostility. And if he now chose to raise his voice again, it was simply to remind us all to take nothing casually, lightheartedly, or for granted. For the Eiger is still as big and mighty as it ever was.

Three days after Hilti's climb two more Austrians started up the Face. They were two Tirolese, the experienced veteran Erich Streng, and a young partner, Robert Troier. No Tirolese party had made a successful attempt since Buhl and Jöchler, though a few years ago Dr. Heinrich Klier and Wastl Mariner came to Scheidegg intending to climb the Face. Finding the conditions unfavorable, the pair did a thing that is increasingly rare among Eiger aspirants: they did not wait, laying siege to the wall at its foot. They just went off on a climbing holiday in the lovely Bernese Oberland. There they did the classic climbs on great north faces, even discovering new, difficult, and interesting routes up mountains already entered in the pages of mountain history, climbed the Schreckhorn, the Finsteraarhorn, the Fiescherhörner and a round dozen other peaks, till their fortnight's leave ran out. All that in a fortnight; but at the end of it both of them looked happier, more relaxed. That was the gift they won from the joy of good, straightforward mountaineering. There was obviously no time left for the North Face of the Eiger.

The two Tirolese who were attempting the twenty-third ascent, however, had no intention of waiting. They knew that if now, at the end of September, the weather should break, it would not recover, but go from bad to worse. In spite of that, they started up the Face and bivouacked at the "Swallow's Nest." It snowed in the early morning, but they went on just the same, and spent the night on the "Ramp." Next morning the weather was even worse; nonetheless, they went on; not because they were featherbrained, but because they knew how to fight, just as Buhl and Jöchler, the five Frenchmen and the brothers Maag had known how to fight, nine years before them.

Again the mountain mustered all its hostile armory; the Face was as hideous as Arnold Glatthard remembered it. They had to bivouac a third time, this time in the Exit Cracks.

And about the hour when the first guests were coming down to breakfast at the Scheidegg hotels, Erich Streng and Robert Troier reached the summit, with four days of hard, admirable struggle behind them. And so closed the history of the year 1961 on the North Face.

In spite of Adi Mayr's tragic death it was a good year—a year of success founded on individual ability and dependable teammates. But 1962 was to show the Face in a new and sadly different light. Admittedly, there were successful ascents, and encounters with men who earned our unreserved respect and sympathy. There were, however, others who, weighed in the balance of fate, were found wanting, and yet returned safe from the wall. And then there were fatalities, shattering, unintelligible fatalities, leaving behind them many an unanswered question.

Nineteen sixty-two was to be no good year on the Eiger.

"I AM SORRY,

BRIAN . . ."

The Eiger year of 1962 was a mad year, unprecedented in its history. Never before had five men lost their lives in one summer. On the other side of the ledger, the entries show equally unprecedented figures: forty-four men climbed the Face and lived to tell the tale. Compared with 1936, the year of Toni Kurz's tragic death, when four men died but no successful ascent was made, one might be tempted to think things had improved over the years. That would be quite a false conclusion, for it must be remembered that in 1952, a year during which conditions were mostly very bad indeed, twenty climbers reached the summit without a single casualty.

Yes, this year of 1962 was an unusual year, a sad year, during which the Eiger ballyhoo reached an unprecedented pitch, sense and nonsense becoming inextricably interwoven. To the layman interested in mountaineering matters, as he read the countless reports, a new meaning to this business of climbing the Eiger's Face soon became regrettably apparent: cash and kudos.

Trenker was making a film on and about the Eiger Face, thus providing a magnet for camp followers, journalists, publicity hounds. Down at Alpiglen there were rows upon rows of tents, at times a veritable village of them. Pressmen moved back and forth between Allmatten and the Scheidegg, clustered around the telescope there, besieged climbers and film personnel, hurried back to the tents down below at Alpiglen. There was little need anymore to ask what this climbing business was all about.

The season had started quite normally, in the way mountaineers like things to go, without sensation and with some good straightforward performances. Even Trenker's cinema activities did not interfere with those of the climbers in any way. First-class climbers and guides, among them a crack team from Styria, led by Sepp Larch and Walter Almberger, worked alongside Trenker's veterans as guides, porters, extras, actors, and doubles, with Wolfgang Görter once again at the cameras. The idea was to take as many genuine shots as possible on "location." There was to be a climb of the Face for the film's special purposes. Toni Sailer, himself no climber, was training flat out to become one; he even managed, with the assistance of Larch and Almberger, to do the "Difficult Crack." The whole lower part of the wall had, of course, been "toned down" by now. There were ropes all over the place: fixed ropes for safety purposes, ropes for film work, old abandoned ropes, ropes from retreats, ropes from attempts. The whole Face was beginning to dry out, though that meant a greater risk from stones.

The favorite place for a first bivouac was by now the "Swallow's Nest," a name suddenly on everybody's lips, in every known language, suddenly elevated to the status of a household word, as though it were an eponym. Even I had forgotten that this bivouac site above the "Hinterstoisser Traverse" had not borne it since time immemorial.

This "Swallow's Nest" was occupied for the first time in 1962 on the afternoon of July 23, by four fine Swiss climbers, Jean Braun, André and Bernard Meyer, and Michel Zuckschwert. The party of four, destined to achieve the twenty-fourth ascent, moved so quickly that they spent the next night at the "Brittle Band." Meanwhile, on the afternoon of July 24, two Englishmen, Brian Nally and Barry Brewster, occupied the "Swallow's Nest." There had been no British ascent of the Face to date. Would this pair be the first to do it?

This summer, there were for the first time some English and Scottish tents at the foot of the North Face. The great Eiger precipice had never appealed to the traditionally conservative outlook of British mountaineers; in their view there is too much unpredictable risk attaching to it and much too much ballyhoo. There was hardly likely to be any great enthusiasm in the Alpine Club if one of its members climbed the Face.

Nally and Brewster, however, were not members of the A. C. Brian, hefty, endowed with the strength of a buffalo, was twenty-five years old; his broad face radiated good health. By and large, he is a fairly un-English type, unusually communicative. It was not long before his fellow climbers of all nations in the tent village of Alpiglen, as well as the journalists, ever greedy for snippets of news and exciting scoops, knew that he was mainly interested in only the biggest climbs of all. Yes, he had already done the North Face of the Matterhorn, the previous summer, with Tom Carruthers, a Scot; the North Face of the Lyskamm too, and the Matterhorn's Zmuttgrat. He had really fallen for the Matterhorn in a big way, had Nally; that was what he called a real mountain. Besides, hadn't it been an English mountain ever since Whymper's day? As a matter of fact, he had had a second go at its North Face—in winter, with "Schorch of Traunstein," Georg Huber.[1] They had been in trouble, but had managed to get clear somehow by way of the Shoulder, and he would be the first to admit that but for Huber he would not have come out of it alive.

So Brian laughed and talked, happy to have an audience, happy too that it believed in his superlative strength, for so did he. Not a very imaginative man, Brian; but not as down-to-earth and stolid as his rustic appearance might suggest, for he, too, had his dreams. And

[1] See n. 1, p. 290.—H. M.

it can be very dangerous to dream of the fame to be won among the high peaks.

So Brian was the man to please the pressmen. He talked and let himself be admired. His whole nature was as cheerful and gay as the name of his club—the Rockhopper Mountaineering Club in London.

Barry Brewster, his twenty-two-year-old companion, was the exact opposite. Tall and thin, with a narrow face full of character and intelligence. He was quiet, almost shy; his ankles and wrists were slight. A student this, a member of the University of North Wales Mountaineering Club, looking much like so many British Alpine climbers, Himalayan mountaineers, explorers, and adventurers—a type wasting little energy on external show but incredibly courageous and tough in moments of difficulty and danger.

The pair bivouacked at the "Swallow's Nest" on the night of July 24, and made fairly slow progress the following day. Barry, the gymnast on Lake District rock, was less at home on ice than Brian; and the house decorator from London, experienced on ice, knew his duty to his friend well enough. Relaxed and comfortable, he cut step after step up the Second Ice Field to provide an easy ladder for Barry.

At the end of the Second Ice Field, at the foot of the steep, brittle rocks that sweep up to the "Flatiron," Brewster took over the lead, moving upwards swiftly and safely. There seemed no doubt that the pair would reach the "Death Bivouac" before the day ended.

Suddenly the watchers at Scheidegg saw Brewster go hurtling down. With him went stones. Late in the afternoon, whole avalanches of stones are apt to come down from the summit precipices and the "Spider" below them. Obviously just such a stonefall had swept Barry Brewster from his holds.

The Times correspondent reported:

One of two British Alpinists attempting to climb the North Face of the Eiger was observed through a telescope tonight to have fallen about 300 ft. from the rock at the top of the second ice field. He is Mr. Barry Brewster of Crawley, who began the climb yesterday with Mr. Brian Nally of New Barnet. Mr. Nally was seen to hold his companion at rope length for some time and then go down to where he was lying in the snow apparently hurt . . .

The journalist had been quite right about what had happened, but wrong about the height of the fall. Nally and Brewster were climbing on a 100-foot rope and as a result of the accident Brewster fell the whole length of it. The pitons through which Brewster had threaded the rope had been jerked out by the violence of his fall; the only one to hold was the belaying peg above Nally's stance. Obviously this made it impossible for the latter to haul in any rope, for Brewster was lying head downward on the Second Ice Field at the end of his fall, at the full length of the rope. All Nally could do was to secure the rope and climb down to his injured friend, under continual menace of falling stones.

Owing to severe shock, exhaustion from his subsequent exertions, and his despair at the disaster, Nally was afterwards quite unable to give a clear picture of the situation. After his rescue, this cheerful talker could not tell his story without frequently contradicting himself. However, it would be unfair to level reproaches at the young man on that account alone. What the house decorator from the Rockhopper's Club said later is not of such importance; it is what he did at the time that matters. And what he did was done under the public's watchful eye.

Brian several times climbed up and down the 100 feet between the upper rim of the ice field and where Barry was hanging. He was clearly fetching provisions, clothing, and the like from his own belaying place to ease the plight of his seriously injured friend. Maybe he had already realised that there was no hope of saving him, but dared not admit it to himself. It seems highly probable that Brewster, during his fall, had shouted Brian's name aloud; it is equally probable that Brewster was unconscious for most of the time Nally was busying himself about him. There is no reason to doubt that during the few, short moments of his return to consciousness Brewster's only words were: "I am sorry, Brian, I am sorry."

You have to know British climbers really well to appreciate their almost inarticulate reticence even in the face of death. Brewster was actually apologising to Nally for the trouble he was causing him.

And this simple young giant whose zeal and passion for mountains somewhat outstripped his experience among them, just would not accept that the man he had always admired as his superior as a human being was about to die. So he simply ignored the stones that showered down on him, obviously finding it unbearable that stones should hit his unconscious helpless friend. Every watcher at the telescopes saw him standing astride Brewster as if to shield him from the stones with his own body, as he strove furiously to hack a bivouac niche out of the ice for his companion with desperate strokes of his axe. At Scheidegg the *Times* correspondent was reporting exactly that on the telephone.

Every mountaineer will know the fearful exertions required to hew a horizontal resting place out of a steep ice slope; a terrible call even on a climber unaffected by weariness and shock. For Nally must have been deadbeat by then. Toni Sailer, who watched it all through a telescope, told me afterwards: "Nally's movements as he hacked at the ice were painfully slow, as if his strength had run out." Nonetheless, Nally managed to hack a bivouac cave out of the ice and, with his last reserves, to drag Brewster up to it.

Obviously Nally had very little knowledge of modern rescue techniques, such as Prusik Knots, block and tackle, and the rest. This lack of knowledge he tried to offset by sheer strength and willpower. Every watcher at the telescopes can testify to that. A doctor among them thought from occasional movements of Brewster's that the injured man was partially paralysed. Spinal paralysis perhaps? At such a distance and such a height differential and through a telescope, even one with a magnification factor of ×72, such things are impossible to diagnose for certain.

Brewster could clearly be seen moving, so he had survived his fall of some 200 feet. He was still able to move next morning when Nally was again seen to climb down to him from his belay. It appeared he was taking him something to drink, tea or soup, which he had cooked on his stance at the dividing line between rock and ice. Then he worked for a long time at the ropes above the ice cave he had hollowed. It seemed as if he were driving in ice pitons and screws as extra belays for the injured man. But was Brewster still alive? Was he moving or wasn't he?

While everyone was watching him, they were also watching the rescue party that had emerged on the Face from the gallery exit at about 4 A.M. It was led by Karl Schlunegger, who had made the third ascent of the Face fifteen years earlier with his brother Hans, and consisted of six other guides from Wengen and Lauterbrunnen, including Hilti von Allmen, at that time starring in the Trenker film, and Sepp Larch, one of the best Austrian climbers of the day. They were in radio contact with the Scheidegg.

Fritz von Almen and his people were also watching a second English rope, consisting of Chris Bonington and Don Whillans, which had just started to climb from the "Swallow's Nest." Neither of them had an inkling of the disaster that had befallen their compatriots, nor of the drama up above, whose outcome nobody could foretell. Up there lay Brewster hanging from his ropes in the ice niche. At about 8 A.M. Nally was seen to climb away from him again, up to the rim of the ice field.

But why? Why not have awaited a rescue party? Later, he said he thought Barry was dead. "I think he died in my arms," he explained, "with the words, 'I am sorry, Brian.'" But what was he doing up there at the ice field's upper rim? Were stones still coming down, as they had done all night?

The watching crowds at Scheidegg noted that the rescue team was making quicker progress than the second English rope. Don and Chris were very experienced climbers, with successes to their credit on high and difficult peaks all over the world. Their climbing was completely unhurried; they used every available means to safeguard their progress.

And then, suddenly, at about 8:45, the crisp rat-tat-tat of falling stones gave way to a dull rushing and thudding on snow and rock. It is a sound which no one who has heard it can ever forget—the downward whirr and thud of a human body as it hurtles to destruction.

Barry Brewster had gone plummeting from the Face, 3,000 feet or more, hurtling out over the heads of the rescue party and striking the Face again close below its eight men. What was left of his body fell to the base structure. Sepp Larch, hardened in a thousand battles with the peaks, is as tough as they come; but hours later when he rejoined his film colleagues his face was still as white as death. Toni Sailer told me: "Sepp is the finest climber I have ever seen; but after Brewster's body flew over his head, he was unrecognisable. It took days before he recovered from the shock. I am certain he was not afraid; he was merely shattered because the man he and others had come to rescue was now dead, had simply fallen off."

How could that have happened? There are many who believe they saw Barry rise upright in his icy niche just before he fell to his death, as if doing something to his belaying ropes; and that he then fell clear, without uttering a sound, just as though he were not roped at all. Was Barry not dead after all, as Nally thought him to be? Could he, unaided, have struggled free of the chest harness, or whatever was securing him to the pitons, realising the helplessness of his plight? Did he undo the belay in a moment of mental disturbance, such as can attack any seriously injured man on a mountain? Or did yet another rock avalanche just sweep him off the Face, the pitons and screws torn from the rotten soggy ice at will by its fury? I personally believe that is what happened. Moreover, it fits in with Brian Nally's statements better than any other explanation.

I do not know Nally personally, but I cannot believe he is one of those men who rise to greater stature when left on their own. I believe it is his rampant spirit of defiance that cushions him from fear. He believed he had done his best for his partner—it is probable that he had. But to see one's more gifted partner go hurtling into the abyss is enough to throw a man's shocked and bewildered senses into a state of utter indecision. So, first he thought he would climb down, unbelayed, across the Second Ice Field under a heavy bombardment of stones; then he thought of turning back and climbing the rocks above—could he perhaps even succeed in climbing the Face solo? He stopped to think it out.

As he did so, far over, where the "Ice Hose" pours into the Second Ice Field, he caught sight of two climbers, who waved to him. He waved back but he didn't shout across to them; and the reason why he didn't shout was his ingrained, deep-rooted horror of making a laughingstock of himself—not so much in public, but in the intimate, purely local atmosphere of the Rockhoppers' Club. For there Nally's image was that of the big, strong climber of north faces. Unbearable to him the very thought that in those circles someone might even whisper: "Nally had to be salvaged from the Eiger Face, you know. . . ."

All the same, they went up and fetched him, for the rescue team had passed to Whillans and Bonington the grim news that Brewster had fallen and it was up to them to fetch Nally in. The two British climbers, well-qualified and safe aspirants for the first British ascent of the Face, did not hesitate to break off their attempt to go to the stranded man's rescue. Meanwhile, the rescue team fixed a rope at the "Hinterstoisser Traverse" to facilitate the British descent. Late that afternoon, the mortal remains of Brewster were brought down, after Frau von Almen had spotted a small tatter of a red anorak at the base of the mountain. . . .

The descent of the three Englishmen was no easy affair, for it was accomplished in a thunderstorm, flash following upon flash, rumble upon rumble, while the crack of falling stones vied with the crash of the thunderclaps. Don Whillans's and Chris Bonington's vast experience had been won in the Himalaya and Patagonia's stormswept ranges as well as in the Alps. Their nerve was quite strong enough to weather the tempest, and they reached the gallery exit safely with their castaway, to be met there by the other members of the British tent colony.

Small wonder that the journalists fell upon Brian Nally, the "Strong Man," who had been the sudden victim of a gamut of despair, grief, anxiety, defiance, hope, the very fear of death, and an utterly unpredictable return home in safety, but without his partner. And if, in spite of some measure of defence, I end by voicing the personal opinion that he was one of those who should not have braved the North Face, I do so simply to reinforce the warning note I have sounded throughout these pages, in the interest of other young men to come, that it is a place for only the very best, by training and by temperament, of those who do battle with the world's high mountains.

JULY 31: START
AND FINISH

Let us paradoxically start with the good finish. On July 31, in the morning, four climbers, two men and two women, returned to Scheidegg. They had come off the North Face after spending three cold nights on it; but there was no trace of struggle, weariness, or the ravages of cold on the faces of the men, nor of hardship, peril, or the notorious terrors of the North Face on those of the women. Their faces, indeed, were neither hardened nor aged, nor marked by the strain of sporting endeavour, but pretty, reserved, and feminine.

The two women were Loulou Boulaz and Yvette Attinger. Mme Boulaz was nearly fifty, which she does not attempt to deny, though her looks would easily allow her to. Her face shows none of the hard lines which usually mark so early on the faces of women who go in for the extreme types of sport. Serene, charming, uninhibited, one would call her, reading the mirror of her face; and one would be quite right. Loulou Boulaz is one of the most successful and famous women climbers of the day, but her ambition burns moderately. True, she had been a member of Claude Kogan's "All Women" expedition to Cho Oyu in 1959; not as a feminist or an exponent of a separate women's movement in mountaineering, but simply because it worked out that way. For Loulou is no "suffragette" type; she prefers to climb with men.

The same is true of Yvette. Her face is perhaps a little more sharply etched, but this is no legacy of tough unfeminine battles, though in the last few years she has reached world-class in the company of Michel Vaucher, whom she has since married.

He needs no recommendation. Every climber knows about the student from Geneva, the top-class climber who, among other things, was one of the party which in 1960 climbed 26,800-foot Dhaulagiri without oxygen and when only partly acclimatised to high altitudes. He looks like the ideal Nordic type, modified by his Gallic charm. Someone once claimed that Michel is the born child of nature. I don't agree; he is just a completely natural human being. Even his climbing is not based on drive and unremitting struggle; he just happens to be so good that he can afford to smile where other climbers are struggling. So he is able to withhold his last reserves for really serious situations and can deal successfully with the worst of them. I do not believe Michel had to call on his reserves of strength on that retreat from the Face; nor did Michel Darbellay, that brilliant young Martigny guide of whom more will be heard later on.

What happened during that first attempt by women climbers, which ended in a safe withdrawal? The Face did its dramatic best to stage a disaster, to the accompaniment of storm and the drumming rhythm of stones. There was no disaster, no high drama. For the two women were two genuinely good climbers; so good indeed that they freely admitted the superiority of the two Michels as the most natural thing in the world. And so they felt safe even in a blizzard; in spite of their own prowess and self-reliance their attitude was that of all good women partners on a climb: "How can anything happen to me, so long as Michel is here?"

The mixed foursome started up the lower rocks on the afternoon of July 28 and camped as low down as the classic bivouac cave between "Shattered Pillar" and "Difficult Crack." Next morning, the weather was uncertain, so they did not leave their little shelter till late. Onlookers at the telescopes, who did not know whom they were talking about but nonetheless offered criticism unasked, shook their heads knowingly: "Fancy starting so late from a bivouac so low down, and in bad weather, too!" But two hours later those same wiseacres were gaping in astonishment; for out of the mists came the Second Ice Field, and on it, unmistakably, were the four climbers.

Yet, in spite of their incredibly quick progress, the movements of the two separate ropes looked less like a race than a gentle stroll. Moreover, they were moving as if they had nothing to do with each other, Darbellay with Loulou and Vaucher with his Yvette. Worsening weather then closed down the curtains; torrents, stones, snowslides could be heard pouring down the Face. Was another tragedy brewing up there? The public, however, could not see the stage.

Behind the curtain things were going steadily ahead according to plan; up the "Flatiron," Third Ice Field, and "Ramp," by afternoon. It would be quite possible to get as far as the Ramp Ice Field, the "Brittle Ledge," the "Traverse of the Gods," or even higher. But that would need the hope of fine weather; suppose it got worse, suppose they were forced to retreat next day? In fact, the party bivouacked at the traditional place on the "Ramp" where, in spite of the cold, their relaxed and cheerful spirits kept depression at bay.

But on the morning of July 30, the weather had deteriorated still further; it was hardly possible to see a rope length ahead, where a wintry scene showed ghostly through the grey murk. The two women were prepared to climb on at once, up the "Waterfall Chimney," but the men did not agree; and their authoritative opinion prevailed. The retreat was on.

Many a withdrawal from such a height on the Face has led to destruction. This time, too, the descent, which—till Hias Rebitsch first laid that bogey—was regarded as a desperate fight for life, was not without somewhat dramatic moments; but nothing more than that—

fugitive haste never came into the question. The two ropes joined up into one, so that a slip on the part of one member would hardly be felt by the others; the danger to a rope of two is, of course, immeasurably greater. All the same, there was danger enough from slippery, iced-over rock, from fresh snow on the ice fields, from falls of stone and avalanching snow. However, the party's great technical mastery, individual and as a whole, avoided anything sensational; nor did they ever have to draw on their reserves.

On the lower part of the Face they had to climb down through veritable cataracts of water till they were soaked to the skin. Darkness fell and still they climbed on through the night, roping down the pitches, plagued by the sodden ropes. The two Michels looked after the two world-famous women climbers, as any male climber will look after a woman companion. At last they reached the bivouac cave, wet and weary and cold to the bone. Next morning, dry again and refreshed, they were back at the terrace in front of the Scheidegg hotels congratulated and admired by all, but seeking no notoriety for themselves.

They must all have slept well up in the cave, for they never heard a thing when early that morning two climbers came up from below and climbed past them on their way to the "Difficult Crack."

That brings us to the story of the good beginning, whose protagonists were two Viennese climbers, Helmuth Drachsler and Walter Gstrein. The names meant nothing to the visitors and reporters at the Scheidegg, nor did the film company take any notice of them, though Walter Almberger and the other Austrians naturally knew enough about their two quiet compatriots not to have any anxiety about them. Walter Gstrein is a modest, reserved man with a face that might almost be described as gloomy; but when he smiles there are dimples in his cheeks—a puzzling contradiction this, but typical of a certain reserved type of mountaineer, as purposeful as it is companionable. Gstrein had already taken part in expeditions abroad, particularly in the Caucasus; he had also done numerous difficult climbs all over the

Alpine chain. Drachsler, however, was hardly his inferior, though the critics, sycophants, and faultfinders were aware of none of these things. Who could these two strangers be, climbing while those two famous ladies and the two even more famous Michels were down here?

They even spared an occasional glance up at them and remarked that they weren't climbing exactly quickly, but then things must be fairly uncomfortable on the Face just now, with water all over the place. But surely they ought not to be taking so long on the easy ground between the "Difficult Crack" and the "Hinterstoisser," using such excessive caution? The two Viennese had, of course, no means of explaining to the public that there was ice on the rocks.

After the First Ice Field they did something unusual. Instead of climbing up towards the "Ice Hose," they moved up towards the rock cliff between the First and Second Ice Field, climbed by Mehringer and Sedlmayer in 1935 on their first fatal attempt. Steep as these rocks are, outward sloping, slippery, brittle, Gstrein and Drachsler hardly used a single piton, as they climbed carefully but with grim concentration upwards. By late afternoon they had reached the "Death Bivouac," and there they called a halt. There seemed to be a slight improvement in the weather. They would need it.

On the morning of August 1 Gstrein and Drachsler were seen preparing to move on. But interest was now focused on something quite different, namely a solo climber said to have been on the Face since yesterday. They had even sited film cameras with telephoto lenses on the shoulder of the Northwest Ridge to await this lone climber on the Face. But he didn't appear. Why hadn't he appeared? Everybody had forgotten the two Viennese while they chewed on that new riddle.

What Gstrein and Drachsler were planning was nothing more or less than a "Direct" climb of the Face, following the line first selected by Sedlmayer and Mehringer, and since attempted by various parties: straight up from the "Death Bivouac" to the "Spider." The day of the "Superdirettissima" had not yet arrived. Men were still thinking on great harmonious lines, proper to mountains and mountaineers alike. The outlook of the pioneers was still in command.

The pair pushed their attempt on the "Direct" farther than anyone before them, till they were little more than a rope's length short of the "Spider's" lower rim; but that short distance beat them, for the rocks were entirely overlaid with ice. It was now past noon and the bombardment of stones was growing from minute to minute. It was a hard decision for them; there was nothing for it but to turn back.

Soon after 3 P.M. they were back at the "Flatiron," tired, depressed, cold through and through, but not defeated; simply the richer by yet another experience. Cautiously they felt their way down across the Third Ice Field, diagonally to the "Ramp"; and there, at the usual bivouac place below the "Silver Trench," they prepared to settle down for the night. It had been a hard and perilous day, but a good one for all that, for they had both given of their best.

On August 2, they climbed onto the "Waterfall Chimney" at a slow pace, dictated by the state of the Face. So icy was the overhang pitch that they were forced to use the difficult variant made by Terray on the second ascent ever. "Brittle Ledge," "Brittle Crack," and the "Traverse of the Gods," all were in an equally bad state. The "Spider" itself was gray, nay black with stone falls that had carved their scores into its ice. No chance of climbing the "Spider" today.

So Gstrein and Drachsler followed the variant opened by the Czechs[1] by climbing its rocky left-hand edge, progressing steadily rope length by rope length. At its top they traversed to the right again and up towards the Exit Cracks, on and on, though darkness had fallen and they had lost their way once and had to rope down some way before climbing again. At last they found a tiny platform on which to bivouac, secured by a couple of pitons through the long hours of a last night that still barred the gateway to freedom.

---

[1] See p. 285.—H. M.

Not only did it bar their escape, it positively barricaded it. The wind blew, it snowed, it froze, as the weather broke completely. In spite of frost and snow a thunderstorm broke on the Eiger, that magnet for storms, continually discharging its flashes and its crashes simultaneously. Many of the flashes ran down the runnels of snow, ice, and cascading water, their blast striking the ironmongery, the drenched clothing, the bodies of the climbers so heavily that the two men were shaken time and again; but they fought off all the perils besetting them, mastering a desperate situation by an effort of untamable willpower.

Their courage and toughness had to endure through the whole of the next day, too, for the icy conditions of the Exit Cracks were grim indeed and the tempest never let up, so that the bitter cold penetrated every protective covering. And still, inch by inch, the gallant pair fought their way up the last 1,000 feet of the Face and reached the summit at about 5 P.M. Then they climbed down through the night to rejoin other human beings, on August 3. This twenty-fifth ascent, which had started on July 31—the day of the good beginning—had been a tremendous performance.

But July 31 was also the day of the bad ending—an ending without a return; for on that same day Adolf Derungs fell to his death. It was the second attempt at a solo climb; like its predecessor it ended fatally.

Adolf Derungs, the stonemason from the Grisons, was no stranger. We knew him as the mason who was so enslaved by the mountains and mountaineering that he had passed the guides' examination; as the man who, with Lukas Albrecht, had achieved perhaps the oddest ascent—the sixteenth—the one in a winter overcoat. What was it that compelled him to try the Face again, and alone? We would have to solve a veritable labyrinth of riddles and questions, the answers to which could range from a pure ambition to succeed, by way of a longing to improve his standard of living, to the very deepest needs of a human soul. The only man who could answer those questions precisely and conclusively is dead. Research, deep, laborious research could possibly build up a theoretic structure; it could equally possibly lead to a completely erroneous conclusion.

There were the usual rumours, opinions, and pronunciamentos, of course. Some clues which could have been right, or utterly misleading. There was endless chatter beforehand, still more afterwards. Everybody knew something, but nobody really knew anything.

It was suggested by some that Derungs only set out to prove that the Face could quite well be climbed solo and that it was not the killer it was reputed to be; and that he, Derungs, was the man to prove it. Maybe he said something of the kind, but I am afraid he did not do so in one of his most sensible moments; for there is every evidence that he was a sensible man.

Wolfgang Görter went up to the start of the climb with him at midday on July 31 and is said to have done his best to dissuade him from his attempt; but who can divert anyone from something he has made up his mind to do?

It is not even clear whether Derungs properly belonged to the Trenker film outfit, even temporarily, as a porter, guide, camera assistant, or extra; indeed, the jobs involved in this mountain film were not so clearly defined. Some said he was, others denied it. Or was Derungs perhaps trying to attract Trenker's attention, so as to get a job with him? The risk would seem excessive, if it was only a question of employment as an extra or a porter. Could Derungs have expected anything better?

How can we know what was in his mind?

Could he have thought of becoming world-famous as a guide and so attracting whole hordes of visitors and climbers in the future? Hardly, I think; for as a clear thinker he must have known that risky stunts are little likely to influence tourists to engage one as a guide. In that context Dr. Ugo Conte di Vallepiana, the president of the Club Alpino Academico, wrote to Kurt Maix to the effect that Walter Bonatti, the most famous Italian guide of his day, was getting fewer clients than he did before he became so well known for his exploits.

There is no point in speculating further why Derungs risked the solo climb of the Eiger's North Face. The few facts are more important. Derungs intended to climb to the "Swallow's Nest" on that day, July 31; on August 1 he would continue, if possible straight through to the summit in a single day. It is a fact that early on August 1 camera teams were waiting on the shoulder of the Northwest Ridge to film the solo climber on the Face. Such shots would certainly have been highly welcome, all the more so because the film schedule postulated shots of a solo climber. They waited in vain, for Derungs never came into their viewfinders. As shown by the spot where his body was found, he fell off before reaching the "Hinterstoisser Traverse."

I think he just slipped on the easy but icy rocks thereabouts, and so fell to his death. It has happened before, a hundred times, in Alpine history. Derungs was, in his way, a remarkable type—from certain aspects, indeed, an example to this all-too-highly-organised world.

THE MASS

ASSAULT

The Face gave the world little time to recover from the shock of Derungs' tragic death; that is, allowing that it needs time for such a recovery.

On August 11, just a week after they found the body of the ill-starred climber from the Grisons, six Italians started up the Face. They were to achieve the twenty-seventh ascent and the first Italian success. I have already described their climb[1] and recorded that the Italian "sixsome"—originally two separate ropes of three—was overtaken at the Second Ice Field by Almberger's party, on their way to the twenty-sixth successful climb.

Almberger and his friends Adi Weissensteiner, Klaus Hoi, and Hugo Stelzig, all from Styria, exhibited a complete mastery in the manner of their ascent; they also proved that overtaking is possible anywhere on this great face, even if you have to pass a rope of six. Almberger, who complies with the English description of "a good sport," had two reasons for his climb. First, he wanted to get to know the Wall in summer conditions (everyone knows he took part in the

[1]See p. 269.—H. M.

first winter ascent) and at the same time to lead the climb; secondly, because "live" shots of climbers on the Face were still urgently wanted for the Eiger film; and Walter belonged to the Trenker film outfit.

Naturally, he climbed the Face of his own free will.[1] To ensure safety, he took his dependable, long-standing friends from Styria with him. Telephotos of the Second Ice Field with climbers at work on it came to nothing; for what was wanted for the film was a sequence of a rope or a single climber on an ice slope, not the image of a playground for rock face exponents which the Second Ice Field presented on that day of August 13, 1962. For there were ten men on it at the same time—above each other, below each other, next to each other!

Almberger, a miner from Eisenerg, and at the same time a great climber and a mountain guide, once again showed himself to be in the very top class of mountaineers. In spite of two uncomfortable bivouacs, at the "Flatiron" and at the end of the "Traverse of the Gods," he brought his party safely to the summit.

One might have thought that ten people on the Face at the same time was something out of the ordinary. Not a bit of it, in this hectic summer of 1962! Between the 19th and the 23rd there were *sixteen* up there on a single day: Swiss, Austrians, Germans, Spaniards, and the first American ever, John Harlin. True, on the 22nd and 23rd, only ten of them got to the top; but there were no accidents. It was proved once again that good climbers can retreat from anywhere on the Face. Six of them did it.

The others gave an example of outstanding good companionship. Though the three ropes of Felix Kühn and Dieter Wörndl (Austria), Konrad Kirch and John Harlin (Germany and U.S.A.), and the four Swiss, Franz and Josef Jauch, Franz Gnos, and Josef Zurfluh, reached the summit separately and at different times, they waited for each

---

[1] He is the only man to have climbed it twice.— H. M.

other all the way up. So their ascent counts as a single twenty-eighth climb of the Face.

The twenty-ninth followed next day, and was accomplished by two careful, competent Austrians, Hans Hauer and Nikolaus Rafanowitsch. If their experience in the Western Alps was somewhat slender and they lacked a little in condition for want of training, that makes their success, entirely unaided as it was and in bad conditions, all the more noteworthy. So we should not grudge them the small celebration laid on by their hometown of Gmunden and its inhabitants after their safe return.

The protagonists of ascent number thirty could not complain of lack of training, for one could hardly do it in shorter time. Only Waschak and Forstenlechner had ever been quicker, twelve years ago; Hilti von Allmen less speedy, last year. The motto of the rope on August 29 and 30 was evidently: "What Hilti can do, so can Paul." For it was led by Paul Etter, who had been Hilti's partner in the winter ascent of the Matterhorn North Face. On the Eiger they were not together, but the new pair, Paul Etter and Martin Epp, both Swiss guides, raced up the Face, too. Starting at first light, they bivouacked at the "Traverse of the Gods"; by noon next day they were on the summit.

How quickly times change! Only yesterday it was the Swiss guides who were furious with everyone who came, over and over again, to attempt the Face, until at long last it was climbed. Today, the Swiss climbers have not only caught up with the "Extremists" of other countries, but the younger generation of Swiss guides is everywhere setting record times. Not achieving them by courting risks, either, but climbing with the utmost skill and safety.

We almost seemed to have established that the Eiger Face is a safe adventure, provided it is done by experts, observing every measure of skill and prudence. We were all bemused by the style and speed of these Swiss speed merchants. Yes, I was, too. But I have skipped a bitter day—a sad day for all climbers of the younger generation, an unforgettably sad day for Viennese climbers. For on August 27 Diether Marchart fell from the Face and was killed. He was the third to attempt the Face solo, the third to perish. On the traverse between the First and Second Ice Fields he slipped and fell, almost carrying away with him a rope of Munich climbers he had overtaken a short time before. He had refused their invitation to tie onto their rope, saying with a friendly smile: "Later perhaps, thank you, when it gets harder." The men from Munich had asked him who he was and where he came from. Again he had smiled as he replied: "I come from Vienna." Just that, but not his name, so that they should not know that he was the man who had climbed the North Face of the Matterhorn alone, who had climbed the South Wall of the Dachstein in winter, who had been one of the first party to climb Distaghil Sar, the highest seven-thousand-meter peak to have been climbed till then, who was, in fact, one of Austria's most famous climbers, though he was only twenty-two.

Nor had Diether entered his name in the Scheidegg hotel register, or everyone would have guessed at once that he had come to climb the Face solo. He wanted no publicity; for he was one of those who generate their strength alone and from their innermost selves, who have to come to terms with themselves before taking a decision. Once they have taken it, they want no words of praise or funeral sermons to embellish it.

Marchart entered himself in the book as "Georg Winkler," which shows what a romantic youngster he still was at heart. For Georg Winkler was the prototype of the solo climber in the classical era of mountaineering, who not only made the first ascent of the sheer Vajollet Tower in the Rosengarten Group of the Dolomites alone, but was swallowed up by an avalanche when climbing the West Face of the Zermatt Weisshorn solo, in 1889, aged nineteen!

Why did Diether Marchart identify himself with this Winkler? Had he a presentiment of his own death, climbing alone? I do not believe it; he was far too self-reliant, too confident in his own great ability as a climber. His kind of lonely pride asked no applause; it is not vanity, which first recognises one's own work when others applaud it.

Kurt Maix, in his memoir, wrote of Diether Marchart:

> He did not climb for sensation's sake. On the contrary, the sensations he caused were to him an uncomfortable by-product of his climbing. This young student, with charming boyish face, with the willpower and judgement of a grown man, with the sensitive nature of an artist, was the true picture of a "gentleman." When Diether had climbed the Matterhorn's North Face solo, three years before, at the age of nineteen, he had at first said nothing about it to anyone. He was afraid that the other members of his club would consider the risk he had taken upon himself harebrained foolishness. But he was not in the least harebrained. His artistic mind was able to foresee all the dangers he would have to live through with the eye of imagination; nor did that gift weaken his resolve, it simply sharpened his presence of mind.

Courage and presence of mind are of no avail to a falling body. His was so battered that it was impossible to identify it till they recognised him by the crippled fingers of his right hand—the result of frostbite incurred on Distaghil Sar. They buried it at Grindelwald.

What a harsh interruption in the list of successful climbs! There was more to come. During the thirty-first ascent, the first to go to a British rope, the climbers' flag was at half-mast once again. For at the same time as our old friend Chris Bonington, with Ian Clough taking Don Whillans's place as his partner, was successfully climbing the Face, a mixed Austro-British party was also on it. They were Egon Moderegger from Hallein and Tom Aston Carruthers of Glasgow. Carruthers had already partnered Brian Nally on the North Face of the Matterhorn; Moderegger was known to have done some notable climbs in the Eastern Alps and had been a member in 1960 of an expedition to the Caucasus. He was a nice young man, but it was doubtful whether he was fit for the North Face of the Eiger. Moreover he knew no English, Carruthers no German; so the requirements for a harmonious partnership were sadly lacking.

Bonington and Clough were very dubious about it, and made it quite clear from the outset to Carruthers that they could take no responsibility for him and his newfound companion. Tom and Egon could climb along behind them if they could maintain the pace; if not, they would have to come along at a slower gait, in keeping with their capabilities.

Tom and Egon found themselves unable to keep up the pace, and—as dictated by their capabilities—fell behind. The distance between the two parties increased on the Second Ice Field, and the mists closed in, not to lift again till Bonington and Clough were on the rocks close to the crest of the "Flatiron." Then they saw the other two almost at the same spot where they had left them, still on the Second Ice Field. There was no use in waiting or even shouting down; it would be impossible to establish intelligible communication. In any case, Tom and Egon would probably turn back very soon.

Bonington and Clough, moving at almost racing speed, reached the "Traverse of the Gods" on the afternoon of that August 30, and there they spent the night. There were other ropes on that part of the Face during those days; they were Werner Hausheer and Paul Jenny, making the thirty-second ascent, while Robert Bögli and Willy Mottet were making sure of the thirty-third. Not one of those four Swiss, nor anyone else, saw a sign of Carruthers and Moderegger. They must have fallen off on August 30. Their broken remains were found close to the "Shattered Pillar." Nobody knows how or why they came to grief.

So 1962 proved a hideous year, even though the tally of successful ascents rose to thirty-seven; but those successes are overshadowed by the disasters.

The members of the parties that notched up ascents thirty-four, thirty-five, and thirty-seven were, by nationality, Swiss, Austrians, and German. And party number thirty-six, when on the Second Ice Field, discovered the desiccated body of Karl Mehringer—just twenty-seven years after he died.

Nineteen sixty-two was a year of great achievement, of much gossip and of many horrors. I, for one, am glad to turn my back on it.

THE YEAR OF
CHIVALRY

One should exercise the greatest caution in the use of flamboyant titles and headings, but I can think of no more fitting word to describe 1963 on the Eiger. Chivalry for me has no connotation of clashing swords and opponents slain; my interpretation rests on manly deeds, courage, reliability, and humanity.

The very first ascent of the year, the thirty-eighth successful climb on the list, awoke splendid memories. One of the Swiss pair involved was called Erich Friedli, a name resounding on the North Face for magnificent rescue work. For one Erich Friedli was in charge of the Alpine rescue center at Thun in 1957. It was that Erich Friedli who volunteered to be let down the Face on a steel cable, to establish the whereabouts of Corti, sole survivor of a tragedy far below—a reconnaissance outstanding as a daring venture in the service of humanity.

The Erich Friedli of the thirty-eighth ascent was his son. He and his partner Arnold Heinen started up the Face before dawn on July 30, made swift progress in the manner of the modern school of Swiss guides, and reached the Third Ice Field, just as the falling stones reached the height of their fury. Normally, there would have been a choice between two courses: to wait, or to accept the great risk of being swept away by the showering rocks. They chose a third. Avoiding the Third Ice Field entirely they traversed on the rocks above it, straight to the "Ramp."

The new route was safe from falling stones, but it calls for the devil's own skill in rock climbing. Then on, over the difficulties of the "Ramp," the "Brittle Ledge," the "Gods' Traverse," at a pace that enabled them to overtake the thirty-ninth and fortieth successful ropes on that high sector of the Face—two Austrians, Max Friedwanger and Friedl Schicker, and the Anglo-Rhodesian pair, Dougal Haston and Robert Baillie. They had been on the Face since early on July 29; Friedli and Heinen, starting on the 30th, got as far as the Exit Cracks before bivouacking. By noon next day they were on the summit, which the other two parties, both exceedingly competent ones, reached during the evening. All three ropes had entered excellent credits for European climbing skill in the Eiger diary.

It was, however, on August 2 and 3 that the first great triumph of a solitary climber on the North Face was achieved. Its greatness lay in its exposure of the myth which had lain upon the Eiger like a curse—the myth that on the Eiger Face it was the solitude that killed all comers. For all the solo climbers who perished there had been brave, highly qualified mountaineers. Even Walter Bonatti, who had challenged the curse with all his skill and willpower, had felt its menace and turned back.

But on August 1, 1963, Michel Darbellay, the Swiss guide from Orsières near Martigny, came back to the Face, unaccompanied by a press agent. He kept his plans strictly to himself, confiding them only to Fritz von Almen and his wife, and in doing so burdened the two presiding spirits of the Scheidegg hotels, those unfailing friends of the climbing fraternity, with serious anxieties. Frau von Almen was pale with misgivings as she prepared the breakfast thermos for yet another aspirant to a solo climb. She thought of Adi Mayr and the others whose remains had been found on the rocks at the base of the wall. And this Michel seemed to her the quietest, the most serious, and the most reserved of them all—a man inspiring the greatest confidence in his ability to succeed, a man whom all would mourn the rest of their lives, should he fail.

Michel left the Scheidegg soon after midnight and started up the Face about 2 A.M. by the pale light of the moon. He climbed so quickly that it was still dark when he reached the foot of the "Difficult Crack," so that he had to wait. At first light he pressed on, moving at tremendous speed. True enough he had much assistance from the many ropes hanging at various points; but all they were doing was to save one of the best climbers of our day precious time which he would dearly need higher up on the most difficult part of the Face.

Fritz von Almen told me that he looked through the telescope very early and failed to see any sign of Michel. When he looked again at about 10:30 he saw a man on the traverse between the two ice fields, but it was not Michel; it must be one of two Germans who had spent the night in the bivouac cave. That was it; for the second soon followed. Darbellay must already be on the Second Ice Field. He looked, but there was nobody there, nor on the rocks above it.

He searched the "Flatiron," in vain. Could the curse of the solo climber have lain on even Michel Darbellay? He searched the Third Ice Field; not a sign of anyone. Then the "Ramp"—yes, somebody was on the "Ramp." And it was Michel! Michel going like a bullet, safe and sure, belaying himself at every difficult place, even though it meant climbing the pitches up, down, and up again.

The two Germans turned back, Michel went on. Not at the same virtuoso pace, now; sometimes feeling his way slowly, never taking the slightest risk, but never hesitating, always the complete master. By early afternoon he had reached the "Traverse of the Gods," then in less than half an hour dealt with the "Spider's" ice, heading for the Exit Cracks. And there he decided to bivouac, though it meant halting his climb in the full light of day.

At 9 P.M. von Almen had another fright. He signalled up to the

Face with a torch, but there was no reply. Derungs, too, was to have answered torch signals, that time; he had not replied, because he was no longer there to reply. Suppose?

But this time it was nothing so sensational. It was merely that Darbellay's watch—evidently unable to keep pace with its owner— was slow. It was 9:30 when he started signalling. He had just the one night more to get through.

Darbellay has said little about what he went through during that night. He battled it out with himself, and endured the loneliness just as he endured the cold and his own weariness. He is not an insensitive, unimaginative man; you have to be sensitive if you are to react instantly in face of danger. But he must have been tough to be able to survive a long, long night without proper bivouac equipment; his character must be strong indeed for him to have borne the utter loneliness and kept fear at bay. I have spoken of the qualities that for me are the marks of chivalry. He must possess them all.

A first solo climb of the Eiger's North Face? The applause of countless thousands? A record in the sporting annals? These are things that fade and pale. The knowledge that he stood the grim test of those icy, endless hours of darkness will endure for him while life endures.

The final success of that summer of 1963, the forty-second, fell to two Germans, Helmut Salger and Horst Wels, on August 2 and 3. They were a splendid pair and their climb, under the menace of falling stones and bad weather, was a fine, courageous performance. They reached the summit at about 7:30 on the 3rd and then did an unusual thing; they climbed down the upper part of the Mittellegi Ridge, in the dark, to the Mittellegi Hut.

The year's tragedy came from a country still held, consciously or unconsciously, to provide the classical pattern of chivalry—Spain. Albert Rabada and Ernesto Navarra started up the Face early on the morning of August 11. They were accompanied at the beginning by a Japanese party, which, however, turned back when the weather threatened to break. They brought back with them the last picture taken of their Spanish friends.

The Spaniards went on, to a first bivouac. The weather grew worse. Still they went on, struggling obstinately upwards, till a second day had gone by. The weather improved only for short moments, parting the curtains of cloud and the veils of blown snow; then everything disappeared permanently from sight. They must have bivouacked a third and a fourth time, this last on the "Traverse of the Gods." On the 15th they were seen on the "Spider." It took a long time to decide whether they were still moving. At first it seemed so—then no, then yes again. One of them was moving very slowly up to the upper rim of the "Spider."

Yet another night. Next morning the two dots were still visible there, one on the rocks at the "Spider's" upper rim, the other about 100 feet lower down, on the snowfield, already half covered by drifting snow. Rescue efforts were put into motion. Plucky friends hurried to the summit, offering to rope down the Face. Helicopters flew so close to the "Spider" and the two men that they risked crashing. In spite of the Devil's din which that awakened in the crannies of the Face, the two men did not move. They were dead.

They had simply passed out. Probably they had really "died" two or three days earlier, and only the compulsion of an inner law had kept them alive—alive and still climbing. Incredibly slowly, utterly exhausted, half frozen, and starving, they had "lived" and climbed on. They had neither admitted defeat nor uttered a cry for help.

"I love the Spaniard and his Pride," runs the poem. That may have been all right in days of mortal combat, man against man. But in the battle against mountains a man has to equate his strength and spirit to a battleground demanding of human beings the greatest endurance and experience. Pride, courage, and dedication to the task are fine things. Everyone conceded and admired those qualities in the Spanish pair. And yet . . .

The true tragedy did not lie in the fact that these two men died of exhaustion or froze to death. The tragic part was that they were both endowed with too much noble courage and spirit, stemming straight from the great days of Spanish chivalry; alas, they matched it with too little and poor equipment, totally inadequate protection against cold, and too little experience among great peaks. In the realm of mountains it is fatal to lose one's sense of the realities. And yet, the regard in which everyone must hold these two men touches us like a gentle breeze blowing from forgotten days across the centuries.

And the closing act of this year of chivalry? No tragedy of knightly daring this, but a carefully planned, clear-eyed, spirited act of chivalry, splendidly carried to its conclusion: nothing less than the complete descent of the Face, during the last days of December. It was accomplished by three of Switzerland's climbing elite, Paul Etter, leading Ueli Gantbein and Sepp Henkel, both of them only just twenty years old. And it was carried out not as a triumph of sporting *bravura*, but as a practical gesture of love for one's neighbour and an act of piety.

They had bivouacked on the Eiger's summit during the night of December 27, in doubtful weather. On the morning of the 28th the trio heard the weather report on their little transistor set. It could not have been better nor more full of promise. Pressure had risen sharply and was still rising: the weather would be fair today, tomorrow, and for some time. All doubts were dissipated.

They descended the topmost sector of the Mittellegi Ridge and then struck down the Summit Ice Field, each carrying a rucksack weighing 50 to 60 pounds; with them they took three 300-foot ropes. Roping down the Exit Cracks, they were at the "Spider" by 2 A.M. There, while Ueli set to work preparing a bivouac, Sepp selected a good stance from which to belay Etter as he climbed down to the dead Spaniards.

Later, he was to write:

It was the most heartbreaking work I ever had to do. The little Spaniard, Navarro, stood leaning backwards in his red down jacket, at the right-hand top edge of the "Spider." He was well secured to a rock piton, still wore his crampons, from which the front points were missing, and his ice hammer was hanging from his wrist. Some hundred feet below him his big, hefty partner Rabada lay across the ice of the "Spider," almost entirely encased in it, and wearing a blue fleece jacket. There he lay, just as if he were asleep. One arm held his ice axe pressed against his breast; he had taken off his crampons, also lacking in front points, and laid them on the ice above him. We could see plainly that neither of them had been injured by falling; they had just died of sheer exhaustion. Rabada was tied to his partner by a taut and well-secured rope, which ran through two ice pitons between them.

It took Paul Etter three hours to hack Navarro out of his armour of ice and lower him down to the place where his onetime partner lay.

The bivouac place where the three men who had lowered themselves down the Face in the bleak grip of winter, on their self-imposed mission in the service of humanity, proved bearable. December 29, the next day, was to exact even harder, more exhausting and depressing work, when it came to freeing Rabada's gigantic body from the ice that encased it. It was nearly midday before they could lash the dead men together and lower them to the bottom of the "Spider" on the ropes.

Hereabouts the rock was almost clear of snow and it was easy to fix pitons. Thus secured, Etter roped down first to a band of ice. There, he hammered in all the necessary rock and ice pitons, before his friends lowered the bodies; nor did Ueli and Sepp come swinging down into the depths till he had firmly anchored the dead men. Another 300 feet down the Face, at the "Flatiron," the three Swiss prepared their second bivouac site; a little way to one side, they hammered in safe rock pitons to which they secured their tragic load carefully with line.

That night, too, was not unbearable; they even managed to sleep a little. When they woke, the bodies were gone. Gone were the pitons, ripped from the rock as if the splitting frost had shattered the rock that had held them. Or maybe a cornice had broken away high above and a whole ice terrace come crashing down to sweep them into the depths.

The three men continued to descend by the usual route. Above the "Hinterstoisser Traverse" they were forced to bivouac a third time. Finally, on the 31st, the Face granted these men, who to the best of their ability and with so much devotion had rendered a last service to their Spanish comrades, a safe escape to freedom. As Paul Etter wrote: "It was the last day of the year, and we felt relieved. We were glad to have made the first descent of the Face, but much more so to have spared the rescue group a commitment which they had for some time been regarding with troubled eyes."

That job of roping down below the "Spider," with its constant threat of avalanches, was more perilous and exacting work than one has the right to expect of any rescue or search party. The three friends, however, had done it of their own free will; and what they achieved was yet another act of chivalry in the context of the mountain code.

MAN, THE

DECIDING FACTOR

Nineteen sixty-three closed on a note of harmony and dignity, if a sad one.

Less than a fortnight later, the blasts of a new Eiger year were already sounding: "Hail to the New Era, hail to the younger generation, hail to the Direttissima!" A new era? That remains to be seen. The younger generation? Paul Etter is still young; his partners just twenty — much younger than this stridently heralded Youth of today. And the Direttissima?

Let us first take a close look at the vertical line up the Face. The route chosen by Sedlmayer and Mehringer all those years ago was an absolute "Direct," which cannot be improved on; they followed it to a little beyond the "Death Bivouac." Gstrein and Drachsler pushed it forward to within a good rope length of the "Spider." If one could reach the "Spider" by the route Etter and his friends took when roping down in their attempt to bring in the two dead Spaniards, that, too, would be a continuation of the direct vertical line; but from the "Spider" onward a diagonal ascent to the left of the Exit Cracks towards the Summit Ice Field and the upper Mittellegi Ridge would not. A true "Direct" would have to continue to the right up the rocky wall of the summit structure and there find a new way out.

The search for such a route, its exploitation, and its eventual mastery would beyond all doubt be a difficult and very dangerous affair. It would certainly not be achieved without the aid of extreme technical devices—probably expansion pitons would have to be used, and hammocks for bivouacs in the cliffs. So even the ordinary Direct Route would demand "the lot." Too much, it seems to me.

But what about this "Direttissima" that, to be sure, does not yet exist, but which they are already planning? Looking through a telescope, one can recognise it, if one's eyes and imagination are good enough; but the light has to be the kind that accentuates wrinkles, embryo ramps, and cracks in the utter smoothness of the wall. Snow, too, which occasionally manages to lie here and there, can help to conjure up the necessary illusion of plasticity. But that cannot have been the reason why Peter Siegert's party set out to do the "Direttissima" in midwinter. They simply wanted to beat the opposition.

Let us return for a moment to this imaginary "Direttissima." Nobody can rob Sedlmayer and Mehringer of its lower part, as far as the Second Ice Field. But what happens higher up? If we follow the upper rim of the ice field, westward to the right, instead of towards the "Flatiron's" rocks, we come to a formation that could, I suppose, be described as a second "Flatiron." Slanting to the left from it there is a crease in the smoothness of the Face which might be designated as a second "Ramp." Higher up still, there is a snowfield embedded in the steep or even vertical rock, which could possibly qualify as a second "Spider"; but above it I can see nothing whatever to earn the title of a second Exit Crack.

Of course, the cliffs up there could be "prepared" to make them climbable; but there could be no question of spending seventeen days on the job; for the Eiger has never yet granted anyone so long a lease of life. It might be possible to climb out to the uppermost part of the Northwest Ridge by a buttress leading to it; but that again would be a crippling defect in the route, for a true "Direttissima" would have to finish straight up the icy face and the great cornice that crowns it.

Would have to, did I say? It *will*, we may be quite certain of that. Even if it were right to try, nothing can stop it now. But the young climbers must heed the warning that the important thing is not "what" they may achieve, but "how" they achieve it.

I am referring here not to the resounding publicity to which they are exposed, but to the fearful self-deception that so many of them practice on themselves when, instead of approaching soberly and in full knowledge of the pitch of competence they have achieved, an assignment, which will have them groping at the uttermost limits of their physical and spiritual endowments, they rely on technical appliances to push precariously forward into a sphere quite beyond their personal limitations. That it is a sphere for which they are not yet fitted can be seen by their very approach to it.

On January 12, Siegert and his three companions started up the frozen Face, following the line taken by Sedlmayer and Mehringer. They ran into plenty of trouble and, three days later, after being almost drowned in snow, had to give in still a long way below the First Ice Field. Eigerwand Station, that haven of refuge, provided an escape hatch.

Their exploit was widely reported in the press. When Lothar Brandler, himself a climber of "Direttissima" routes, ex–film amateur, now Director of Films in a Television Station, wanted to film them and ask a few questions, they played the "don't quote us" game and wanted a fee. Though if they had in fact already sold the exclusive rights of the story, it would have been somewhat unethical to accept one!

Naturally, the first man to do the "Direttissima" on the North Face of the Grosse Zinne wasn't going to pay the first aspirant to an Eiger "Direttissima" anything at all. The incident caused a good deal of quiet amusement, not only along the approaches to the Eiger; unfortunately there was also many a malicious smile as people whispered—"Well, you know, when these climbing people get together. . . ."

But even if you are a genuine "pro," it pays to pay regard to the so-called mountain code. More than ever if you are a "pro"; for your good name is then your capital.

Siegert, Kauschke, Bittner, and Uhner need not have been in such a tearing hurry. As I write these lines in mid-July 1964, the "Direttissima" has still not been achieved. Most people forget that the summit cliffs alone are as high as the whole South Face of the Marmolata and quite as sheer. Between July 2 and 4 two parties were up on the Face with the "Direttissima" in mind. One consisted of John Harlin, the American whom we have already met in 1962, and two French friends; and they started up the Sedlmayer-Mehringer route. Two Austrians went up by the Hinterstoisser variant to the foot of the supposititious "Direct" above the Second Ice Field. Both parties had to turn back before they got very high. Both aroused sympathetic interest for the quiet way in which they went about things; nobody even knew the names of the two Austrians.

They turned back; but the day of the Direct climb is at hand. Let no one doubt it: the one or the other route, perhaps both, will be climbed. We will all hope that the inevitable series of attempts will not bring death and disaster in its train. It is a safe bet that the guides will decide not to go to the assistance of anyone so idiotic as to attempt such a harebrained adventure; it is equally predictable that, if the need arises, they will nonetheless go to the rescue, all the more so because the most successful performers on the Face in recent times have been young Swiss guides. But we will still hope, and we will utter yet another warning, in the hope that further tragedies may be avoided.

To start with, what about the many useless ropes hanging all over the lower part of the Face, simply inviting even moderate climbers to start up it? Surely, everything which does not belong there, according to strict Alpine rules, should be removed? I put forward just that suggestion and later discussed my proposal with Fritz von Almen.

"Of course you're right," he said, "but it just can't be done. None of them want it done—not the guides, nor the rescue teams, nor the Cantonal Authorities back in Berne. Not only to help rescue operations, but because they know that everyone has by now heard that the sting has been taken out of the lower part of the Face, so everyone insists on starting up it; if, when they got there, they found none of the aids, it would only mean an increase in the number of accidents."

Fritz is probably right, and the guides, too, and the authorities. Nonetheless, all this fantastic litter of pitons, ropes, slings, lines, and whatnot decorating the lower third of the Face is totally irreconcilable with the "how" of mountaineering, which I mentioned above. The intention of this book has never been merely to relate the sensational history of this great Face, but to reveal its true beauty—a beauty which, one cannot reiterate it too often, is not for the average man.

The hotel guests at Kleine Scheidegg are avid for more ventures. Not only they, but the guides, too, want something new; and something new will certainly happen.

What novelty is there left, other than the "Direttissima"? When I first penned these lines there was still the first ascent by a woman. Now only a month or two later even that record has gone. For on September 1, 1964, Daisy Voog, a thirty-two-year-old Munich secretary, and Werner Bittner, aged twenty-six, an electrician from Saxony, now resident in Munich, started up the Face. They bivouacked three times, once at the "Swallow's Nest," once on the "Ramp," and the last time only 200 feet below the summit, which they reached safely in the morning sunshine of September 4 and immediately descended by the normal route.

I have already mentioned Bittner in connection with Siegert's first winter attempt on the "Direttissima." He is an experienced climber, belonging to the group known as the "Munich Saxons," and had made the first winter ascent of the Matterhorn's North Face with him and Kauschke, incurring severe frostbite in the process. There can be no doubt that both he and his fair companion—to whom has fallen the sought-after prize of the first ascent of the Eiger Face by a woman climber—are pretty tough customers.

What else, then? The first winter ascent, straight through, without a break on the way; and any number of freak "firsts" which I, certainly, do not propose to detail.

Kurt Maix, once again my spiritual rope mate in the compilation of these additional chapters, interrupts the thread of dismal conjectures when he says: "With so much senselessness about in the world generally, how can one expect the Eiger's Face to escape its share of senseless excesses? Isn't the real point that on it we have met so many splendid young men, right through from your own pioneering days to the present time? They are still coming and they will continue to come—these splendid young men of every nationality, brave men all of them."

It may be that climbing on so incomparable, so immense, so desperately lonely a face as this is in truth an advanced school and supreme testing place of a man's worth as a human being. If so, everything depends on "how" the questions set in that examination are answered.

And that "how" will in every case be conditioned first and last by the character of the man who comes to take the examination.

ROUTE GUIDE

TO THE

NORTH FACE

(Compiled by Heinrich Harrer)

H eight of the Face: 5,900 feet.
To the right of the "First Pillar" three rope lengths up through a system of chimneys and cracks, then a traverse, right, to a large patch of snow. Follow the left-hand edge of this and from its top left-hand end up over successive ledges in a zigzag line to the foot of the "Shattered Pillar." Then as far to the right as is necessary to find a favorable continuation of the ascent. (At this point two pitches of about 15 feet can be reduced in difficulty by the use of étriers.) Now traverse horizontally leftwards to the top of the "Shattered Pillar." Straight up an easy rib to the "Wet Bivouac Cave" at the foot of the vertical wall. Upward for a short rope length, then traverse 150 feet to the right to where a small knob surmounting a pillar indicates the start of the "Difficult Crack." The crack is 80 feet high. (Piton s V) It is followed by a 70-foot gully. From its head about four rope lengths of ascending traverse to the left until a platform is reached. This is the start of the "Hinterstoisser Traverse."

Move up a few metres to several pitons.

Fix the rope necessary for the 130-foot traverse. From the stance at its far end a vertical crack runs straight up for about 70 feet to the "Swallow's Nest." A short traverse to the left to the "First Ice Field." (Inclination 55°.) Two rope lengths straight up to the foot of the perpendicular cliff separating the First and Second Ice Fields. The best line is now 50 feet to the left of the "Ice Hose" up a 40-foot rock pitch (IV) to a stance. Then diagonally to the right to the "Ice Hose" and up it to the "Second Ice Field." When there is much ice, the "Ice Hose" can be climbed in its entirety. Diagonally leftward to the top of the "Second Ice Field." (Inclination 55°.) Using the assistance of the rift between rock and ice, traverse to the left till about 130 feet before the reentrant this side of the "Flatiron." (Ring piton below an overhang.) A short 50 feet up towards the left with a small overhang and piton (−V) up to a ledge. Three easy rope lengths' traverse, horizontal at first, then gently upward onto the crest of the "Flatiron." (Heavy risk of falling stones.) One rope length up the crest to a stance under an overhanging cliff. (The "Death Bivouac.") Horizontal traverse of the "Third Ice Field" (inclination 60°) to reach the next projecting rock buttress. Slight descent to the start of the "Ramp." Five rope lengths up the "Ramp," with difficult pitches (IV) to a chimney. (Waterfall or ice.) There is a good bivouac site here. Up the chimney (IV +) for one rope length. (Variant, Grade VI, to the right of it.) Stance at the top. Traverse 6 feet to an edge and 35 feet upwards (−V) to a stance. Up a 50-foot ice gully to the "Ice Bulge." Up it, or better turn it to the left on rock (Piton, IV +), to the Ice Field in the upper part of the "Ramp." 170 feet straight up it (inclination 55°) to the start of a "Brittle Ledge" running out to a small platform on the right. This is the first opportunity to get off the Ice Field to the right and must be taken, if the "Traverse of the Gods" is to be reached. Sixty feet farther on horizontally to the start of a difficult crack (V) 130 feet high where the rock is bad. At its top start the "Traverse of the Gods" (III) to the "Spider." Up the "Spider," keeping to a bulge in its middle, up to its left-hand edge at the foot of a prominent couloir. (It is the second couloir, counting from the left: the first peters out into the ridge.) One rope length up the prominent couloir to a step of black rock about 50 feet high, at its right-hand side. Up this concave pitch (piton, V), after which the slope of the gulley eases off. Avoid going straight up to the left into a cul-de-sac at this point, but curve away gently for two rope lengths up the main couloir to the start of a crack of white quartz. Follow the crack to a 130-foot overhang. At the top of the overhang (IV +) traverse across smooth slabs to the left into a shallow gully. Climb it for 25 feet to a stance. Now not straight up, but about 30 feet to the left to a clearly defined pulpit. From the pulpit a short diagonal *abseil* to the left onto a ledge below a steep gully. (Water or ice.) Four rope lengths, very steeply at first, up the gully, then gradually less steeply to a ridge in somewhat low *relief*. Four rope lengths upward to the right of this over downward stratified rock (or ice, according to the conditions) to the top end of the rocks (ridge) that forms the junction with the Northeast Face. Then diagonally to the right up to the Mittellegi Ridge and along it to the summit.

Note 1: The assessment of standard of difficulty is based on the natural formation of the rock and does not take temporary conditions into account.

Note 2: It is advised most urgently that the 130-foot rope be left in position at the "Hinterstoisser Traverse," in case of an eventual retreat.

ATTEMPTS AND SUCCESSES ON THE NORTH FACE

August 22–25, 1935
> Max Sedlmayer
> Karl Mehringer
>> Frozen to death at the "Death Bivouac" (10,800 feet).

July 18–22, 1936
> Edi Rainer
> Willy Angerer
> Andreas Hinterstoisser
> Toni Kurz
>> All killed while retreating down the Face.

August 11–14, 1937
> Ludwig Vörg
> Matthias Rebitsch
>> Withdrew safely from the "Death Bivouac."

June 21, 1938
> Bartolo Sandri
> Mario Menti
>> Fell near the "Difficult Crack."

July 21–24, 1938 First Successful Ascent
 Anderl Heckmair
 Ludwig Vörg (killed on the Russian Front, 1941)
 Fritz Kasparek (fell when climbing Salcantay, Peru, June 6, 1954)
 Heinrich Harrer

August 16–17, 1946
 Edwin Krähenbühl (fell on the Engelhörner)
 Hans Schlunegger
 Bivouacked and withdrew safely from the upper end of the "Ramp."

July 14–16, 1947 Second Ascent
 Lionel Terray
 Louis Lachenal (fell into a crevasse on Mont Blanc, 1956)

August 4–5, 1947 Third Ascent
 Hans Schlunegger (killed later in an avalanche accident)
 Karl Schlunegger
 Gottfried Jermann

July 22, 1950
 Karl Reiss
 Karl Blach
 Withdrew safely after a hand injury at the "Difficult Crack."

July 26, 1950 Fourth Ascent
 Erich Waschak
 Leo Forstenlechner
 Climbed the Face *in a single day* (18 hours), bivouacked on the summit.

July 25–27, 1950 Fifth Ascent
  Jean Fuchs
  Raymond Monney
  Marcel Hamel
  Robert Seiler

July 22–23, 1952 Sixth Ascent
  Pierre Julien
  Maurice Coutin

July 26–27, 1952 Seventh Ascent
  Karl Winter
  Sepp Larch

July 26–28, 1952 Eighth Ascent
  Hermann Buhl (killed June 26, 1957, when a cornice on Chogolisa
    in the Karakorum broke)
  Sepp Jöchler
  Sepp Maag
  Otto Maag
  Gaston Rébuffat
  Paul Habran
  Jean Bruneau
  Pierre Leroux
  Guido Magnone

August 6–8, 1952 Ninth Ascent
  Erich Vanis
  Hans Ratay
  Karl Lugmayer

August 14–15, 1952 Tenth Ascent
  Karl Blach
  Jürgen Wellenkamp (fell to his death in the Bregaglia, later)

August 15–16, 1952 Eleventh Ascent
> Karl Reiss (died of pneumonia in a high camp on Saipal, in the Himalaya, 1954)
>
> Siegfried Jungmeier

July 26–28, 1953
> Paul Körber
>
> Roland Vass
>> Reached the "Death Bivouac"; killed by a fall from the Second Ice Field during a retreat after a break in the weather.

August 20–22, 1953 Twelfth Ascent
> Uly Wyss
>
> Karlheinz Gonda
>> Fell to their death from the Summit Ice Field on the third day after completing the climb of the Face. Recognition of this successful ascent, withheld for a decade, was finally accorded in 1964.

August 25–27, 1953 Thirteenth Ascent
> Albert Hirschbichler
>
> Eberhard Riedl
>> (Hirschbichler died in the Karakorum 1959.)

August 8, 1956
> Dieter Söhnel
>
> Walter Moosmüller
>> Fell to their deaths to the left of the "Difficult Crack," almost bringing down with them the rope behind them.
>
> Lothar Brandler
>
> Klaus Buschmann
>> Who then climbed down again safely.

August 4–8, 1957 Fourteenth Ascent

The disaster to:

Günther Nothdurft

Franz Mayer

Died of exhaustion during their descent of the Western Flank after completing the ascent, leaving the two Italians on the Face unable to proceed.

and Stefano Longhi

Claudio Corti

Longhi perished on the Face, all rescue attempts from above having failed. Corti was rescued by Alfred Hellepart, who was winched 1,000 feet down from the summit on a steel cable and brought him up strapped to his back.

August 7, 1957

Wolfgang Stefan

Götz Mayr

Safe retreat from the First Ice Field.

July 31–August 1, 1958

Hias Noichl

Lothar Brandler

Herbert Raditschnig

Safe withdrawal from the "Death Bivouac" on the second day, after Noichl had been injured.

August 5–6, 1959 Fifteenth Ascent

Kurt Diemberger

Wolfgang Stefan

Originally rated as the thirteenth ascent, but now established as the fifteenth, owing to the recognition of Wyss and Gonda, and the discovery that Nothdurft and Mayer had in fact perished on the way down *after* completing the ascent.

August 10–13, 1959 Sixteenth Ascent

Adolf Derungs (killed in July 1962 during a solo attempt)

Lukas Albrecht

These two Swiss, masons by profession, had both great luck and strength of will. Their equipment was very primitive: Derungs wore four shirts, one on top of another, as protection against the cold in bivouac; Albrecht carried an old overcoat with him as far as the Spider and threw it down the wall after the third bivouac. The pair, brave to the point of rashness and very tough, descended by night by the dangerous Western Flank.

September 13–14, 1959 Seventeenth Ascent

Peter Diener

Ernst Forrer

Two Swiss again achieved the ascent; moreover, in the same rapid time as Diemberger and Stefan. Both distinguished Alpinists, they were to take part in the Swiss Dhaulagri Expedition in 1960. On the Face, they had to put up with very cold nights (it was September) and stiff ice conditions, and their achievement is therefore even more remarkable.

March 6–12, 1961 Eighteenth Ascent: first Winter Ascent

Toni Hiebeler

Toni Kinshofer (killed on a practice climb in 1964)

Anderl Mannhardt

Walter Almberger

This most remarkable ascent was achieved under severe ice conditions that compelled the climbers to spend six nights on the Face, at temperatures dropping to 14°–23° F. They spent most of the previous year training in the eastern Alps, and prepared elaborate equipment (50 lbs. per man), including a 600-foot nylon rope for a double-rope descent in case they were forced to retreat, and special ice hammers instead of the ordinary long-handled ice axe. They said afterward that the most difficult part of the climb had been the ramp leading up to the Traverse of the Gods, though they never took off their crampons the whole climb. Despite the conditions and the enforced slowness they never appeared worried or flustered and climbed with the greatest assurance and skill.

August 27–28, 1961
Adolf Mayr (*first solo attempt*)
Fell to his death from the "Silver Trench."

August 30–September 2, 1961 Nineteenth Ascent
Radovan Kuchař
Zdeno Zibrin
The first East European team to make the ascent (Czech).

August 31–September 1–2, 1961 Twentieth Ascent
(Sept. 2) Leo Schlömmer
Alois Strickler
and (Aug. 31) Stanislaw Biel
Jan Mostowski
and Kurt Grüter
Sepp Inwyler
Another example of the "International Rope." Of the six men who teamed up into one party on the Face, three were Swiss, one Austrian, and one Polish.

September 19–22, 1961 Twenty-first Ascent
Gerhard Mayer
Karl Frehsner
Georg Huber (died on Cho Oyu in 1964)
Helmut Wagner

September 23–24, 1961 Twenty-second Ascent
Hilti von Allmen
Ueli Hürlimann
> On the 24th they climbed from the "Swallow's Nest," to the top in 14 hours—the first of the lightning climbs by the younger generation of Swiss guides.

September 26–29, 1961 Twenty-third Ascent
Robert Troier
Erich Streng

July 23–25, 1962 Twenty-fourth Ascent
Jean Braun
Bernard Meyer
André Meyer
Michel Zuckschwert

July 24–25, 1962
Brian Nally
Barry Brewster
> The first British attempt. Brewster fell from the rocks above the Second Ice Field and died of injuries. Nally was rescued and brought down by Chris Bonington and Don Whillans, who abandoned their climb to save him.

July 28–31, 1962
Michel Vaucher
Yvette Attinger
Michel Darbellay
Loulou Boulaz
> This strong Swiss party, including the first two women to make a serious attempt on the Face, was forced to withdraw at the "Ramp" by appalling weather, after three bivouacs, and made the descent safely.

July 31, 1962
  Adolf Derungs (*second solo attempt*)
  Derungs fell and was killed on the lower part of the climb.

July 31—August 3, 1962 Twenty-fifth Ascent
  Helmuth Drachsler
  Walter Gstrein
  A tough four-day effort in very bad weather conditions.

August 13—15, 1962 Twenty-sixth Ascent
  Walter Almberger
  Klaus Hoi
  Hugo Stelzig
  Adolf Weissensteiner
    Almberger, a member of the Hiebeler team that made the first
    winter ascent in March 1961, returned to lead this successful sum-
    mer ascent.

August 11—18, 1962 Twenty-seventh Ascent
  Pierlorenzo Acquistapace
  Romano Perego
  Gildo Airoldi
  Franco Solina
  Armando Aste
  Andrea Mellano
    The first Italian ascent, by a team of six who spent seven days
    with six bivouacs over the climb.

August 19—22, 1962 Twenty-eighth Ascent
  Felix Kuen
  Dieter Wörndl
  and John Harlin
  Konrad Kirch
  and Franz Jauch

Josef Jauch

Franz Gnos

Josef Zurfluh

These three parties, the first Austrian, the second composed of the first American to climb the Face and a German, and the third all Swiss, joined to form an international "eightsome" on the Face, though they all reached the summit at different times.

August 19–23, 1962 Twenty-ninth Ascent

Nikolaus Rafanowitsch

Hans Hauer

A relatively inexperienced pair who triumphed over bad conditions.

August 27, 1962

Diether Marchart (*third solo attempt*)

Marchart fell to his death crossing from the First to the Second Ice Field.

August 29–30, 1962 Thirtieth Ascent

Martin Epp

Paul Etter

A very fast ascent, by another pair of young Swiss guides. Starting at dawn, they bivouacked at the "Traverse of the Gods," and reached the summit by noon next day. Etter later on led the first descent of the whole Face, December 27–31, 1963.

August 29–31, 1962 Thirty-first Ascent

Chris Bonington

Ian Clough

The first British ascent. Bonington who, with Don Whillans, had broken off his first attempt in order to rescue Brian Nally a year earlier, returned with a new partner to achieve a very fast climb, bivouacking at the "Traverse of the Gods."

August 30, 1962

> Tom Carruthers
>
> Anton Moderegger
>
>> After being overtaken by Bonington and Clough and later seen to be in difficulties, fell to their deaths from the Second Ice Field.

August 28–31, 1962 Thirty-second Ascent

> Werner Hausheer
>
> Paul Jenny

August 29–31, 1962 Thirty-third Ascent

> Robert Boegli
>
> Willy Mottet

September 2–3, 1962 Thirty-fourth Ascent

> Otto Wiedmann
>
> Walter Spitzenstätter

September 2–3, 1962 Thirty-fifth Ascent

> Otto Wintersteller
>
> Kurt Walter

September 2–3, 1962 Thirty-sixth Ascent

> Claude Asper
>
> Bernard Voltolini
>
> Christian Dalphin
>
> Roger Habersaat
>
>> At the Second Ice Field they found the remains of Karl Mehringer, twenty-seven years after his death there.

September 3–5, 1962 Thirty-seventh Ascent

> Alfred Brunner
>
> Edwin Brunner

July 30–31, 1963 Thirty-eighth Ascent
Erich Friedli
Arnold Heinen
> Another lightning climb by the young Swiss school, having over-taken the next two parties and reaching the summit in the morning.

July 29–31, 1963 Thirty-ninth Ascent
Max Friedwanger
Friedl Schicker
> Reached summit at noon on 31st.

July 29–31, 1963 Fortieth Ascent
Robert Baillie
Dougal Haston
> This rope of a Rhodesian and a Briton reached the summit in the evening.

July 31–August 1, 1963
Walter Bonatti (*fourth solo attempt*)
Withdrew from his first bivouac in safety.

August 2–3, 1963 Forty-first Ascent: First Solo Ascent
Michel Darbellay
> Darbellay, a young Swiss guide from Orsières, started up the Face soon after midnight on July 31 and, climbing with great speed and certainty, bivouacked early in the afternoon in the "Exit Cracks." He completed the climb early next morning in only eighteen hours of climbing time.

August 3–4, 1963 Forty-second Ascent
Helmut Salger
Horst Wels
> This determined attempt succeeded in spite of a break in the weather. The pair reached the Summit at 7 P.M. and took the

unusual course of climbing down the Mittellegi Ridge to the Hut in the dark.

August 11–15, 1963
Alberto Rabada
Ernesto Navarra
The two Spaniards battled on through ever-worsening weather till after four bivouacs they reached the "Spider," where they both died of exhaustion and exposure.

December 27–31, 1963 First Descent of the Face: and in Winter
Paul Etter
Ueli Gantbein
Sepp Henkel
The three Swiss guides, of whom Etter had participated in the thirtieth ascent fifteen months earlier, descended the whole icy Face, bringing down with them from the "Spider" the bodies of the two Spaniards who had perished there in August.

1964: The year of the first unsuccessful attempts at a "Direttissima."

January 21, 1964
Siegert
Bittner
Kauschke
Uhner
Withdrew after three days, without reaching any great altitude.

July 2–4, 1964
Two ropes, among them John Harlin, equally unsuccessful in achieving any altitude.

July 25–27, 1964 Forty-third Ascent
Michl Anderl
Gebhard Plangger

July 26–27, 1964 Forty-fourth Ascent
Hans-Peter Trachsel
Hans Grossen

July 26–29, 1964 Forty-fifth Ascent
Karlheinz Werner
Ernst Mahner
Pit Schubert
Rüdiger Steuer

July 30–August 1, 1964 Forty-sixth Ascent
Franz Häppl
Herbert Kettner

August 4–7, 1964 Forty-seventh Ascent
José Anglada
Jordi Pons
  The first successful Spanish team.

August 4–7, 1964 Forty-eighth Ascent
Wulf Scheffler
Gert Uhner

August 5–7, 1964 Forty-ninth Ascent
Dietmar Bachstein
Georg Ostler

September 1–3, 1964 Fiftieth Ascent: First Ascent by a Woman Climber
Daisy Voog
Werner Bittner
  This climb was successfully accomplished after three bivouacs by
  a Munich secretary and her experienced companion who has
  already been mentioned in connection with the first unsuccessful attempt on a "Direttissima."

Editor's note

Up to the time of writing there have been nearly fifty more successful ascents. Despite the resulting accumulation of experience, the North Face of the Eiger remains an important yardstick of ability for ambitious alpinists.

Some of the more notable of the recent climbs are listed here.

February 23–March 25, 1966 First Ascent of John Harlin Route—the "Eiger Direct"

Dougal Haston

Jörg Lehne

Günther Strobel

Roland Votteler

Siegfried Hupfauer

Harlin was killed when a fixed rope on the face below the Spider broke during the summit push.

July 28–31, 1968

Kristof Cielecki

Tadeusz Laukajtys

Ryszard Szarfershi

Adam Zyzak

A new route crossing the North Pillar and finishing up the Lauper Route, opened up by four Polish climbers, and hence known as "the Polish route."

July 29–31, 1968

Reinhold Messner

Günther Messner

Fritz Maschke

Toni Hiebeler

A new route on the North Pillar, crossing the Polish route, and climbed the following day.

July 15–August 15, 1969
Ms. Michiko Imai
Takio Kato
Yasuo Kato
Susumu Kubo
Hirofumi Amanao
Satoru Negishi
> Six Japanese climbers, one of them a girl, made a new route up the right side of the Eigerwand taking several weeks, using siege tactics and many bolts.

December 24, 1969–March 21, 1970
Jiri Endo
Nobuyiki Ogawa
Takao Hoshino
Yukio Shimamura
Ryoichi Fukata
Masaru Sanba
Yukio Takaku
> The second ascent of the Harlin Route using siege tactics. The party used bolts on some of the crucial pitches but, having reached the summit, they retreated down their fixed ropes, retrieving them as they descended and leaving the route clean.

January 1970 Second Winter Ascent of the 1938 Route
Masaru Morita
Masaru Okabe
Yuuji Hattori
Tetsuo Komiyama
Kenji Kimura
> Kenji Kimura fell in the Exit Cracks and broke his leg and was rescued by being winched up to the summit and taken off from there by helicopter. The others reached the summit three days later, after nine days on the face.

January 20–25, 1970

    Hans-Peter Trachsel

    Peter Jungen

    Otto van Allmen

    Hans Müller

    Max Dörfliger

        An all-Swiss team made the second ascent (and first winter ascent) by the Japanese Route, again using siege tactics.

July 28–30, 1970 Third Ascent by the Japanese Route

    Hans Müller

    Hans Berger

        They avoided using siege tactics.

June 12–July 31, 1970

    Ian Maceacheran

    Ken Spence

    Bugs McKeith

        Three young Scots found a new route, the North Pillar Direct. This is a very hard rock climb with long artificial sections in the lower half. The upper half consists of difficult mixed climbing. Siege tactics were used to the third pillar and the trio completed the route from there.

September 5–10, 1970

    Cliff Phillips

    Pete Minks

    Eric Jones

    Leo Dickinson

        Four British climbers climbed the 1938 route in six days, making a television film in the process.

September 1971

Peter Siegert

Martin Biock

> After a series of delays they were storm-bound at the "Death Bivouac" and signalled for rescue. A helicopter succeeded in lowering a line to the Flat Iron and the climbers were rescued unscathed. The first helicopter rescue from the face.

March 1972

Sylvia Kysilkova

Jiri Smid

Zbynek Cepela

Lubos Novak

> Attempt by a Czech team at a third winter ascent of the 1938 Route. Cepela and Novak retreated at the Rote Fluh, but the others got as far as the top of the Second Ice Field. There they were rescued by helicopter. This helicopter rescue and the one mentioned above have reduced the commitment of the normal Eigerwand route, as pilots are now well trained to pick climbers off the face.

Winter 1972–73 Third Ascent of the North Pillar: First All-female Ascent of the Face

Wanda Blaszkiewcz

Danuta Gelner

Stefania Egierszdorff

> Three Polish ladies made perhaps the most difficult Alpine climb so far achieved by an all-female team. It is not clear whether they followed the Polish Route or the Standard North Pillar route.

January 1973

Hans Von Kanel

Hansjorg Muller

> Third winter ascent of 1938 route in six days. First winter ascent of the face by a two-man team.

August 1973

Juek Kotnik

Franci Verko

> A remarkable variation by two Yugoslavs. They took the Japanese Route to level with the Fly, found the top section too difficult, traversed into it, descended the Harlin Route to the Spider, and finished by going up the Exit Cracks on the original 1938 Route.

August 14, 1974

Reinhold Messner

Peter Habeler

> The fastest ascent of the face. The pair started the climb at 5 A.M. and completed the 1938 route in just ten hours, descending to Kleine Scheiddegg on the same day.

March 1975

Joe Tasker

Dick Renshaw

> Fourth winter ascent by two young British climbers in six days.

February 19–March 5, 1976

Martin Novak

Leos Horka

Petr Gribek

Jan Martinek

Milan Motycka

Vladimir Starcala

> Second winter ascent of Japanese route, again using fixed ropes.

Summer 1976
> Jiri Schmid
> Sylvia Kysilkova
> Josef Rybicka
> Petr Plachetsky
>> A new line to the right of the Japanese route, climbing the right-hand side of the Rote Fluh and then the steep pillar above. Siege style was again employed, during 26 days.

August 3–9, 1976
> Petr Bednarik
> Pavel Cicarek
> Pavel Sevcik
> Jindrick Sochor
>> The first summer ascent of the Harlin route, always considered a suicidal proposition in summer. The first time any of the direct routes was climbed without fixed ropes. (Muller and Berger's ascent of the Japanese route made use of ropes left over from the winter.)

January 16–February 26, 1977
> Jaroslav Flejberk
> Josef Rybicka
> Jiri Smid
> Miroslav Smid
>> Another sieged new route, this time to the left of the Harlin route. The Czech team spent ten days on the overhanging section near the ramp.

October 13–17, 1977
> Alex MacIntyre
> Tobin Sorenson
>> The second summer ascent of the Harlin route by a young English and young American climber in excellent clean style.

November 1977

Fernandez Jesus Domingo

Miguel Perez Tello

Perez broke both his legs in the Ramp. Nonetheless, these two young Spaniards were plucked off by helicopter, thus finally proving that rescues are possible from just about anywhere on the face.

January 17–21, 1978

Jiri Benes

Jan Krch

Second ascent of the Scottish North Pillar route.

March 3–9, 1978

Tsuneo Hasegawa

First winter solo of the 1938 route.

March 7–12, 1978

Ivan Ghirardini

The second winter solo of the 1938 route. He also soloed the Croz Spur of the Grandes Jorasses and the North Face of the Matterhorn in the same winter season.

Summer 1981

Uehli Buhler

He soloed the 1938 route in a record 8½ hours.

August 26–27, 1981

Hans Howald

Christel Howald

Marcel Reudi

A rock climb to the right of the Rote Fluh. A rather minor new route on the face, finishing on the West Flank.

INDEX

Index

Seven Years in Tibet

HEINRICH HARRER

foreword by His Holiness the Dalai Lama

In this vivid memoir that has sold millions of copies worldwide and that was made into a feature film, Heinrich Harrer recounts his adventures as one of the first Europeans to enter Tibet. It is the extraordinary true story of how a young Austrian adventurer became tutor and friend to the Dalai Lama.

In 1943, Heinrich Harrer, a noted mountain climber and skier, made a successful escape from an internment camp in India through rugged Himalayan passes to the Forbidden City of Lhasa in Tibet. From destitute vagabond, he rose to position of tutor and confidant to the fourteen-year-old Dalai Lama until their parting in 1950, when the Chinese Communists overran the country.

Seven Years in Tibet is a timeless story that illuminates Eastern culture, as well as the childhood of His Holiness the Dalai Lama and the current plight of Tibetans. It is a must read for lovers of travel, adventure, history, and culture.

Return to Tibet

Tibet After the Chinese Occupation

HEINRICH HARRER

The *New York Times* best-seller *Seven Years in Tibet* told the incredible story of an idyllic life on the "roof of the world," before it was destroyed by the invading Chinese army. Now Austrian adventurer Heinrich Harrer revisits the people and places he left behind, in the extraordinary *Return to Tibet,* appearing for the first time in paperback. A compelling mix of history, religion, and travel writing, his book bears witness to the suffering and perseverance of this ancient civilization under Chinese rule.

Against a backdrop of ruined monasteries and the beautiful, mysterious Himalayas, Harrer vividly evokes both a free Tibet, in which religion and faith were central features of daily life, and the present-day occupied nation, in which a profoundly spiritual culture is threatened with disappearance. He reflects on the country's problems, and in a reunion with his former pupil the Dalai Lama, discusses ways of preserving the Tibetans' national character and their homeland.

Like *Seven Years in Tibet,* this is a timeless story of Eastern culture that beckons readers to a land of majestic mountains and a religion that has endured forever.

JEREMY P. TARCHER/PUTNAM

A MEMBER OF

PENGUIN PUTNAM INC.

$12.95 (ISBN 0-87477-925-1)

ABOUT THE AUTHOR

Heinrich Harrer was born in 1912 in Carinthia and studied at the University of Graz, where he distinguished himself both in geography and athletics. His skiing prowess won him a place in the 1936 Austrian Olympic team, and in 1937 he won the World's University Slalom Championship. He was in the party that first ascended the notorious North Wall of the Eiger in 1938. *The White Spider* is the story of that expedition, and of previous attempts to make that terrible climb. Harrer is perhaps best known as the author of the classic *Seven Years in Tibet*, also available from Tarcher.